THE EDUCATIONAL ODYSSEY OF
A WOMAN COLLEGE PRESIDENT

D1528017

THE EDUCATIONAL

ODYSSEY *of a*

WOMAN COLLEGE

PRESIDENT

Joanne V. Creighton

DISTRIBUTED BY
University of Massachusetts Press
AMHERST AND BOSTON

Copyright © 2018 by Joanne Creighton
All rights reserved
Printed in the United States of America

ISBN 978-1-62534-398-7 (print)
ISBN 978-1-61376-647-7 (e-book)

Designed by Kristina Kachele Design, llc
Set in Alegreya HT Pro

Cover design by Kristina Kachele Design, llc
Cover photograph from the collection of Mount Holyoke College

British Library Cataloguing-in-Publication Data
A catalog record for this book is available from the British Library.

This book is a memorial to the little-postage-stamp
world of northern Wisconsin of my growing
up years and the alma maters which shaped
my itinerant educational odyssey. It is also a
testament to the formative role of my family.
In appreciation of their abiding love and support.
I dedicate this book to them.

CONTENTS

ILLUSTRATIONS

PREFACE

My Educational Odyssey

"How did you become a college president?" I have been asked this question frequently, sometimes by young women who think it would be a pretty desirable career ambition, and other times by empathetic observers who, appalled by the demands of the job, cannot resist blurting out, "I wouldn't have your job for anything in the world!"

It is not a question easy to answer, and my life has taken surprising turns over seven decades. I certainly never wanted to be a college president when I grew up, nor was it likely given my origins. My earliest career ambition was to be a cowgirl, rather like Dale Evans, who rode off into the sunset with Roy Rogers (before he metamorphosed into a restaurant chain). Soon books, not movies, stirred my imagination. I was delighted to realize in college that I could major in reading novels, and, later, even better, that I could make a career of it as a teacher and scholar of English. I thought I had found my life's perfect fulfillment.

Only inadvertently, reluctantly, and with great misgivings, was I talked into taking on my first administrative assignment, "for one year only," a fateful step that changed the course of my life and led to college presidencies. At that time, in my faculty-centric view, I thought an administrator was the alien "other" in academia. After doing administrative work for a while, though, I had to admit to myself that I was energized by it, especially by working together with others in common cause. Still, I resisted the role, telling myself that I was doing it only "temporarily"; my real job was scholarship and teaching. But after years of this rationalization, I had an epiphany one day that reconciled me to this work: I realized that I approached an administrative task in much the same way as a scholarly one. In both I was taking an inductive "reading," using the analytical skills I had honed in literary analysis. And I was asking questions: What are the themes, conflicts, and characters? How do the parts fit together into a whole? What are the external forces, contexts, and traditions? "Reading" an institution, like reading a novel, is seeing it in all of its complexity and uniqueness, testing common understandings with others, and bringing out incipient potentialities (or "plans") for discussion and debate. Maybe, doing administrative work wasn't a radical career shift? Maybe there was some continuity to my life and work, after all. "Reading" the institutional culture was the foundation of my approach to academic leadership as I moved up the administrative ladder from associate dean to dean, provost, interim president, and president.

To be sure, I didn't always love academic leadership. In addition to the drudgery of bureaucratic tasks and endless meetings, there were dark days on campus. For instance, when students outside the window were chanting: "What do we want?" *"Answers!"* "When do we want 'em?" *"Now!"* I wished to be somewhere else, anywhere else, than in the president's chair. Yet I must also admit that I can't imagine a job with greater rewards than that of college president. One of the great pleasures—that more than makes up for its great pains—is the vista, the bird's-eye view, afforded by the position. A college president is likely to have occasional moments of seeing the college steadily and seeing it whole, to borrow a phrase from Matthew Arnold.[1] It is a perspective that one doesn't always have on the ground when engaged in the day-to-day business of administration. To be sure, these transcendent moments don't last for long. The president has to come down from the mountain and hear about the excesses of last night's parties, the warring factions in the history department, the budget overruns, the itinerary of the visiting dignitary, among other routine affairs.

Nonetheless, those visions from the mount, as it were, provide great surges of adrenalin. To see an educational institution from that lofty perspective is to appreciate its multifarious complexity, energy, and excellence. It is to see the enterprise as a single organism, diverse yet ineluctably bound together by implicitly shared values, habits of mind, and attitudes towards knowledge. It is to see the common ground and common values that bind the college community together in common purpose.

From the broadest vista of the presidency, one appreciates with special acuity how extraordinarily valuable colleges and universities are in advancing knowledge and passing on to successive generations the accumulated learning and wisdom of humankind. Closer up, a president encounters countless students, parents, and alumni full of appreciation for the institution and eager to express their thanks. Indeed, another rewarding part of the job is that a president is often the recipient of these profuse thank-yous. And there are many more of them than there are complaints. Colleges and universities are transformative. They make an enormous difference in people's lives, and they express their appreciation in praise and in support.

But lest one think that all this positive feedback would give the president a big head, let me add, hastily, that the presidency is also a humbling job. A college president can declare, as Secretary of State Alexander Haig did when President Ronald Reagan was shot in March 1981, "I'm in charge here"—but do so with equal *credibility*. So many others—students, faculty, administrators, trustees, alumni, and the surrounding community—make up the fabric of the place as well as its accumulated history, customs, policies, and traditions do. Yet, despite all of this diffused strength, presidents also see the fragility of the institutions they serve. Colleges and universities are not self-sustaining. They need our undivided attention, our most inspired imagination. They are worthy of our best effort. Is there a better job than that?

This book chronicles my life's journey from its inauspicious beginning in a small village in northern Wisconsin through successive schools, universities, and colleges en route to three (albeit two interim) college presidencies at distinguished eastern liberal arts colleges. Most notable was the traversing of custom and expectation contingent in place and time and in family, class, and gender that this journey entailed. What did I learn? Is my journey illustrative and endemic?

I use pieces of my life idiosyncratically as points of departure for reflection about issues of importance to me. I go backward and forward in time, for, as William Faulkner says: "There is no such thing as *was* because the past *is*. It is part of every man, every woman, and every moment. All of his and her ancestry, background, is all a part of himself or herself at a particular moment"[2] I cut across the same time periods from different angles because this book is about the strands of influence that make up a life.

This story is my world as I remember it, as I "compose" it through the faulty and creative mechanism of memory. While the first three chapters are a kind of *bildungsroman*, my account of that time is now retrospectively intermingled with books I have read and influenced by the example of others I admire, prominent among them former Smith College president Jill Ker Conway's three volume memoir, *The Road from Coorain* (1989), *True North* (1994), *A Woman's Education* (2001), and Mary Catherine Bateson's *Composing a Life* (1989). Their works demonstrate the way that successful women "compose" a life out of the discontinuities of their experiences. I am interested in tracing the influence that particular places and people—family members, teachers, friends, and writers—have had on me and the course of my life.

This is a woman's book in part because much of my journey is about coming to terms with myself as a woman contending with gender expectations imposed by environments within which I lived. I include the word "woman" in the title because the gender of a woman who assumed a position of leadership was almost invariably remarked upon, perhaps because it was so uncommon. Commenting on the way women writers are segmented off from the mainstream of literature, Joyce Carol Oates—with whom I have had a long personal and professional relationship—says, "A writer may be afflicted with any number of demons, but only a (woman) writer is afflicted with her own essential identity." The same can be said for a woman who becomes a dean, provost, or president and enters what has been for centuries the all-male establishment of higher learning. How to deal with this insistent categorization and exclusion, asks Oates: "With resilience, with a sense of humor, with stubbornness, with anger, with hope." The "ghetto," after all, is "a place to live."[3] The ghetto of female identity as well as other defining parameters in my life is what this book is exploring. When I became president of Mount Holyoke, I felt that I had come round full circle to embrace the world of women, which I had discounted on my way to making a success in a man's world.

This is also a book about higher education as seen through the shifting perspectives of my changing position as a student, professor, dean, provost, and president on my fifty-year itinerant journey through large public and private universities and progressively smaller liberal arts colleges, both coeducational and single-sex, during a time when the educational landscape and the position of women within it changed dramatically. It is a story about academic culture, shared governance, and academic leadership, containing many lessons from the field that I learned over my long career, and about the strengths and weaknesses of liberal arts institutions and the challenges facing them in particular.

I examine at length some events at Mount Holyoke that tested my leadership and shook the fabric of the college community: student protests and takeovers of academic buildings; a rupture with the alumnae association; and a highly publicized scandal involving a distinguished professor. These experiences tested process and principle, toughness, and ability to withstand public scrutiny, but ultimately my presidency was strengthened, and, with that, I had a good run for over fourteen years. The College experienced a dramatic revitalization and restoration of institutional confidence. In this book, I isolate key components of that transformation and the abiding strengths of the institution.

I spent over twenty years in leadership positions at three distinguished private liberal arts colleges–Wesleyan University, Mount Holyoke College, and Haverford College—which have much in common but house distinctively different campus cultures. Originating in the nineteenth century, these mission-driven institutions had been pioneers in advancing educational opportunity and upholding high standards of academic excellence and ethical seriousness. Were they still relevant and sustainable in the twenty-first century in the face of many competitors and challenges? This was a particularly salient question for Mount Holyoke College, since women's colleges have declined precipitously in numbers. Yet liberal arts education is of inestimable value. An educated citizenry is quite literally our civilization's best hope, especially in the face of a distressing onslaught "of alleged false news," "alternative facts," conspiracy theories, and dismissal of science in recent public discourse. I feel enormously blessed by having spent so much of my life working on behalf of these learning communities dedicated to truth, principled critical inquiry, and the intellectual and ethical education of young people.

THE EDUCATIONAL ODYSSEY OF
A WOMAN COLLEGE PRESIDENT

PART I

My Odyssey Begins

Pound, Wisconsin, Roadside Sign
Photograph by Patricia Schutte

1

PARENTS

There is no such thing as *was*, because the past *is*—
William Faulkner in James B. Meriwether, *Lion in the Garden*

Before the bypasses of recent decades, city folk from Chicago and
Milwaukee driving straight north on Highways 41 and then 141 had
to slow down, sometimes to excruciatingly slow speeds, as they
passed through one tiny village after another en route to the lakes
and woods of northeastern Wisconsin. I doubt that they took much
note of the life that went on behind the ubiquitous gas stations,
greasy spoons, seedy taverns, and sundry other local services strung
along the highway to tempt the commuting vacationers and local
residents.

Thirty miles to the north of Green Bay stood Lena, amid dairy
farms, one of which was cheek-by-jowl with the highway that ran
through the center of the village. Lena was notorious not only for its
malodorous Frigo factory out of which a mighty cheese empire grew
but also for being a speed trap, its twenty-five-miles-an-hour limit
catching many an irritated driver. Lena was at the southern edge of
the terrain that formed the cultural and social fabric my childhood
and adolescence. Only on occasion, such as the exhausting, tension-
filled, clothes-shopping trip with Mother, would my family venture
farther south to the big city of Green Bay. My schoolmates and I travelled by bus to rival high schools in Lena and other small towns for
football and basketball games from our school in Coleman, which
was ten miles farther north from Lena on Highway 141. Just two
miles beyond Coleman, past the swimming hole created by the dam

on Little River, was Pound, my hometown, which announced its 354 residents on a highway sign at the edge of town.

Then, looking northward three miles beyond Pound was Beaver, where my mother grew up on the family farm and worked in the family store. Near Beaver a highway wayside designated the spot as precisely equidistant between the North Pole and the equator. As if in acknowledgment of that geographical distinction, the glacier receded from there millennia ago, its retreat evident in the abrupt transformation of farmland into the rugged, sandysoiled, lakestudded northern woods, now in its second growth, since loggers and would-be farmers of the nineteenth century had depleted the virgin forests.

Seven miles farther north on Highway 141 sat Crivitz, the site of another rival high school and the self-proclaimed "Gateway to the North." It developed over the years into a burgeoning tourist center catering to the visitors who streamed north in growing numbers and populated the modest cottages and campgrounds that popped up in the woods, on the shores on the dozens of spring-fed lakes, or on the banks of the Peshtigo River, a vast watershed harnessed by dams and replete with beautiful expanses of serene water as well as rushing rapids over ragged rock beds. Its countless, sprawling tributaries and small lakes flowed throughout the forested terrain of the region. One of them, Left Foot Creek, the outlet of Left Foot Lake, ran through the thirty acres of land my parents purchased when I was in college. On this land, they fixed up an old house ("the damned shack") and later built a lovely homestead, a place now suffused with memories of innumerable family gatherings during their retirement and declining years.

But Pound, where I grew up, was the epicenter of "my own little postage stamp of native soil," as Faulkner calls his fictional Yoknapatawpha County. Tiny as it was, Pound did not feel remote and isolated there on the highway to the North, but interlinked to town and country, farm and forest, and a social and cultural network of other towns on either side of it. To a child, the village was a complete world unto itself with the ranger station where my father worked and we first lived, a baseball field, three grocery stores, five churches, three taverns, two gasoline stations, a bank, hotel, barber shop, dime store with soda fountain, two feed mills, a hardware store, furniture store, variety store, post office, car dealership, doctor's office, grade school, car repair shop, and my mother's beauty shop—most sited either along Highway 141 or on Main Street (County Highway Q), which intersected it. I traversed the length of Main Street at least four times daily during the school year, walking back and forth for lunch at home, sometimes in the bitter cold of northern winters, with my saliva-soaked scarf frozen to my face. The farms, creeks, woods, and lakes surrounding the town, where I freely roamed on bike or foot, were also as much part of my world as the houses, businesses, and denizens of the village.

The geography of childhood is a palpable "electrocardiogram of her childhood, a map of her past," finds Frances Wingate when she returns years later in Margaret Drabble's *Realms of Gold*.[1] So too for me is this backcountry terrain of northeastern Wisconsin, still powerfully evocative and redolent with memories and influences that took root in my being. I, too, like Thomas Wolfe, learned that "you can't go home again."[2] Indeed, my "home" no longer exists, yet for me in some fundamental ways, it still *is*.

And so too is the emotional terrain of family. Mine was composed of three powerful and domineering family members: father, mother, and older sister. I struggled to define myself in relationship to them, and at different points they have each evoked a range of emotions in me, from rage to love. But with the mellower retrospective of later years, my dominant response is one of admiration for these willful, self-made, capable individuals. In such a family, I was the youngest, smallest, and seemingly "dumbest," and it was sometimes hard to be assured of my own self-worth, although if willfulness is the core ingredient of the Vanish family identity, I seem to have gotten a goodly portion of that quality.

FATHER

One of my father's favorite stories was about how he won a battle of wills when I was an infant. One night, I stood up in the crib and screamed for attention. My mother couldn't deal with the squalling anymore. My father took over, calmly and silently, lying me down each time I stood up. Eventually, this display of patient paternal willfulness overtook my rebellion, and I was too exhausted to rise and scream again and so succumbed in ignominious defeat. This was viewed as an important lesson in "breaking my spirit" and instilling

Bill and Bernice Vanish in front of Newly Built Ranger Station in Pound, Wisconsin, ca. 1938

obedience. It was also a lesson in the implacable supremacy of male authority, a lesson I refused to learn then and later. The body was weak but the spirit was undaunted.

My father, Bill Vanish, was a forest ranger, a profession that people romanticize, although its main responsibility, firefighting, is dangerous and hard. Nonetheless, he was indeed a romantic, albeit a gruff and often-taciturn one. One dimension of that romanticism was his deep communion with nature. Another part was in his sensitivity to language and poetry. Most fundamentally, however, he, along with my mother, embodied the romanticism of the American dream, building a life through drive and determination, resourcefulness and resilience. First-generation Americans, they sprang from modest immigrant stock and worked their way into the lower middle class. Shaped inexorably, as so many of their generation were, by the Great Depression, they endured and prevailed through hard times and travail, and through tensions and incompatibilities in their marriage, and created full lives deeply rooted in place and community.

Bill was the eldest of seven children born to an impoverished family in west-central Wisconsin. His less-than-exemplary father, Peter Vanish, had emigrated with his family from Bohemia when he was five years old. He was variously a self-taught surveyor, a tavern and grocery-store keeper, a beekeeper, a drunk, an unfaithful, abusive husband, and a domineering and willful father. While I barely knew my grandfather I did learn that my father had had a stormy relationship with him and had at times tried to defend his mother, who was, it seemed to me as a child, a wholly admirable grandmother. Of Irish/German origins, Anna Kennedy (distantly related, we learned, to President Kennedy's family) was the only one of my grandparents who was born in this country.

Our paternal grandparents and the extended Vanish clan were somewhat remote from our daily lives, since we visited their modest, slightly seedy homestead in Mosinee, which was about two hours away, only periodically and briefly. Grandma Vanish always greeted us cheerfully, saying that she would add water to the soup simmering on the black cast-iron, wood-burning stove in the kitchen. These visits contrasted sharply with the family dinners of my mother's relatives, which were always filled with daunting amounts and varieties of food: turkey, chicken, pork chops, and sausage were "the meat," along with soup, several kinds of vegetables, potatoes, salads, cakes, pies, cookies, and ice cream. They also were noisy affairs with squalling infants, squirming children, and adults loudly and rapidly gesticulating in an amalgam of Polish and English.

In the Vanish household, in contrast, not only was the food comparatively spare, you could hear the clocks ticking and the rocking chairs creaking. Taciturn and introverted, my aunts and uncles would typically sit silently doing crossword puzzles, smoking, drinking, or staring into space. They weren't unfriendly, only uneasy with visitors and apparently unaccustomed to filling up time with talking. They communicated sporadically in wry quips. Our visits were filled with my gregarious mother's chatter punctuated by brief rejoinders and long silences. I was fascinated and puzzled by these exotic and unknowable relatives who seemed to occupy a different realm than the one we inhabited. Only later did I realize that we had inculcated the values, customs, and style of a homogenizing, aspiring middle class, whereas the Vanishes still had some of the vestiges of the pioneer about them: they lived on the edge of society—solitary, self-sufficient, and without much practice in social graces.

One of the vivid memories of my childhood was a visit when I was about eight years old. Grandma Vanish confided to Mother that she had an open wound on her side, she presumed it was cancer, and she was having difficulty bandaging it. Shocked, Mother demanded to see it and then vociferously expressed her concern and sympathy. Counterpointing Mother's exclamations was the grim commentary of my grandfather, sitting in his rocker in the living room: "You're going to croak! You're going to croak!" With a family history of cancer, my grandmother thought that she did indeed have a death sentence and didn't think that money should be spent on doctors and hospitals. Eventually, though, she did agree to consult with our local doctor, who talked her into having the surgery that prolonged her life but did not finally arrest the cancer. She spent a month or so recuperating in our house—a rare opportunity to get to know her a little better and to appreciate her ever-present cheerfulness, resilience, and wit.

Dedicated to his mother, a self-described "angry young man," Bill told off his father and left home when he graduated from high school in 1928. He moved around the country, doing odd jobs, working in a factory in Milwaukee, and becoming a migrant worker following the crops out West. Eventually, he joined the Civilian Conservation Corps and so began his career that led him into the Wisconsin Conservation Department, first as a tower man and later as head of the Ranger Station in Pound. Tall and handsome, the new ranger was a stranger in a community where everyone knew everybody and their family history. He met my mother at a local dance in 1935 and promptly asked her for a date. She said no; she didn't know him. Not to be deterred, he found an acquaintance who vouched for his character. Finally she said, "Well, I'll take a chance," a comment that became a joke between them over the years. She took a bigger chance and married him in the fall of 1936, and they began a marriage of over fifty-five years and a long sojourn in the town of Pound.

The Pound Ranger Station was home for my first eight years. An imposing stone building surrounded by a manicured lawn, it stood adjacent to the town's baseball field on one side and to old Mrs. Prue's house with chickens and cats and an irresistible junk pile on the other. Backing onto woods, fields, and railroad tracks, the Ranger Station was a wonderful place for a child, if you include as a positive the ghastly spectacle of Mrs. Prue's periodic beheading of chickens. We had the "living quarters" up the concrete stairs above the ranger station, while downstairs was a large garage with a fire truck, a caterpillar, and an impressive number of hoses, spades, shovels, and other firefighting equipment, along with my father's meticulous office. The "crew," two or three hired men, were usually kind and friendly to the two little girls who hung around. "Go tell your mother that Kelsey wants a cookie," said one, helping us get contraband goods. Bob Shout, young and handsome, forever washing his beloved car, used to call up the stairs when we were singing as we washed dishes: "Could you turn that radio down up there?"

Tower men out in the districts called in reports of "smokes" to the station. Their sightings were tracked with marking pins on a wall map in Daddy's office, and he dispatched fire equipment to the scene. The ranger station also issued burning permits and fishing and hunting licenses, and during hunting season a steady stream of hunters brought their slain deer to be registered. Doing double duty as a game warden, Daddy would also surreptitiously roam the byways in his green pickup, looking for poachers and violators to "pinch."

Maintaining the beekeeping tradition of his father, our father set up, in addition to the hives out in the back of the ranger station, a glass hive in his office so that we could watch the bees at work. I spent many an hour fascinated by the queen and her attendants, although I wasn't delighted to have bees on the premises, given that I was strung more than my fair share of the time. Daddy, in contrast, would move gracefully among the bees buzzing around him, untouched and unharmed. Even to the bees, our father was intimidating and unapproachable.

Silent, moody, introspective, acerbic, our father was a formidable presence in the family. I don't remember ever being really comfortable talking with him. It wasn't until I was much older that I realized he was congenitally incapable of facile conversation with anyone. But I admired him tremendously and tried to please him and to spend time with him, which often meant tagging around while he performed the countless chores and activities that made up his day. "Why come?" I would ask, even though my sister imperiously mocked my improper usage.

Sometimes Daddy would patiently explain what he was doing; other times he brusquely dismissed the question or belittled the questioner: "Don't you know nothin'?" I often wished that I had been a boy, not out of any real desire to be one but because my father should have had a son, it seemed to me. His interests and talents were so clearly "masculine," and here he was placed so unfairly in a family of women. I tried to take an interest in hunting and fishing, but when my sister and I accompanied our father on such expeditions, we were clearly relegated to a subordinate role, taggers-on rather than fully franchised participants. In those prefeminist days, daughters were not accorded the rights and privileges of surrogate sons. We did not shoot any weapons. We followed in Daddy's stealthy footprints on forays into the woods, trying hard not to step on twigs that snapped or to make other errors in hunting etiquette that would disgust him. We did often go fishing with him, yet when it came to the masculine sport of fly-fishing, we were just observers, for weak-armed girls couldn't be expected to cast properly. Nonetheless, it felt like a privilege to be out with our father in the woods or on the water, where we could appreciate the graceful competence and cool mastery of a man fully in his natural habitat.

Self-taught, our father mastered many trades, often times necessity being the mother of invention. He was especially skilled at woodworking, and for Christmas and birthdays he would present us with handcrafted chairs and tables, rocking horses, dollhouses, and cradles as well as brainteasing puzzles, for he himself loved a mental challenge, posing a problem and coming up with a solution, often an ingenious one. In fact, one of his favorite activities was taking things apart, including a piano, out of sheer curiosity. The piano provided numerous pieces of valuable stuff that could be repurposed in another form. Indeed, most notable was his tendency to press discarded materials into surprisingly new service.

He was an inveterate "shopper" in the dump. He would stockpile recovered junk, which he called his "jewelry," in neat piles in the woods. It was a great blow to his custom when the dump was closed to scavengers. Many a discarded object found its way into one of my father's inventions: the motor from an old washing machine powered the lawn sprinkling system he designed; and the old windup telephone became a pencil sharpener. Before the days of central car locks, he fashioned a paddle with a custom-fitted notch that would open the doors on the opposite side of the car. He also kept everything in the house in working order. There was no need to discard any appliance; he could always "fix it" or anything else for that matter. My parents used the toaster they got for a wedding present, for over fifty years. Some years later, when he would visit me in my various adult residences, my father would bring along his tools so that he could fix the many leaky faucets, loose door handles, and broken fixtures that cluttered up a life without a live-in handyman.

While he had only a high school education, our father retained much of what he learned and an avid appetite for intellectual stimulation. He enjoyed mathematics and taught himself trigonometry and advanced algebra for the fun of it. At age eighty, he learned how to operate an antiquated, castoff computer and enjoyed typing out poetry that he had memorized as a child. The melodious rhymes of Longfellow were particular favorites. His sensitivity to language, like that of others in his family, expressed itself in addiction to crossword puzzles and witty playfulness. He was a writer of memorable letters, simple, direct, specific, thoughtful, and wryly amusing. He could turn out effortless and witty doggerel as well. Written expression unlocked a natural eloquence that was not apparent in the terse conversation of this taciturn and introverted man.

Daddy's quick intelligence was not always the best teacher. He could be impatient if you didn't "get it" right away, and he might resort to humor and belittlement. "Ask your father," my mother would always suggest. Sometimes I appreciated his help with my homework; more often I would stubbornly stick it out on my own. Daddy could be a tease and wield cutting humor (or other kinds of playful putdowns such as tickling) as a weapon; sometimes he wouldn't stop until the badgering squeezed tears from his younger daughter. Occupying the bottom rung in the family ladder, I could be the butt of jokes that often provoked the rage of indignity and helplessness.

But he was fundamentally kind and sensitive. I never doubted his love and usually appreciated his humor. One time, my sister didn't want her little sister hanging around with her and her friends, so she pushed me away, hurting my arm. I went screaming to my father with my wounded arm and bruised ego. "Show me your arm," he said. I held out my unblemished limb. He quietly took out his colored pencils and drew an impressive black-and-blue mark on me. I ran back to my sister in triumph to display the damage, but, of course, by that time I was completely cheered up by our small act of collusion.

Our father was strong and seemingly invincible, and so it was hard to see him in any situation that diminished him. We all conspired to keep his clay feet from showing, but he had them. He could be a man of dark moodiness and deep depression. He worked for years for a mean-spirited boss, who seemed to enjoy the exercise of bureaucratic small-mindedness. Daddy always assumed that he would get the district rangership when his boss retired, so he stuck out this tense, unhappy situation rather than accept a similar position that he was offered in another town and would necessitate a family move. But when his supervisor finally retired, there was an open competition for the position, including a group interview of the finalists. Our father was always tongue-tied and ill-at-ease in social situations, and thinking that silence was more becoming than empty-headed garrulousness, he apparently said little while his competitor confidently chattered on and dominated the interview. All we knew was that he came home from the interview angry, defensive, and deeply humiliated. Moreover, he lacked a college degree and military service, and both "counted" in a kind of point system for the finalists. In the end, he did not get the job, a disappointment that sunk him into a deep funk.

Then, and at other times in his life, he resorted to booze, for he shared the Vanish family's fatal weakness for alcohol. Our parents, young adults during World War II, engaged in the heavy social drinking habits of their generation; they were part of a circle of couples who regularly partied, drank heavily, and played cards. We heard about one evening when our father, high on drink and feel-ing invincible, yanked the table cloth off out from under the dinner dishes at the house of their friends. Fortunately, the dishes remained in place. But he was also a solitary and secretive drinker. True to type, he would hide bottles in his back office, woods, or basement. We said nothing when we found them buried in bureau drawers,

Bill on One of His
Many Woodpiles

for our mother feared the "disgrace" should our father's drinking become known by others. But, of course, those "others" were aware. Drunks deceive no one, not even themselves, although they work hard at self-deception. This recurrent and intractable problem wore at the fabric of my parents' marriage and exacerbated unspoken tensions in the family.

The terrible thing about problem drinking is that it is so degrading. Loosening inhibitions, it can bring out a nasty side of the personality. Our father, I am afraid, could be a sometimes mean, maudlin, or sentimental, but always off-putting drunk. Of course, he pretended that nothing was wrong or that he was in complete control—he certainly did not drink too much or he could stop if he wanted to. So he told himself and us. It was so painful to see my father, a man with so much natural dignity and pride, reduced to such a debased condition.

His problem with drinking ebbed and flowed. It wasn't until I was college age and he was in another of his dark depressions and drinking heavily, that the situation reached a crisis point. Home for a visit, I went with Mother to the doctor for some routine matter; he told us that Daddy was "killing himself": something had to be done. Mother told him about this conversation at lunch that same day. Deeply mortified and defensive, shocked that such a topic would be raised in front of his daughter (for my parents had by this time put on "company manners" with me and kept the dirty linen carefully hidden), he vehemently denied his condition, although his speech was slurred; he suffered a bout of unstoppable hiccups and was unable to eat. His condition must have been painfully obvious to him. With resolution and desperation, Mother swallowed her pride, joined Al-Anon, and tried to cope with her own unwilling complicity in the crisis. Our father, a loner, found groups like the AA abhorrent.

But eventually, through an impressive act of willpower, he stopped drinking. He had occasional brief lapses after that, but the last decades of his life were mostly sober years, and he achieved a measure of health and inner peace that had eluded him earlier. Although he had abused his body with alcohol, he had a tenacious will to live. Indeed, he said, not infrequently, that he wanted to live to a hundred years old. He ate well and loved fresh vegetables. He used to say only half-jokingly that he wanted us to get the water boiling on the stove, run to the garden, pick the vegetables, run back, cook them right away, and eat them before the vitamins had time to run out. Even at eighty years of age, he spent every day doing hard manual labor, chopping countless cords of woods on his Left Foot Lake estate. He planted thousands of trees in his impressive plantations, made innumerable birdhouses, grew a productive garden, and dreamed up dozens of ingenious inventions. Never idle, he retained an avid interest in the world. He quite literally communed with nature: roaming the woods; observing the birds, animals, insects, plants, and trees; drawing deep sustenance from the life teeming around him. He was thoughtful about politics, proud of his daughters and grandson, content with his life, finally.

Although he died before I became a president, he was alive when I served as vice-president and provost at Wesleyan. In a letter taking note of my forty-eighth birthday, he wrote:

No one in our families has ever reached anywhere near the accomplishment you have. And don't think we aren't proud. You should just hear your mother's glowing account of our young- est. Guess you aren't so young anymore. 48 is it? You haven't reached the midpoint (50) yet. After that it gets easier. If you live to 80 and enjoy life as much as I have, you should see nothing but joy ahead. Really, life is pleasant . . .

Your Dad 79¾

I'm glad that he was proud of me and that he felt a sense of content- ment his later years. But it was a cruel fate that he died only three years later. He thought it was a rotten trick that, like so many of his relatives, he got cancer after all. At age eighty-three, he thought he had evaded that ominous family destiny. It was a very short, painful, and sad few months between the startling diagnosis and his death. This dreaded illness is one thing I hope *not* to inherit from my father, but I see the outline of his face in mine (my son Will eerily resem- bles him), and I feel his temperament in my bones: his deep reserve, his love of language, his irreverent wit, his strength of will. Although I could never match his masterful problem-solving, his meticulous orderliness, or his ingenious inventiveness, I am my father's daugh- ter all right, just as I am my mother's. Indeed, played out in me are the jarring incongruities of my paternal and maternal inheritance.

MOTHER

In Kate Chopin's "The Story of the Hour," a woman experiences an instinctive flash of joy on hearing that her husband is dead.[3] (It turns out he is not dead.) I always thought this was a wickedly hon- est rendering of how a person in a less-than-fully-satisfactory mar- riage might feel in such a circumstance. I'm positive, though, that joy was not what my mother, Bernice, experienced upon hearing of my father's death. An openly expressive person, she felt a torrent of grief, sorrow, and deep anguish. She had been a loyal and dutiful wife for nearly fifty-seven years, and to the end, she was a solicitous nurse, doing all she could do, then grieving and burying her man with all proper respect, and surely missing him as well.

Nonetheless, I couldn't help but observe that Mother seemed to be a happier widow than she was a wife. After the initial mourning period, an unmistakable lilt lifted her telephone voice. She had a

Mother, Judy, and Joanne (and Topsy) at the Ranger Station in Pound, Wisconsin, ca. 1944

new-found resilient cheerfulness, without a trace of that telltale self-pity, and an intrepid hardiness, an acceptance of whatever would come with a new philosophical calm. She was animated by a new self-confidence and proud self-reliance.

Why was this so? I suspect that Bernice, at age seventy-eight, found a kind of independence that she had not openly and fully enjoyed before. Better late than never, I thought. I liked this version of Mother, with her strengths at full sail, not held back with a begrudging kowtowing to cardboard male authority. Indeed, without Daddy, whom we all deeply loved and admired, we metamorphosed into a new family constellation, a circle of energetic, independent, cheerful women: my sister, my mother, and me. Undoubtedly I grew to appreciate Mother, but she grew to a new calm, a self-acceptance of herself as a pretty "smart" person too.

As I think about it, so much of my family history is about being "smart" or not. Bernice Blachowiak, with a goodly portion of natural intelligence, was from a very early age taught to devalue herself, a lesson she could never quite stomach, and so she lived in conflict with herself and her heritage as a woman, although she wouldn't allow herself to face the conflict openly. Indeed, in many ways my parents were each raised in prototypical gender roles: my father was the eldest son and my mother the youngest daughter in large families. Each was expected to follow a traditional gender pattern—and each did.

Mother's parents were Polish immigrants who came to this country around 1900 and ended up running a farm in Beaver, Wisconsin. When they retired, they moved to a house in Pound, just a few doors away from the Ranger Station where we first lived, so my sister and I saw them fairly often. When our parents took winter vacations, she and I stayed with them. Of sturdy peasant stock, both grandparents lived well into their nineties. To me, my grandfather was a genial old man who could speak only broken English and who seemed to spend most of his time either sitting in a rocking chair or puttering around the yard. (I did learn some impressive Polish swear words from him.) Grandma, in contrast, spoke heavily accented English well, and although she had never received any formal schooling, she taught herself to read and write in English. She read the newspaper, kept up with politics and world events, and bustled about with great energy.

But I know my mother had great affection and admiration for her father. A risk-taker, he had been pretty lively and adventuresome in his day. In fact, he and my grandmother had come to America twice around the turn of the century, going back to Poland when he inherited a farm. In danger of being conscripted into the Russian Army for a second time, he left Poland again after a couple of years in a great hurry, taking as subterfuge a load of potatoes into Germany and fleeing from there. Always the competent one, my grandmother was left to sell the farm and pack up the family. They moved first to Chicago where my grandfather worked in a factory and my grandmother as a seamstress. But fond of trade and barter, my grandfather eventually traded his house in Chicago for a farm in Wisconsin, sight unseen, where my mother was born. Apparently it was rather a bad bargain since the farmhouse in particular was in a sorry state.

Later he traded that farm for another in Beaver, a short distance from Pound, where my mother lived most of her childhood.

Bernice went to the grade school across the street from their farm, followed lovingly for a time by a young pig that had formed an attachment to her, because she nurtured it after its own mother rejected this runt of the litter. Eventually, to her grief, this pet was slaughtered and found its way to the family dinner table; sentimentality about animals had no place on a working farm. I've come to view this story as emblematic of my mother's fate (especially as she self-pityingly saw it): her pleasure was readily sacrificed for the welfare of others.

Although she loved school, she was not allowed to go to high school, even after begging and pleading, because her parents thought education was wasted on girls. Ironically, her brothers were forced to attend, against their own strong disinclination, and frequently played hooky. Undoubtedly, Bernice was shaped and scarred by the unapologetic sexism within her family that favored boys and put down girls, this dismissal of the importance of her "mind," this imposed gender classification and limitation. On one level she internalized, accepted, and conjoined this sexism with a generalized ethnic devaluation: she was nothing but a "dumb Polack." On the other hand, she rebelled against it. She was embarrassed by her limited education for the rest of her life, but that didn't prevent her from having strong opinions or from airing them vociferously.

Put down or not, she made the best of her opportunities. Displaying the adventurous spirit in her genes, she took off for Chicago at age fifteen, finding work as a housekeeper, making just enough money to afford the weekly dances featuring the music of the big bands. She loved this life and was disheartened when she was called back to Beaver by her parents, who wanted her to help out with a new venture, a grocery store, just down the road from their farm in Beaver. But a dutiful daughter, she obeyed the summons and joined her brother Frank in running the country store. Freedom and independence were only temporary—girls were expected to serve their parents and their brothers, and eventually their husbands.

Unwisely playing favorites among their children, Bernice's parents had special fondness for Frank, to whom they intended to give the store when they retired, just as Johnny, another son, was to have the farm. For some reason, the store papers were made out in Frank's name from the beginning. Guided by some evil impulse, Frank decided that he wanted the store right away, rather than later, and he stole the papers from the homestead and later took his parents to court. Bernice testified for her parents, but it was to no avail: Frank perjured himself and contradicted her testimony. The store became his alone, much to the chagrin of his family, none of whom would have anything to do with him for decades.

Many years later, shortly before my grandmother died, Frank begged for and received her forgiveness, and cool relations were established among the brothers and sisters after that, but I don't think my mother ever truly gave Frank her full love and trust, although she tried. The two of them were the last surviving children in the family of eight siblings. In an act of reconciliation, she invited Uncle Frank, Aunt Stella, and their children to her eightieth birthday celebration, and that was the first time I ever talked with two cousins, Don and Elmer, who were then well into middle age. What a loss, for they seemed to be well worth knowing and lamented the family schism as well.

Bernice was twenty when she met Bill Vanish at Bogard's dance hall. She was tall and attractive, popular and gregarious, never wanting for dance partners (by her own proud recording). It's no wonder that my father singled her out. While he didn't go in for polkas, jitterbugs, and other fast dances, he could do a slinky, long-stepped waltz. Together they were very striking partners; in fact, in later years they won prizes for their dancing more than once. They married in 1936 and settled down to raise a family. But Bernice was told by the doctor that she couldn't have children. So, deciding she would have a career as a beautician, she studied beauty culture. Fortunately for my sister and me, she persisted in her wish to have children, and after a minor surgical procedure, she got pregnant, birthing Judy first, then me two years later.

But having entertained the idea of a career, Mother was not content to spend her life raising children. Before I started grade school, she opened Pound Beauty Shop in the old hotel on Main Street; later, after my parents built a house at the end of Main Street, she set up shop in its upstairs. As a toddler, with my sister in school, I would go with my mother to the beauty shop and hang out listening to the ladies talk. Often I would sit on the curb, watching the world go by. Mother was a very successful beautician: she worked on volume, setting a number of heads into production at various stages: washing, cutting, curling, crimping, setting, drying. Her shop was a cheerful place full of bustle, gossip, and chattering ladies. "Bea" was loved by her customers, and she, in turn, loved the work. She didn't say so though; instead, she complained a lot. She worked flat-out—sometimes until her fingers bled from too much shampooing and contact with chemicals—and then she came home. Exhausted and crabby, she'd say, "I work my fingers to the bone for you!" She claimed that her working was for the welfare of the family, that she made possible the lifestyle that wouldn't have been possible without it. This is no doubt true. It is also true that she drew identity, purpose, energy, and self-esteem from this work.

She also got great sustenance from her friends in Pound. A number of women came together casually for "coffee clutching" and more formally as "the Club," which met every Thursday evening to play cards, dress up, drink, talk, eat, and generally have a good time, and that they did. Club night at one's house meant that husband and children cleared off while the high spirited ladies gathered in the living room, emitting periodic gales of laughter. Sometimes we would surreptitiously listen to the innuendo and try to piece together the fascinating, taboo gossip. The Club also had special outings, usually at "the lake," White Potato Lake, where many of the families in the town had summer cottages. Members of the Club went "treeing" every Christmas season, visiting each other's houses, and they threw birthday parties for each other. Lasting more than fifty years, the Club was a model of affectionate, tenacious female bonding and friendship; the ladies saw each other through the good times and bad; through pregnancy, childbearing and all the stages of child-rearing; through accidents, illnesses, infidelities, a suicide, and death of children; and finally through the stages of old age, widowhood, and death.

I've always envied these deep and sustaining friendships, this rootedness in the nurturing soil of multigenerational community. This is what I lost when I moved away and the deprivation is not inconsequential. By birthright, however, I'm a legacy of the Club and of the larger community from which it is drawn. Until our mother's death at age ninety-seven, when she was the last living member of this group, my sister and I were tenuously linked to this world by our deeply connected mother, who gave regular reports about Pound denizens and their children, grandchildren, and great-grandchildren, determined, as she was, to maintain the ties that bind.

When we were children Mother set up Father as the authority, the smart one, who could solve any perplexing school lesson. His was the standard that supposedly ruled the house: "Ask your father"; "What would your father say?!" In contrast, she characterized herself as a "dummy." Although she apparently felt it was her duty to express this deference, her heart wasn't in it; she couldn't suppress herself, couldn't resist putting in her two cents or taking charge of most things, including just about all aspects of our upbringing. She was a stern taskmistress. She ran the family like a general. Having been beaten herself as a child—in fact, she had to go out and select the stick that would be used for beating—she was quick to slap, shout, and punish. Under her command, Judy and I from a young age were expected to contribute to the household. Every Saturday morning, we had to thoroughly clean the house and "bake something." Every day we set the table, peeled the potatoes, started supper cooking, and washed the dishes. Regularly, we mowed the lawn, weeded the garden, picked the vegetables, cleaned the basement or garage, went to the store, and carried out the countless other tasks given to us by our Chief Executive. It seemed that other children had much more time to play; we always had our "work" to do first.

Did we carry out Mother's orders obediently? Yes, we could do no less, because she exacted our obedience. Did we do so cheerfully? Not always. But she tolerated not even a modicum of resistance: "Don't look at me in that tone of voice!" was one of her frequent expressions. My sister mastered the art of the nonresponse, passive aggression, which was as effective as it was maddening, just as she intended it to be. Always more passionate and willful, I sometimes provoked a battle of wills. For example, Mother would demand that we eat everything put on the table. I happened to loathe liver and peas. I would count out twenty peas—the minimal acceptable number—and try to down them, but I would invariably gag on the liver and frequently run into the bathroom to spit it out. Then I would come back to the table and be forced to try again to eat it, and so the ritual was repeated until my plate was clean. In the battle of wills, my parents always won, but not without strengthening the resolve and covert rebellion of the subjugated. "I'm going to run away from home!" I swore to my sister more than once. Of course, it was an empty threat.

Mother was very concerned with appearances and propriety. No surprise, I suppose, from someone in the beauty business. Judy and I were told many times (is everyone?) that we must put on clean underwear "in case we were in an accident." But church evoked the most-scrupulous regime of keeping up appearances. Mass was, I sometimes thought, a fashion show where you wore your Sunday-best and looked around to assess what everyone else was wearing. Child of my mother, I long retained excessive self-consciousness about my appearance. Facing the public required careful primping.

Not only were we expected to dress properly, so too should our house pass inspection; no slacking off was allowed. Never was an unwashed cup or glass left on the sink or the dishes drying on a rack. Housecleaning never made the grade if the mopboards were not thoroughly dusted and the furniture was not moved and vacuumed. House rules took precedence over all else. In high school, I was responsible for making Friday-night dinner and cleaning up before I could go out, because Mother worked that evening. I remember vividly my boyfriend, who was captain of the basketball team, hurriedly helping me do the dishes right before a big game.

Mother valued being attractive to the opposite sex, so she was pleased that I had boyfriends. But she was a worrier. She would lay awake at night waiting for me to come home. If I was slow getting from the car to the house after a date, she challenged me when I came in. If I dated one person a long time, she feared I would "come home with a bundle" or would get married, and she fretted that my boyfriends were usually not Catholic. Of course, I had no intention of marrying any of these boys; I lived in anticipation of life in college.

She conceded the territory of academics. This was an area where her smart husband and her daughters clearly held the high ground. "I don't know nothin' about that," she would say with self-effacement. "I'm just a dumb Polack." But just because we were allegedly smart didn't mean we were good. "Don't think you're so smart," she would frequently say. Being good was far more important than being smart. But Mother was proud of Judy and me and beamed over our sterling academic records in particular. She would bore her friends and customers with tales of the accomplishments of "her girls." She was an unfailing booster club, attending all school events. And I must say that her appreciative, unmistakable laugh was always reassuringly distinguishable in the audience.

Later, when I was dropped off at college for the first time, I remember looking out the window of my new dorm room to see my mother disconsolately crying. I didn't share her grief at the time; I was elated to have finally gotten away from home and entered a world of new adventures. But Mother got her belated revenge; I found myself sharing her sentiments when, thirty-four years later, we dropped our son off at his dorm.

I see now that Mother got a great deal of vicarious pleasure out of my high school activities, experiences she was denied in her adolescence. Of course, releasing the last child from strict parental control is hard to do, and it is an understatement to say that she had a lot of advice and prescriptions for proper living to offer. My sister was exceptional: she was very smart and very tall; she was likely to have a life that didn't fit into an ordinary mold. Therefore, I should fulfill Mother's more traditional ideas of success. She thought I should go to college, to be sure, but with carefully prescribed aims. Learn a nice respectable occupation such as school teaching and then get married, have lots of children, settle down close to home, and live a "normal" life. But the more my mother pushed me in one direction, the more the rebel arose in me, the more fervidly I resisted.

Over the years, she became increasingly alarmed as I went for one academic degree after another. She feared I would be both uprooted from my origins and, worst of all, unmarried. Her ominous warning was: "Men don't like women who are too smart." This remark became an ironic epigram in my consciousness over the years, but my mother knew its truth in her heart, having been confronted with it all her life. These old wives' tales had some measure of truth for me too; that's why they were so irritating. Well into my middle age, Mother continued to worry and fret and try to tell me what to do. She was deeply suspicious of the university culture with all those hippies, free-thinkers, and atheists dominating the scene. She was terribly upset when I (and my sister) stopped going to church and tried through various self-dramatizing means to instill the guilt that would effect a change in our behavior and faith: "I'm going to hell because of you"; "I don't know how I could have been such a terrible mother."

Once I finally got married, she was upset that we didn't have children for a number of years. In happy anticipation she had even had my father build a sandbox on their property. "What's that for?" I asked one day. "For the grandchildren," she said sheepishly. Long before the advent of our son William, seven years after getting married, the box had been sadly dismantled. Again she has her revenge. I, like my mother before me, am still poignantly waiting for my first grandchild. Now, I understand what she felt.

When my parents visited my adult residences, I would go into a frenzy of housecleaning, knowing that I could never meet my mother's standards but trying nonetheless. But inevitably, some items needed correcting. Often she thought my appearance, especially my hair (or Tom's or William's), not "right." A topic that I tried to avoid but often couldn't was politics. I was committed to liberal values (as was my sister), while Mother became an increasingly outspoken conservative, whose reactionary views were fueled by her dedicated watching of Fox News. She would go into diatribes about how, when she was young, she *worked*, not like those lazy welfare free-loaders. Invariably, she would lambast candidates whom Judy and I strongly supported: George McGovern, Bill Clinton, and Barack Obama aroused her visceral repugnance. I used to joke that no one needed to take opinion polls to learn what Middle America was thinking: just ask my mother. Daddy was often silent and enigmatic during these conversations. It was hard to know what he thought: Mother always dominated the discourse, but that didn't mean that she necessarily ruled the roost. She not only had recalcitrant children to deal with but lived with a bullheaded husband who did things *his* way.

My leaving for college was soon coupled with another major life transition, my father's early retirement. My parents sold their house in town and built a new one on Left Foot Lake, about ten miles north of Pound. Mother didn't retire herself but instead set up a beauty shop in the basement of her new house. Although she continued to see her friends and go to the Club, she experienced the pangs of physical and psychic separation from town and the social fabric of the life she had known. This move was one of her many self-pitying "sacrifices" to accommodate the wishes of my father.

Gregarious, chatty, high spirited, my mother liked being around people. Reclusive, introverted, reserved, my father was uncomfortable in social settings and craved the solitude and the sustenance of nature. While absorbed in the life they created at Left Foot Lake, Mother would nonetheless sometimes feel oppressed and depressed by the daily routine and isolation away from stimulating social interaction of town. Daddy never wanted to "do" anything. I knew from the tone of her telephonic voice, moreover, that sometimes old tensions surfaced in their relationship; they achieved only temporary truces, not sustained compatibility. Not even the celebration of their fiftieth wedding anniversary relieved the tension. They renewed their marital vows and were feted by dozens of friends and family, but in the car driving home, Daddy responded to some concern she was expressing: "Oh shut up, you old battle axe!"

I have often puzzled over their temperamental incompatibilities. How did they get together? Why did they stay together? It wasn't easy. They got under each other's skin and bickered unpleasantly over small things. They got deeply angry with each other and shouted mean-spirited invective that would terribly upset me as a child. But they were Catholic, they had vowed to stick together through better or worse, and that they did. They stuck it out, with strong wills clashing, with deep-seated differences rubbing raw, with some pretty tough times, including the tortures and indignities of Daddy's alcoholism, weighing heavily.

But clearly bad times were interspersed with good. They showed a strong attraction and abiding respect for one another in spite of everything. When one of them was ill, the other quickly and generously assumed the role of solicitous and caring nurse. They had a storehouse of shared memories. Their lives were intertwined with friends, church, community, and, of course, "the children" and, in later years, their beloved grandchild, William, who gave them great joy. They had a grandchild to cherish at last, and I'm so glad his life was enriched by their deep rootedness in place, history, and family.

In addition to their strong wills, Daddy and Mother had more in common than might first be apparent. Neither was content with "doing nothin'." They had a congenital need to keep busy. They each had a deep capacity for "work," not only because it was necessary but because it was engaging, challenging, and satisfying. They both had more energy than could be absorbed in routine work, so Daddy occupied himself with woodworking and beekeeping, repairing and inventing, reading and learning, and Mother, with sewing and handicrafts, painting and ceramics, cooking and canning, garden-

Bill and Bernice
in Retirement

ing and decorating. Together and separately they tackled innumerable home-improvement projects, for they both invested themselves deeply in the making of "home."

Not surprisingly, Mother and Daddy maintained the home at Left Foot Lake like a well-run country estate. They were proud of their self-sufficiency, living off the land to a large extent. My father chopped the logs on his own land and fed them to their wood-burning furnace. They ate seasonal berries and apples from the wild and vegetables from the garden—fresh, canned, and frozen. They cut their Christmas tree from their own plantation, and they kept the house and grounds in impeccable order.

But then Daddy died. Mother seemed distraught and unlikely to carry on alone at Left Foot Lake estate, which was so much to manage. While she considered relocating, what she immediately moved out the house was Daddy's presence—his clothes and other possessions. "He's got so much stuff all over the place, there's no room." Soon she took over his chair: "It's so much more comfortable than

Judy and Joanne with Mother, Age Ninety-Five

mine." Although she professed her eagerness to get rid of all his tools and equipment, she gradually started using them: "They're so handy." Before long she was driving his truck, hauling wood, and mowing the lawn on his riding lawnmower. She confronted problems around the house that he had dealt with in the past, either fixing them herself with solutions sometimes more elegant than any Daddy had devised (at least in her view) or hiring someone to tackle them. She took pride in her competence and gained confidence in her self-reliance. Well into her eighties, she undertook daunting tasks: she got up on a ladder to paint the trim and clean the gutters on the house, she raked and hauled the leaves, she shoveled the snow. She got more pleasure out of solitary self-sufficiency than she or anyone else might have expected. Perhaps she had grown to be like Daddy, after all. Certainly she seems deeply rooted in the place on Left Foot Lake, which they had made home for over twenty-five years.

But her social side was not quelled. Whereas Daddy had always balked at going on trips, she was always more ready to take off, and now she indulged her whim, planning visits to her daughters and to her niece and joining overnight trips sponsored by her church. She stepped up her community-service activities. And, while never heavy, she lost weight, adding to her svelte appearance. Always a very attractive woman, she continued to turn heads well into her nineties because she dressed impeccably and moved with such energy and verve.

She was an impressive woman, my mother, more impressive in her later years than when she was trying unsuccessfully to hold herself back. She always had incredible strength. She had faced more than her fair share of illness, cheerfully surviving many surgeries and battling multiple disabilities including macular degeneration; uterine, colon, and skin cancers; heart disease; high blood pressure; neuropathy; broken bones; and more. Repeatedly, she came out a survivor; she was indeed "a tough old bird," as my father called her, and that toughness remained well into her eighties and nineties, fortified by her newfound independence. During those nineteen years after Daddy's death, she was, for the first time in her life, truly on her own, without others to look after and to tell her what to do or to hold her back.

And she relished it. She was proud of herself and I was proud of her. She earned the freedom to be unapologetically and imposingly herself. And, indisputably, she continued to be proud of Judy and me. She never tired of bragging about "her girls." While in earlier years she had tried to dissuade me from pursuing an academic career, she applauded my achievements and was present for milestone events such as my inauguration at Mount Holyoke and the celebration of my presidency marking the end of it. She was undoubtedly my most enthusiastic and reliable cheerleader. I could always count on her abiding interest, concern, and support.

But, of course, Mother couldn't go on forever. Nor was her proud independence without shortcomings, including its painful loneliness and increasing impracticality. "I don't want to be a burden," she said, and she was not, soldiering on alone while we were hundreds of miles away, living separate lives, calling her once a week, and seeing her typically only two or so times a year. But in her nineties, she started to slow down, to experience more and more episodes of illness requiring emergency trips to the hospital. The cruelly debilitating blindness that accompanied macular degeneration narrowed and darkened her world, making it increasingly impossible for her to live without daily assistance, even though she belligerently clung to living alone and keeping her house.

She was the last surviving member of her family and her circle of friends, although ever gregarious and charismatic, she attracted new, younger friends who visited often and watched out for her, especially neighbors at the lake. She could not have survived living alone as long as she did, however, without the loving services of Pat Resch, who was on call night and day. She was handywoman, housekeeper, nurse, driver, shopper, cook, bookkeeper, loyal and trusted friend, and even surrogate daughter, much more attentive than her own daughters were.

Mother was thrilled when her beloved grandson, at age thirty-five, was finally getting married in December 2011. She was determined to be at the wedding. So she, a legally blind ninety-six-year-old, intrepidly flew on her own to Washington, D.C., and then joined Judy in driving to Charlottesville, Virginia, for the wedding and travelled afterward to my home in Philadelphia for Christmas. There was no faulting her courage, spunk, and high spirits, and it was wonderful to have her at these festivities, making the celebration complete. All the time, though, she was teetering on the edge of functionality. Even so, she made it back home, chattering away, as usual, with newfound friends on the plane, thoroughly enjoying her outing, and then settling back into living on her own at Left Foot Lake.

It became an annual ritual in our family to gather in Wisconsin for the celebration of Mother's birthday on June 21 and Will's on June 22. We faithfully convened in June of 2012 for a celebration that was made even better by the perfect summer weather of beautiful northern Wisconsin, the presence of Lisa, Will's wonderful new wife, and the bittersweet realization that these family rituals could not go on forever. It was sad to see how chair-bound Mother had become, she who had been forever popping up, never sitting still. Still, she gamely joined in festivities, even continuing to play Crazy Eight with color-coded cards and gigantic numbers she could barely make out. Near the end of our visit, she suddenly seemed confused and unable to control her limbs. Of course, we called Pat who immediately came over and dealt with the issue, administering an antidote that got her back to normal.

Little did we know, though, that Mother's period of well-being was to be so foreshortened. During a hot spell in mid-July, she got dehydrated and delirious and ended up in the local hospital in Marinette. Hospital staff put Mother into a regular room, not the ICU, and apparently they failed to monitor her closely. Sometime during the night, she must have attempted to get up. She was later found lying on the floor and unconscious with a head injury. No one knew how long she'd been there. She was rushed by ambulance to a larger hospital in Green Bay where, my sister observed with horror, the staff's inept attempt to hold down our hysterical mother resulted in the x-ray machine banging hard against her head.

This second blow was too much for her. She never regained consciousness. The doctors told us that she had significant cranial bleeding and could not recover without irreparable damage. We made the painful decision to move to palliative care and began the death watch, which went on for several days. Our tough, old mother clung to life even then. I was glad to be there for her last few days, even though she was unconscious. I got a chance to tell her I loved her; I hope she understood. I know a big smile flashed on her face when grandson Will spoke to her on the phone. I was holding her hands when she quietly stopped breathing, peacefully relinquishing her hold on life, not on our hearts and minds.

Mother had been a formidable presence in our lives, and she remains so even in death. But death is only the beginning of the process of closing out a person's life. We had the funeral to plan, her possessions to sort through, her homestead to dispose of, the legal issues to resolve, including, not incidentally, the culpability of both hospitals in her head injuries. But we were advised we could do nothing about the catastrophic carelessness of the hospitals. We felt terrible that we could neither protect nor avenge her when she was most helpless and in most need.

The Left Foot Lake house seemed empty and bereft without her, even though her presence was everywhere instantiated in the kitsch and "old things" she loved to collect and display. She and Daddy had lovingly constructed and maintained the Vanish homestead; they made it distinctly their own. But, putting sentiment aside and with the pressure of time, we set about the process of deconstruction, disposal, and divestment, taking only a few things and then, in a surprise development, selling the house and grounds and all the contents as a single package to a lucky buyer before the week was out. It took us longer to dispose of the "damned shack" down the road, which our parents rented out. When it too was sold within a few months, our tangible connection to the world of our parents was rapidly coming to an end. But abrupt and hasty as all of this was, it wasn't an end easy to make.

I saw William go around the homestead and take last mournful views of the rushing "crick" where he so often went swimming, the shimmering lake across from the house, Grandpa's towering tree plantation, and all the other memory-filled places of good times with Grandma and Grandpa and friend Bennett during those splendid summer vacations of his childhood and, over the years, annual birthday celebrations with the family. For me and, I suspect, for Judy, the resonance was even greater, because the roots were deeper. Mother had been the glue that bound us together, connecting our childhood and our adulthood, our past and our present, even our lives to one another. She was still wound into the fabric of the close-knit community we had left behind. She maintained ties to extended family and friends, and their children and grandchildren, to church, and to rootedness in place. However frayed and attenuated those connections were for us, it was still comforting that she held them together in her mind and we could be drawn back to the place where she was so much at home.

Indeed, her world was the only constant locale in my life, a place I found so limiting and dull when I left home at eighteen years old. Needing room to grow, I, like Joyce's Stephen Daedalus, attempted to "fly by the nets" of family, gender, class, culture, and religion.[4] With an implicit faith in books and learning, I gave my allegiance to *alma maters*, and found, to be sure, much fulfillment in this life. Looking back now, though, I am more poignantly aware of how much I gave up, and I am grateful to Mother for insisting on a connection for so long. But clearly, maintaining that connection would not be possible without her; thus, we were doubly bereft, losing not only our mother but also our "home." Now, we really can't go home again. When we drove away, we knew we would probably never come back. Indeed, we did not want to see the changes that would inevitably set in when the formative Vanish presence *vanished* from "the little postage stamp of native soil."

Judy and Joanne around Ages Six and Four

} 2 {

SISTERS

She was my sister, my fate, my example, her effect on me was incalculable—
Margaret Drabble, *The Waterfall*

I didn't come into a *tabula rasa* world: it was already inhabited by my sister, Judy, two years, two months, and two days older. My sister's presence was one of the most significant defining dimensions of my early life. Anything I did, she had done first, charting out the territory and serving as a guide to it. Sometimes I appreciated her formative example; other times I rebelled against it, trying to find my own space, my own separate self. Only with decades of trying, did I finally succeed.

Sisters close in age are as children likely to live in a "merged" world where much is shared, and sometimes it is difficult to sort out what is mine and what is thine. Nancy Chodorow discussed this phenomenon in her post-Freudian analysis of the "permeable boundaries" between women.[1] Of course, most centrally Judy and I shared our parents and the way they shaped and circumscribed our world. In some ways we were a unit, "the Vanish girls," whose purpose, it sometimes seemed, was to shed credit on our parents. Our behavior was expected to be exemplary in every way and everyday, and if it was not, we were scolded, slapped, or issued a punishment. It was a given that we should be smarter, better behaved, cleaner, more polite, and harder working than other folks' children. It was never clear why that should be the case. It simply *was*. Ingrained early and deeply was the view that we were contributing members of the household who were expected, cheerfully and without question, to carry out the tasks authoritatively assigned to us by our mother.

Most of the time Judy and I accepted these orders with reasonable cheerfulness and set about to accomplish our tasks with dispatch. Little did we know we were honing the administrative skills that would serve us well later in life. We early discovered the efficiency of the division of labor: Judy would wash and I would dry; she would vacuum and I would dust. We also learned that work could be made more palatable if it had built-in rewards, so she would mow once around the lawn while I lounged and vice versa. We didn't exactly whistle while we worked (I could never master it), but we did sing while doing the dishes on many days. All in all, we learned quite a bit about sharing from our shared fate.

We painstakingly saved money from our weekly allowance, our earnings selling apples and pine cones, and other enterprises, and then we splurged on a special treat. But given the limitations of our finances, it was a special shared treat. Our first big purchase was a scooter. Next we moved up to a bike. More than a year later, we finally accumulated enough cash to purchase a second bike. Until then we managed sharing one bike and one scooter well enough, and although we found a great deal to argue and bicker about in the general course of events, I don't remember any arguments over our chief goals—those on which we had broad areas of implicit agreement.

Our sharing was not limited to our working life. We shared a room, a bed, and most of our leisure hours, which we filled with "structured" activities. As children of our parents, we were never comfortably idle but always "doing something." When we weren't drawn into activities with other kids in town, Judy and I still had each other for playmates and companions. We read a great deal, including complete series of Cherry Ames, Nancy Drew, and the Bobbsey Twins books, among many others. We were looking in literature for models of how to live a girl's life. But we weren't narrow feminists. Our comic book collection was dominated by the usual male heroes: Superman and Batman with a few copies of Wonder Woman thrown in. And we regularly traded what we owned with other kids in the town.

Judy and I keep "secret" journals of our creative writing in an attic hideaway. We were also aficionados of games. We had an impressive collection. One box had forty-eight different games in one; we tried them all. And we perfected our skills through innumerable contests. When friends came over to play our games, one of us almost always won, not a very companionable thing to do. I still remember the day

Bonnie picked up handfuls of letters from Scrabble and threw them all over the kitchen in frustration at losing again.

But it was not really share and share alike; the cards were stacked against me. My sister, after all, was older, bigger, and smarter. In truth, she usually won the games (although I won when she didn't play). She could and did boss me around. "Get me the milk," she would imperiously say when we were at the dinner table, and dutiful little sister that I was, I would obey her—then wonder why. It was, I suppose, out of habit, for in so many ways she was the pioneer and I was the follower. I was used to being at least one-down in this family of strong-minded individuals.

More times than I can remember, I bore the brunt of family jokes, and sometimes Judy joined in belittling me. I remember that after my first day of school, I told the family about our first test. The teacher asked a series of questions, and new pupils were supposed to circle the right picture to answer. For the question, "What goes fastest?" the choices were a plane, a car, and a horse. In truth this was the most-puzzling question of all to me. At home I told my family hesitantly that I circled the horse. "Oh, no!" my sister burst out in derisive laughter. "You are going to flunk first grade!"

Judy was the first to go to school, of course. She was three years ahead of me because of a December birthday. (Mine regrettably was in February.) I looked with envy at this exciting world she had entered, while I was cooling my heels on the curb in front of mother's beauty shop on Main Street. Judy tried to satisfy some of my yearning by playing teacher with a small blackboard easel our father had made. When I finally got to school, I already knew the lessons and was rather bored. Somehow I missed the freshness of the first-hand experience, a situation that would repeat in other instances in my life as well. Eager to get ahead, I vicariously shared my sister's experiences, but my own became somehow secondhand and seemingly second-best.

Not only were my adventures not really new, they were not applauded with the same enthusiasm. So I started school. So what? It was a terrain already charted by Judy. So what if I got all A's; isn't that normal from the "Vanish girls"? Each new experience or honor she had already experienced, and the fanfare was dimmer for me. How could I earn respect and gain self-confidence with this achiever always blazing the trail before me? As exasperating as this problem was, in truth, I admired my sister and sought to emulate her. She was my model; she set a standard; I wanted to match her.

I was well into my adulthood when I discovered the novelist Margaret Drabble. I noticed that she too was working her way through a relationship with a sister. No one needed to tell me that Drabble was a younger sister; it takes one to know one; I could read it in her novels. When Jane Gray in Drabble's *The Waterfall* says about her cousin Lucy, "She was my sister, my fate, my example, her effect on me was incalculable," I understand perfectly what she means.[2] Imitation is the sincerest form of flattery. But later, when I read *The Game* by Margaret Drabble's older sister, A. S. Byatt, I was surprised and disturbed by its depiction of the elder sister's point of view. In 1987 I wrote an academic paper comparing how the sisterly bond was presented in the fiction of the two Drabble sisters (both have acknowledged their vexed sisterly relationship).[3] Subsequently, Judy and I used this paper to try to understand each other's perspective. Not an easy thing to do.

As children we would sometimes divide up pieces of our shared world in noncompeting halves. In jewelry, I liked silver, Judy gold. In chicken, I liked wings, Judy drumsticks. Sometimes we angrily asserted the division: "Stay off of *my* side of the bed!" "Don't mess with *my* things!" But more important aspects of experience were less easily divided. Judy thought that she was Father's special child and I was our Mother's, but this didn't seem the least bit satisfactory to me. I wanted Daddy's love too, and I'm sure she wanted Mother's. In fact, I don't think that our parents played favorites in this way; at least they tried not to. But as a child, I took on myself responsibility for any apparent diminishment of my father's regard. If he didn't respond to me with quite the same respect he had for Judy, I somehow missed the mark, was unequal to the standard of "smartness" she exemplified. Our mother had a different way of dividing up the pie: Judy was the "smart" one; I was the "pretty" one. Judy would succeed through academic achievement; I would conquer through my social value. Of course, this was unsatisfactory too. I wanted to be "smart," and Judy wanted to be "pretty." It wasn't enough to have half a pie; we each wanted it all.

Yet what I hadn't fully appreciated until I read Byatt's *The Game* was how an elder sister might feel about her sister's incursions into *her* territory. To be sure, I was aware that my sister sometimes found me a nuisance and didn't always want me to join in the tête-à-tête she had with friends her age. But I presumed the territory ahead was big enough for two. But in Byatt's *The Game*, Cassandra, the elder, recoils snake-like: "Like certain reptiles she had learned to survive by leaving in Julia's hand the dead stump of the tail by which she had been grasped. One could even, she thought, sacrifice a more necessary limb, a hand, a foot, which would not grow again, and still survive. One could do this forever, so long as one was not touched to the quick." Cassandra's method of coping with her sister—perfected in childhood—is to withdraw and then to obliterate consciousness: "After a time she could usually reduce herself to being conscious of nothing, blank space in the head." My sister too had mastered the art of impassivity and silence, maddening not only Mother but me as well, just as she intended to.

As she got older, Judy would more often slip away from me into the deep silences of adolescence, which I could not penetrate. Sometimes, she miserably cried herself to sleep. I knew some of the causes, and my heart went out in sisterly sympathy. She may have gotten more glory for her accomplishments than I did, but she also experienced more pain. If her life was more exalted than mine, it was altogether more demanding. She had the high road; mine was lower. Judy was very smart, very tall. But she was misplaced both academically and socially in Coleman High School. A fretful parent and tough disciplinarian, Mother forbade Judy simple adolescent enjoyments, like going to "The Hut," a local hamburger joint, after football games. Her friends, preoccupied with boys, easily abandoned her as the odd girl out. Fortunately, the principal of the high school recognized Judy's academic abilities and asked my parents to let her try out for a Ford Foundation early admission scholarship. This was an experimental program that let exceptionally able students skip the final two years of high school and enroll directly as freshman in college on full scholarship. Judy won the scholarship, and after a great deal of angst and indecision in the family, she enrolled at only age fifteen in the University of Wisconsin.

This seemed to me to be an incredibly exciting new adventure in an alluring new world that brought Judy local fame and glory as well. She wrote ecstatic letters describing her experience and joy in college. I was happy for her and basked vicariously in her newfound happiness. But now, she was five years ahead of me in school, although only two years older. Judy's leap to university put a great deal of distance and psychological space between us. Still, where she led I wished to follow.

Whatever my misgivings, Judy dropping out of high school let me make its halls my territory. At first, though, her shadow still inhabited the ground. I was "Judy Vanish's sister," that "brain" who went to the University of Wisconsin. Her celebrity gave me some visibility and engendered a certain respect. On the first day of high school, much to my surprise, I was made president of my class of nearly one hundred students, even though I only knew the eight kids who came from my elementary school. I had, I suppose, a kind of reflected glory. The teachers remembered Judy with pride, and constant comparisons were inevitable.

Yet my experiences at Coleman High were much happier and more fulfilling than Judy's had been. Although I excelled in academics, I also became part of the social fabric in a way that had eluded my sister. I was tall, but not so tall that ruled out all the interesting boys in the school. I knew how to negotiate the culture, and I had a goodly measure of popularity, boyfriends and fun, experiencing the joys and trials of "normal" adolescence. I rebelled against excessive parental restriction and worked my way towards greater freedom and relaxation of strictures and a more comfortable relationship with my parents than my sister had enjoyed.

Moreover, I had teachers who took a strong interest in me and promoted my welfare. One, Mr. Slaney, knew of my intimidation by my sister. He tried to assure me that I was smart too. He looked up our IQ scores, and although he didn't reveal what they were, he said that mine was higher. I always suspected that he misread or misreported the results. I did tell my sister what he said, though, out of some ignominious need for her opinion or validation, never thinking how this might hurt her, until it was too late and I saw the effects. When I read *The Game*, I understood how the younger sister, Julia, needed Cassandra to know of her experiences and value. Byatt writes, "Julia needed to tell her [Cassandra] the details because whatever they had done was not real or finished until she had been made to be the audience, fully informed."[5] But it was one thing to strive to equal a sister's accomplishments; it was another seemingly to surpass them. I could not "top" my sister (or seem to) without guilt or denial.

To differentiate myself from Judy, I considered going to a different college, but no place was quite as alluring as the University of Wisconsin, and that's where I wanted to go. Judy and I shared a lot of tastes and appetites; I wanted the same things. She was the pioneer, but if she had not been, I'd like to think I would have done the same things myself. In my heart I knew, however, that wasn't quite true. I suspected she set a higher standard than I would have on my own.

The summer after my graduation from high school, I moved to Madison and lived with my sister in an apartment (and so, as was so typical, began my college experience before it actually began). Judy was finishing up her master's thesis, and I began working as an IBM key punch operator in the registration office of the University, a job that, of course, Judy had found for me and that employed me throughout college. We shared a companionable summer, and I gladly played the role of admiring and supportive younger sister, reading and typing her thesis and encouraging her to finish the thing. It was reminiscent of old times when we accomplished a task collaboratively and companionably through determined effort and a clear division of labor. At the end of the summer, she flew off to the University of Bristol in England on a Fulbright scholarship, and I set about the task of forging my own separate identity in the expansive university world, which was much more daunting than any place I had encountered before.

Judy had taken a two-year general-education program called Integrated Liberal Studies (ILS), which she loved, but I deliberately took a different curriculum. That first semester, I enrolled in a political science course that, unbeknownst to me, was taught by someone who had known Judy. As he read the roll, he stopped and asked, "Are you Judy Vanish's sister?" Later, during the class, after I made a remark, he observed, "You have a voice like your sister." After class, when I went up to the front to have him sign my program, he commented, "You have hands like Judy, too." The next day I dropped the class, determined not to play out my college experience as "Judy's sister."

And my university was not the same as Judy's. In fact, we had different academic interests and aptitudes. I majored in English, she in political science. I liked "big picture" thinking; Judy grounded herself in empirical analysis. But I was drawn inexorably over the years towards an academic career, just as she had been before me. Meanwhile, she fell in love and got married, and this experience, too, I looked upon with rapt curiosity and empathy. I was very pleased for Judy; she seemed to achieve in her young adulthood the "normality" and happiness that had eluded her as an adolescent.

I spent the summer between my junior and senior years in Berkeley, California, where my sister and her husband lived. I worked in the psychology lab at the University of California doing IBM key punching, again a job that my sister had found for me. I lived just down the street from Judy and Dick, saw them everyday, and observed close up both the pleasures and the tensions of their marriage, much like Jane observes her cousin Lucy's marriage in Drabble's *The Waterfall*: "I inspected their cutlery, their furniture, their wooden floors" for "the secret of matrimony, the secret key to being a woman and living with a man."[6]

But this scrutiny revealed that all was not well. Studying the same academic field as her husband, Judy seemed to feel that she should drop out of the competition and leave the field to him—lest she "beat" him at the game. While he was finishing his dissertation, she stopped working on hers. In retrospect, this inclination to "let go" of the territory was strikingly similar to Cassandra's releasing the "snake skin" in Byatt's novel, to try to protect her identity. Instead of doing her academic work, Judy took up other interests: she became a potter; she painted; she cooked. And, when not happily engrossed in these activities, she withdrew into herself. I didn't know how to help, and I left Berkeley, worried about her.

After I graduated from Wisconsin, I went to Harvard for a master's degree. Judy and Dick had meanwhile gone to Yale, where he began as a new assistant professor. The move exacerbated the fault lines in their marriage, and soon after, they separated. Struggling through a difficult transition of my own in Cambridge, I empathized with my sister and tried to keep in touch with her. But her way of coping was to cut me off—our parents too—creating tremendous anxiety and grief in the family. Like Cassandra in Byatt's *The Game*, Judy slipped away, leaving me to hold the snake skin while she was somewhere else. When visiting her, I was taken aback by her suppressed rage. "Don't you know that I am knitting my anger into this sweater?" she asked at one point. I hadn't, and I didn't know what to say.

For several years, Judy and I experienced a painful, tense, and inexplicable separation. She needed to sever all family connections. So I had no choice but to forge my way on my own, but our separation was not complete, only held in a curious lacunae. I continued on my inexorable march towards an academic career, much to Mother's dismay. Judy eventually returned to California, finished her degree, and took a teaching position. But, after a few years, she gave up her academic career and moved into public service, a fortuitous change that led to a distinguished thirty-three-year career at the Department Housing and Urban Development in highly responsible positions. The work clearly absorbed her attention and brought her much satisfaction. Sometimes, Judy articulated reasons for why she made the career shift: she liked the collaborative work of government; she disliked the petty politics of academia. But, in that painful sorting of our relationship occasioned by my essay on the Drabble sisters, she startled me by saying, "I gave up my academic career for you."

I tried to understand that view. She stressed how "motherly" she had always felt towards me, how much love and solicitude she had given me, how much pride she had in my development and achievements. This characterization surprised me, because I hadn't thought of her as a mother but as a model, a companion, a rival, a friend. I strove towards equality in our relationship. I wasn't looking for another mother, nor did her withdrawals and relinquishments feel like sisterly love. I wasn't without my baser motives. I admit to wanting to compete and sometimes even to win as a validation of my own right to be smart. I certainly suffered from the pangs of sibling rivalry, overlaid as it was with admiration and respect. Finally, though, I didn't accept that I was the cause of Judy's career shift. A piece of my newfound separation was having the courage to challenge the authority of my sister. She didn't "own" the whole territory of academia; there was plenty of space for both of us. We couldn't divide Mother and Daddy between us; we couldn't divide the world of experience either. We had to learn to share the space.

After I made the shift into college administration, it didn't occur to me that this career move too could be seen as an intrusion into my sister's world. Judy had already staked out the administrative territory, and there I was invading again. I suppose there is some validity to this view, but the dying eighty-five-year-old Pearl Tull in Ann Tyler's *Dinner at the Homesick Restaurant* gets it right when she asks about her middle-aged sons locked in sibling rivalry: "Honestly . . . wasn't there some statute of limitations here?"[7] I think there has to be, and over time and with work, I think Judy and I have built a mature separated relationship. Now we are each free to take a step without worrying about how it will affect the other. Our relationship, while still complicated by symbiotic tensions, is fueled by shared interests in books and politics, and a merged history, and it achieves, at times, the kind of equality and reciprocity that I aspired to all along.

But I have worried about whether this memoir is not again eerily duplicating Julia in *The Game* by writing about pieces of our shared world and so violating my sister's privacy. Julia justifies her action by thinking of her novel as "a way of coming to grips with Cassandra, but also of detaching us. It would be way of seeing her as a separate individual. Knowledge, after all, was love. A lighting up of the other." It is also an attempt to detach herself decisively from the symbiotic bond to her sister: "All her own efforts had been directed towards making the guilt real, weighty, binding. Because if it was real, then she was responsible. And if she was responsible she had a choice— her acts were her own. She could be detached from Cassandra."[8]

There are undoubtedly serious moral problems to ponder in the use of real situations and other people in published texts. It may well be that "writing is aggression . . . an imposition . . . an invasion of someone else's most private space," as Joan Didion puts it.[9] Yet I believe that, in the end, a woman must act assertively to claim her right to her territory, however "merged" and interconnected with others that space is. Sometimes women think that "to be good" is to be selfless and self-effacing. But our lives necessarily interpenetrate with others and that selfless "goodness" can be both unloving and self-annihilating. "When my sister was born, I lost my Garden of Eden," says Adrienne Rich.[10] But for Rich's younger sister, there was no Edenic "sister-less" world. She had to find identity in this merged space. The fictional worlds of both Drabble sisters demonstrate that a certain amount of guilty self-assertion, appropriation, and willingness to compete and to win are essential to psychic health for sisters. Neither isolation nor innocence is possible in the growth towards a separate identity.

In writing about the complexities of our "sisterly symbiosis," I'm trying to understand not my sister but myself (I'm sure my sister would write a much different account), and more generally, I'm trying to understand the polarities of female identity played out in the dynamics of sisterly relationships. It would be hard to overstate the formative power of the sisterly bond, which has caused me to think a great deal about girls' and women's relationships with one another and about gender identity in general.

Judy and I didn't live in an isolated world of two as we puzzled through the issue of gender. Our mother was a formidable presence, and the large circle of women in her world impressed ours as well. Our mother and, to a lesser degree, our father tried to school us in the ways of patriarchy. In the culture Judy and I inhabited, gender stratification was omnipresent. Yet because we had no brothers, we likely experienced less gender categorization at home than some girls. Mentors and friends helped to shape the gender expectations of our world.

An early mentor was our next door neighbor Jean Rentmeester. Judy and I were the "special girls" of this stylish, generous, and educated woman, and we spent many hours over at her house. She became our Girl Scout leader, helping to inculcate in all of us girls a spirit of adventure, self-reliance, and fun. Packed several layers deep into Jean's open convertible, the Pound Girl Scouts went on many joyful camping trips, marking circuitous trails through the woods, cooking over campfires, sleeping out in the open, skinny-dipping at midnight, and enjoying the pleasures of female *esprit de corps*.

In our pre-adolescent days, we comfortable hung out with other kids, both boys and girls, in the town. During summer, we often played softball (I was one of the last ones chosen) or trekked down the side of the highway to the swimming hole. In winter, we often gathered around the bonfire at Waller's brook for ice skating, or sledding or skiing on their hill—and avoiding the treacherous barbed wire fence at the bottom.

But our close, intimate relationships were with other girls. I had a best friend, Karen. She and I spent a great deal of time together, often sleeping over at one another's houses. Karen's mom, Dorothy, was one of Mother's closest friends but so unlike her in temperament. Invariably clutching a cigarette and cup of coffee, Dorothy calmly presided over a brood neighborhood kids who would stop by her house after school to help polish off the cake she had just taken out of the oven.

Later, almost conterminous with Judy's moving to college, Liola moved to town. She resided just a couple doors down the street when we were both in the eighth grade. We became fast friends and, it turned out, had a great deal in common. We were excellent students, preoccupied with boys, and soon became deeply involved in high school activities. We rode the bus together, shared a locker, took the same classes, and often double-dated. It was a friendship at once companionable, affectionate, and rivalrous, and clearly it replaced for me the sisterly relationship that was in abeyance while my Judy was away at college.

But one day during our junior year, Liola didn't respond to my greeting as we boarded the bus in the morning. Later, as we rushed to put our coats in the locker and get to class, I again tried to wish her good morning and she still didn't respond. At the beginning of our first class, I said rather emphatically and humorously, "Well, hello, Liola!" and she burst out with "Don't you talk to me! I'm never going to talk with you again!" and she didn't, at least not in any consequential way for the next twenty years. I was stunned by her rejection and clueless about what caused it. I tried several times to get her to tell me what was wrong; so did several of our mutual friends; Liola would not talk. I felt mortified and guilty although I didn't know what crime I had committed. I obsessed on the problem, trying to locate the terrible thing I might had done, but I couldn't fathom it.

Throughout the rest of the school year we coexisted in awkward silence broken only when we had to communicate about some matter. Then, compounding the mystery, she inexplicably moved away at the end of that year and finished up her last year of high school in another town. She left her mother and lived with relatives. What would motivate such sudden, dramatic leave-taking—almost flight. I surmised that it had something to do with our impasse. All I knew was that I felt somehow responsible.

Over the years, Liola's angry renunciation of our friendship and inexplicable departure remained a painful and troubling enigma in my life. I heard nothing until we both showed up at our twentieth high school reunion. She initiated a conversation with me: "You know, that time I was so mad at you, I was trying to remember what it was about. I think it was because at a basketball game I kept asking you what Allen [her boyfriend who was on the other side of the court] was doing, and you got tired of telling me and said, 'Oh, you're so blind, why don't you put on your glasses and look for yourself.'"

Was that it! The sin that had exiled me to twenty years of rejection from my "best" friend? I was impatient and rude that time, but my aggravation hardly deserved her devastating rebuke. I was nonplussed by Liola's explanation. How could she have shunned me over such a trivial irritation? But years later, I now see the lesson about the acute sensitivities, even anguish, over appearance that afflict so many adolescent girls and, more pointedly, about the potency of female rivalry. I suspect that Liola, like most young girls (including me), was deeply insecure about her looks and really hated wearing those damned glasses. Competitive with me, she envied my better eyesight, an advantage I didn't maintain for much longer. I was also a somewhat better student and worked less hard than Liola, while she fretted about her academic work. But I wasn't so confident of my edge over Liola. In many ways, I envied her too: she was pretty and popular and not inconveniently tall like I was—all advantages with a lot of social value and symbolic power in our high school.

So perhaps Liola's perception of my advantages, combined with my impatience and insensitivity, so enraged her that she dropped me as a friend. Perhaps she dropped out of the competition altogether and relinquished the field of Coleman High to me. Withdrawal, as I knew from my sister's practice, is a powerful passive-aggressive way to inflict pain and to gain the upper hand in a merged relationship. My ruptured friendship with Liola was another lesson about the difficulties of sisters sharing the common ground. Girls know in their hearts that boys don't have a monopoly on competition, although we play the game more covertly and its stakes are usually more elusive.

But later Liola explained the real sources of her jealousy toward me: the stability of my home, my parents, and my ordinary life. That was a surprise. In the narcissism of youth, I hadn't seen what was most obvious and what I took for granted. Her life was far from ordinary or stable: she lived in the rectory with her often-moody and embittered mother, who was the parish priest's housekeeper. Liola's move was probably compelled by these complicated family dynamics and, as she also noted, by worry about how she would afford college and not by our relationship. But all I knew at the time was that this breach with her was painful and formative for me.

Why does an undercurrent of jealous competition often undergird girls' and women's sisterly friendships? I think women share a common insecurity about identity, one that manifests during adolescent years, when girls first feel the potent double binds of gender identity and when they learn to tread through the minefield of gender-laden inhibitions and prohibitions. I think that both Liola and I had successfully split our pretty side from our smart side, and both of us tried to keep these two halves chugging along in our lives on separate tracks. Where they intersected was in our relationship; there we were each attempting to construct a whole identity from these disjunctive parts. We modeled ourselves on one another and watched enviously to see how the other was doing at that difficult task. Girls make their way in the world in part by observing and emulating other girls and women. We look to each other for how to live, how to be.

I don't wish to overstate the negative aspects of this relational identity. Before Liola angrily terminated our friendship, I found our relationship sustaining, stimulating, and satisfying. And through the next stages of my life, I continued to find great sustenance and pleasure in close friendships with other women. Together and separately, as we evolved and established our lives, my friends and I were also working through the complexities of female identity, just as my sister and I had done.

As is evident from my narrative, formative "sisters" weren't limited to women I knew; they also included female authors and memorable women characters. I admired and emulated Dorothea Brooke, Isabel Archer, Jane Eyre, Emma Woodhouse, and a whole host of others. I absorbed women's lore drawn from fairy tales, literature, and popular culture. And my professional work wasn't chosen disinterestedly. Before I discovered Margaret Drabble's younger-sister perspective, I studied Joyce Carol Oates. For me, she functioned as a mysterious but alluring older sister who blazed a trail that I tried to understand and document as a literary scholar. Her background and experiences paralleled mine in many ways. Her fictional Eden County in upstate New York evoked in me the northern Wisconsin of my childhood. She too grew up in a Catholic, working-class family in a backcountry region and traversed class and gender lines using her talent, brains, and willpower in a single-minded act of self-definition. She too made the university her chosen home. After her undergraduate years at Syracuse University, she attended the University of Wisconsin; in fact, we arrived there the same year, 1960. Afterward, she lived formative years in Detroit, just as I did, and that is where we met. In her fiction Oates examined repeatedly the difficulties of constructing a selfhood from the dualities of being and amid the dislocations of American culture and experience.

My professional work on Oates interfaced with our personal relationship during our Detroit years. Joyce and I were brought together by mutual friends and occasionally had lunch or dinner together with husbands, but our friendship, while pleasant, was constrained by the fact that neither of us could forget that I was the symbiotic critic writing about her work. She was at once generous in discussing literature, modest about her own work, and guarded about her private self. I, in turn, was deferential, intimidated, and careful not to intrude. My first book on Oates's work, while highly appreciative, contained some critical comments as well, since I felt compelled to maintain my integrity as a critic and write an honest appraisal of her fiction. By the time that the book was published, Joyce had moved to Princeton. I sent her a copy of the book, but she never replied. I sensed and regretted her disapproval and withdrawal, a response I had experienced before in my sisterly relationships.

Several years later, as I was leaving Detroit, I received a postcard with a disturbing message:

Dear Joanne: I heard, by a mutual acquaintance of ours, that you are in the habit of saying rather malicious, if not frankly slanderous things about me—for what reason, I can't guess. As a one-time guest in my house and a person to whom I did give an interview you might, I should think, at least exercise some common discretion and courtesy. If you dislike both me and my books so much, perhaps an enigmatic silence might become you better.

Joyce Carol Oates (July 10, 1985)

I was shocked by Joyce's angry accusation and completely at a loss about the cause. The situation was eerily like my earlier experiences with Liola and my sister. Abruptly and inexplicably, I was found guilty and condemned. But what was my terrible crime? I surely didn't know.

After puzzling over this matter, I replied to Joyce that I had examined my conscience and could find no culpability. I didn't hate her work; I had devoted much of my career to it. And I had the deep-

Joanne and Joyce
Carol Oates at
Mount Holyoke
Commencement,
May 2006

est respect for her; indeed, I saw her as a kind of sister, and I wasn't
in the habit of saying anything personal about her, especially since
I didn't know very much. She wrote me a gracious note: "We have
both been slandered. I'll think of it no more" And that was the end of
that, but I couldn't help but see playing out in this episode the same
older-younger sister dynamics that Drabble and Byatt write about.

Years later, when I wrote a second book on her work, Joyce generously read the manuscript and offered detailed, helpful, appreciative commentary. And over the years, we maintained a friendly,
if intermittent, connection. I was pleased when she agreed to be a
speaker at my inauguration as president of Mount Holyoke and to
receive an honorary degree and deliver the Commencement address
several years after that. At the latter occasion, she and her husband,
Ray, stayed with Tom and me at the president's house and the four
of us enjoyed reminiscing about our life in Detroit. It seemed as
though we were life-long and cherished friends.

I think that Joyce and I successfully worked through a symbiotic bond just as my sister and I did. In both relationships, I was for a time perceived as the young sister, the "aggressor," appropriating a piece the elder sister's world and hurting her in the process. But, after painful rapprochement, both older sisters acquiesced to my right to share the territory and to be independent, and both generously reinstated the relationship on a new, more-equitable plane of acceptance and understanding. I continue to admire Joyce Carol Oates, this pioneering older sister, a brilliant woman of letters, a great and good friend.

Margaret Drabble's work interested me not only because I could identify with her younger-sister perspective but because she too was finding her way through complicated issues of female identity, including relationships to parents, sisters, husbands, lovers, children, and work. She said about the experience of growing up female in the twentieth century: "We do not want to resemble women of the past, but where's our future? It is an uncharted world. We have whole new patterns to create."[11] Because the territory is "uncharted," the paradigm is changing while we live. We look around anxiously, curiously, and sometimes enviously to see how other women are doing.

I felt fortunate that my maturation as a young woman paralleled the development of the women's liberation movement. I read Betty Friedan's *The Feminine Mystique* (1963) during the summer I spent in Berkeley before my senior year in college and started to see the world through the first glimmerings of a "feminist perspective." While the more-strident "women libbers," the so-called "bra-burners," were something of an embarrassment, I also knew that their angry protests were opening doors for my generation, allowing us to have a much easier time of it. They were pioneer sisters leading the way. I'm reminded of a comment by Margaret Drabble, who, coming to terms with her complicated and painful relationship with her mother, put it this way: "My mother ground her teeth and everyone said 'how unattractive'—and I was in a position because of circumstances of education and money to be able to profit from her having ground her teeth twenty or thirty years ago."[12] I thought of my other mother's equivalent "teeth grinding," and how I too profited from her not-always-attractive insistence on being herself.

Knowing of my mother's distress over the denial of even a high school education, I was always acutely aware of the shallow, even tenuous roots of female education. One doesn't have to go back very far in time to see how recently women were invited into the male academy: only a generation or two have entered. Virginia Woolf's *A Room of One's Own* (1929), a powerful book on this subject, had a formative influence on me as on so many other women. She poignantly describes the cruelty and destruction of sexist exclusion, a subject she knew in her heart, for she suffered throughout her life the pain and stigma of being forbidden a university education. In contrast, many women of my generation had the opportunity to break into male-dominated worlds, including the academy. When we crossed those thresholds, we had to learn to think and act like males, at least in part. Even though the playing field may not have always been even, we aspired, we competed, we achieved, and sometimes we won. And, I might add, we got a lot of satisfaction out of participation in this world. Our female progenitors who were refused our opportunities sometimes suffered from their subjugation; they split themselves and went underground. They tried to school us in the ways of patriarchy, but they were not always able to hide their resentment, bitterness, and disappointment. Who can blame them?

Feminist scholars have looked back at women authors and characters with new eyes. In *The Madwoman in the Attic*, for example, Susan Gubar and Sandra Gilbert notice that there is a disjunctive split of female identity, an unholy sisterly counterpart in most nineteenth-century stories and novels written by and about women. For every Jane Eyre, there's a Bertha Rochester, a mad woman in the attic; for every Snow White, there's a wicked queen. For every angel, there's a witch. For every submissive woman enshrined in domesticity, there's a dark sister, a fiendish embodiment of "Female Will."[13] Conterminous to the dominant story of female triumph and success are other stories of female rage, defeat, duplicitous and subversive acts of revenge and escape, and madness and self-destruction. In other words, standing alongside or behind every good woman are other women, sisters, who sometimes embody the dark side of female identity—will and rage. Neither in literature nor in life are we without our progenitors. We too may have our Berthas in the attic or in our family tree, or, more pointedly, in the contradictory impulses within our own psyches. Our symbiotic bonds to sisters are often external manifestations of dualities within. This relationship is vividly portrayed in the fiction of Joyce Carol Oates with its omnipresent "doubles" including Monica and Sheila in *Solstice* (1985) and in her pseudonymous double, Rosamond Smith, who "authors" several novels about twins and doubles, and dualities of being.[14]

We are not singularly extraordinary women who have risen through our own efforts alone, although we sometimes like to think of ourselves that way. Rather, we are standing in the evolutionary stream of our grandmothers, mothers, and sisters, as well as all those real-life and fictional progenitors who have come before and led the way. Their life stories are a history of large and small victories, and sometimes of compromise, self-sacrifice, rage, and defeat. We cannot so easily slough off these "sisters" as irrelevant, nor can we help but notice that the space within most private and public institutions is still a man's world.

Professional success is defined most often by validation in the eyes of the father or the male establishment. Vying for that favor can lead to divisive competition with and disparagement of other women. Success is public recognition as the exceptional woman who can make it in a man's world, and sometimes that achievement is all the sweeter because it is enjoyed by so few other women. But such a spurious rationale often bears loneliness, suppression of the "female" in ourselves, and closing off potentially nurturing bonds with other women.

The consequence of our mixed inheritance is that we women are likely to have complicated, conflicted psyches, and we may well find ourselves alternatively at odds with the so-called "female" and the "male" traits and traditions within ourselves. While Virginia Woolf said in *A Room of One's Own* that "a woman writing thinks back through her mothers,"[15] actually she must think back through her fathers as well. We must work out our relational identity not only with other women but with the men and the male institutions in our life. In subsequent chapters, I'll trace the significant influences in my gradual acculturation into the gendered world up to and including my assumption of the presidency of Mount Holyoke College, a watershed moment in my coming to terms with the female side of my inheritance.

Joanne in Second-Grade School Photo

} 3 {

SCHOOL

....

> I reckon I got to light out to the Territory ahead of the rest.
> —Huck Finn in Mark Twain, *The Adventures of Huckleberry Finn*

I finally started school at age six and a half, and I've never left. School was second only to my mother, father, and sister in shaping my character. For better or worse, education was the vehicle with which I negotiated the barriers of custom, class, and gender, shucked off the world of my upbringing, and embraced the world of letters. I now see the process was not without the pains of deracination. "Once you pull up that old tap root you can't put it down again," said a fellow traveler on the academic administrative circuit. Yet what was the alternative? A life lived out in Pound, Wisconsin? I could never quite imagine that. What's a young girl with ambition and brains to do? Go to school, of course.

I spent my first eight years of education at Pound Elementary School, a square brick building with three classrooms and a music room (distinguishable by its sole instrument, a piano) along with a small gym in the basement. My grade over the years was small, between eight and ten pupils. Like generations of students before us, first through third grades were in Mrs. Beaudoin's room, then fourth and fifth grades were with Mrs. Kleiner. In a break with matronly authority, we were taught by a succession of three young and inexperienced teachers in sixth through eight grades.

Near summer's end, we made forays to the local store to buy shiny new school supplies and gave anxious attention to our wardrobe of "school clothes." My Proustian memories of school are suffused with the unmistakable odor of waxed hardwood floors spiced with eraser and book dust. There were the telltale barn smells from the farm kids who milked cows before coming to school. The unmistakable pungency of oranges, peanut-butter-and-jelly sandwiches, and other less-identifiable and unappetizing foods wafted from lunch boxes. Like other children from the village, I walked home for lunch, feeling superior to these "country bumpkins," for we certainly had our social hierarchies and prejudices. I recall my discomfort with the filthy, wax-filled ears and the occasional smell of urine that emanated from Glen, the boy who sat in front of me in first grade. In the sixth grade, I was equally put off by the blood-smeared skirt of Carol, a girl from a disheveled, impoverished family.

I suppose I was a goody-goody student. My unbroken series of gold stars and A's earned me special privileges as the teacher's pet from grade to grade. Often I oversaw the room's bulletin boards and decorative borders or ran errands. Finishing the lesson quickly left me with a lot of time on my hands, so I got to sit in the back and read books in the small library. We had to wait around until our class was invited to the front of the room to recite our lessons, then wait again for the slow readers to stumble through the text. Despite the snail's pace and the monotonous, uninspired, rote curriculum, I liked school and learning. And I got a lot of satisfaction from doing well.

Moreover, school life had welcome diversions. Everyday, we bundled up for recess and rowdily played "Annie, Annie over," "red rover," "captain, may I," "fox and goose," softball, jump-rope, tug of war, and many other games passed down in the schoolyard from generation to generation. Every year, a Christmas play absorbed hours of class time in rehearsals; our mothers created the sets and costumes. And every holiday—Halloween, Thanksgiving, Easter, Valentine's Day, May Day—entailed cut-and-paste "art" projects and usually inspired a party or production of some sort. Karen and I once went to the Halloween party as "Old Gold King Size" and "Regular." We slaved over and proudly wore our box costumes only to be deflated by some boy's dismissive comment, "Look at those two jerks in boxes." I must admit it wasn't much fun to party stuck inside oversized cigarette boxes.

Valentine's Day was always a special occasion. We deposited valentines in a decorated "mail box," then, after their delivery, counted up our cards to quantify our popularity, reading—even analyzing—the messages carefully for clues to how our classmates esteemed us. Some messages were heavy-handed insults slyly sent to appropriate individuals. In the third grade, I received a valentine quite unlike the standard cheap little ditties we generally got. It was an expensive, individually purchased card, with a puffy red heart on the cover and gushing sentiments, including "I love you," inside. It was unsigned. I was deeply embarrassed and flattered. Who was my secret admirer? There weren't a lot of possibilities; most of the boys were short, nasty, and unthinkable. Could it have been Johnny?

He was a lively kid and a good student. His merit was evident in his casting as Santa Claus in the school play one year. (I was Mrs. Claus.) He used to pull my scarf and throw snowballs at me and engage in other kinds of attention-getting behavior as I walked back and forth past his family's store on the corner of Main Street and Highway 141. My father used to tease me about him: "Got a boyfriend, Johnny." This seemed preposterous to me. Johnny was a pest, and besides I wasn't interested in boys—yet. And he moved away before I was.

By the time I was in eighth grade, elementary school was confining and suffocating. My new friend Liola and I anticipated high school with its four hundred or so students with considerable enthusiasm and relief. School was then and always an exciting new world. And it included all those interesting boys.

In chemistry class, three "smart" boys (Rusty, Chuck, and Allen) and I were told to sit together at the back of the room and to proceed at our own pace. This was just as well because the teacher, Mr. Douglas, was the coach of the championship wrestling team and spent a great deal of class time talking about wrestling technique and strategy. Our chemistry instruction was pathetically inadequate (and without a laboratory to boot), but the four of us enjoyed good fellowship, had fun, and learned a little chemistry, while our romantic interests were elsewhere. I had a weakness for handsome athletes, I admit. Sports were the central social activity of the school, and the boys with cool charisma and high prestige were the varsity players on the football and basketball teams.

Friendships with girls were more personal and intimate relationships, without the raucous good humor and witty badinage of the boys. As I explained in the last chapter, my relationship with one friend, Liola, was particularly fraught with the complex dynamics of sisterly companionship and competition. In many ways, however, our high school was without strict gender stratification; we spent a lot of time in and out of class in mixed groups; our teachers were both male and female. And except for sports, which were clearly the province of males alone (girls watched and cheered), we were a well-integrated, coeducated community.

I see now that the extracurricular activities I crammed into my schedule honed skills for my later life. I recall with some embarrassment that I was the drum majorette. While twirling a baton, I took the band out into the streets of Coleman and put them through their paces, trying to get all those left feet rising off the ground at the same time. What better preparation, in its combination of discipline and exhibitionism, I now think, for a future academic leader? I also took drama and forensics, acted in plays, and delivered solemn and "original" orations, platitudinous sentiments delivered ponderously with studied gestures. Little did I know then I was practicing for the innumerable real life "dramas" that would embroil me and for the "original orations" that I would deliver later as a dean, vice-president, and president. As class president for two years, representative on the Student Council, and delegate to Girls' State, I was apprenticing for a future of campus activism and academic leadership.

I also took typing in high school. "Being a secretary is always something you can fall back on," Mother advised. Indeed, typing came in handy when I worked as an IBM key punch operator in the registration office at Madison to help finance my education. But I didn't aspire to secretarial work; I never doubted that I would go to college. I thought I might major in English since I liked reading novels and writing papers, despite the uninspiring English instruction in my school.

In fact, I was able to challenge and intimidate one young English teacher, who always deferred to my confident assertions of the "right" answer, be it a point of English grammar or literary interpretation. I remember the odd sense of control and embarrassment I felt in this relationship. I knew the balance of power was inappropriate but enjoyed it all the same. I wasn't necessarily right all the time, but she didn't know that, or at least she was too insecure to challenge me and set me straight.

I wasn't the only obnoxious kid in her class. Others openly undermined her authority, playing practical jokes or leading what amounted to class insurrection. One day the entire class played hooky by going to the lunch room and then, when she finally found us, pretending she told us to do so. At other times, students sang out the answers to quizzes when her back was turned. Clearly, our English class lacked discipline and compassion; it also, like many other courses at Coleman, lacked any discernible pedagogy. When we read Shakespeare, the approach was a communal read of *Julius Caesar* or *Macbeth* with one person after another taking turns. We suffered through the stammering English of our classmates without any discussion whatsoever of the play. Then we would do an art project on the work. I made a shadow box of Brutus killing Caesar. We read aloud a few works of the Romantic poets and recited the first fifteen lines of the *Canterbury Tales*, pronouncing them however we wished, without a glimmer of understanding or discussion about Chaucer's meaning or artistry. Still, imperfect as my education in English surely was, the subject had a certain allure for me.

When my high-school home economics teacher, Mrs. Brown, learned of my inclination towards English, she was horrified, thinking it would be a shame if I ended up doing something as dull as teaching English. Mrs. Brown, though, was the Miss Jean Brodie of Coleman High School, and her views were not lightly brushed off. My mother came to dread the moral authority assumed in the phrase, "Mrs. Brown says. . ." One of the school's best teachers, a woman with style, confidence, and conviction, Mrs. Brown imparted aphoristic wisdom to her "girls," and she thought I was one of the special ones destined for some kind of greatness if I didn't mess up and aim too low. She had ambitions for me, the winner of the "Home Economics Award." She thought I should somehow combine home economics and television, rather like Betty Furness, who opened refrigerators with panache and proclaimed, "You can be sure if it's Westinghouse."

I appreciated Mrs. Brown's effort to imagine a career for me that would somehow combine gender expectations and glamor into one happy package. Under her influence, I briefly entertained the idea of majoring in home economics, but my heart wasn't in it. Even so, I was fortunate that Mrs. Brown was my teacher and I went to Coleman High. The school—its staff no less—undoubtedly nurtured me, and I developed a sense of self-worth, self-confidence, and competence. And I felt that I was part of an extended community providing identity, support, and continuity.

But by the time I was a senior, I was determined to move on. All that community solicitude started to feel cloying and confining. And

I wanted to prove myself "out there." I learned that girls as well as boys could distinguish themselves through academic merit, but I wanted to go on to the next step, the next challenge. It was one thing to be valedictorian in a class of eighty-six students, quite another to succeed in a university of over eighteen thousand students. That was a challenge worthy of an ambitious young woman. Like Huck Finn, I reckoned it was time to "light out for the Territory."

It seemed to me that at each new stage of my life, the way forward necessitated a repudiation of what had come before, a clean slate, a fresh start. Lured on by the bigger, brighter world of the university, I disparaged the claustrophobic and homogenous little world of my childhood and sought to identify myself with all that the university represented. Only much later did I realize the toll of that repudiation and sought to dust off and value the pieces of myself that were nurtured in the northern Wisconsin soil.

UNIVERSITY OF WISCONSIN

"Look to the right of you, look to the left. Next fall only one of you will be here," said the grim orientation speaker in September 1960, acknowledging the Darwinian way the University of Wisconsin coped with open admissions. Intimidating? You bet! But from the very first I was dazzled by the diverse, vibrant, and expansive culture of the university and was determined to be a survivor. Wisconsin was a composite of many different cultures, and I sampled several, first that of the dormitory, Elm Drive A, a lakeside residence, where I met girls to hang out with. Mary, my roommate, became a life-long friend. In the coed dining hall (doubling as study hall) we developed casual friendships and sometimes found boys to date. I always remember the way that Mary's head would bob up from her books in the dining room study hall that first year each time the door opened; she didn't want to miss any interesting opportunities to pursue her social interests. Everyday, we trudged along the winding trails along the lake and over often-icy hills to our classes. As I became more immersed in my studies, I felt the need for space to think and be alone, and I moved across campus in my second year to another dorm, Barnard Hall, where I could have room of my own. And so did Mary, who like me, went on to get a PhD.

A young woman at college felt conflicting pulls on her life. Studying was important, but so was having a social life. Always at the back of my mind was the thought that college was the place where a girl was supposed to find a nice man to marry. Between the conflicting push and pull of solitary intellectual development and gregarious social life, I pledged the same sorority my sister had belonged to earlier. But I felt distinctly un-Greek. From the first, I was appalled by the ritual of "pledge night" and the forced sentiment; "sisterhood" was not so easily taken on, in my view. I remained skeptically detached and critical, especially when I was increasingly influenced by the aspiring "intellectuals" I interacted with in the honors program. After a few months I dropped out of the sorority; I would find my sisterhood and social life elsewhere.

I became no less disenchanted with the fraternity boys and the beer bashes that were integral to the Greek scene. I remember a "formal" weekend that included "the brothers" and their dates picnicking at Wisconsin Dells. My date, steeped in the traditions of chivalry, wanted to help me, the fair damsel, over the rocks. I finally blurted out, "I'll do it myself!" breaking the courtly illusion and casting a pall over the rest of weekend festivities.

While I graduated in spring 1964, before the great waves of civil unrest and student activism took over the Madison campus and many others, I took deep draughts of the liberal politics and culture of the Madison campus. My education at Wisconsin was as much expanded by the liberating culture as it was by the academic curriculum, although I was not always totally comfortable. I would get snowed under by papers and exams, and sometimes, especially in the summers, I stayed on to work in the registration office and experienced excruciating loneliness and a feeling of exclusion. But I thought such suffering was a normal part of the struggle to grow, to be worthy of greater expansiveness, intellectual seriousness, and eclectic sophistication. Wisconsin seemed to me the prototype of what a university should be, and I fully embraced it as my alma mater.

However strong I tried to appear, the intellectual discourse and the eccentric people who practiced it sometimes intimidated me. A particularly nerve-wracking experience was taking honors logic from Professor Pratt. Invariably dressed in all black, he darkly urged students to drop his course, warning how hard it would be, how fast paced, how intolerant he was of slackers and dullards. I hung on tenaciously but fearfully as we raced through the logic book in six weeks, and then Professor Pratt told us about the new symbolic logic system he was developing. He engaged in abstruse dialogue about it with the math majors in the class while we humanists hung back in silent misery. For the final exam, he said, "I'm introducing a new connective into my logistic system." Then he wrote two formulas on the board. "Say something interesting about it," he instructed. We could go anywhere, consult anyone, including PhD students in philosophy, but we should come back in two hours with our exams.

I wandered off disconsolately, unable to make any inroads into this assignment, distraught over my limited aptitude in symbolic logic. Two hours later, I went back to the classroom only to find no one there. Finally, after wandering around aimlessly, I ran into someone from the class. "What am I supposed to do with my exam?" I asked in panic. "Turn it in at the KK," he said, as if everyone should know this. And so I went to the local pub and submitted my exam to Professor Pratt, who was having beer with my classmates.

It was no surprise that I loved my English classes, especially when professors knew something about the topic and could teach with some passion. I sweated over my freshman comp essay into the early hours of the morning, each week. My instruction in high school had been primitive to this point; I had never heard of a thesis. I thought you just wrote from inspiration. Mr. Mitchell was one of the first instructors who taught me not to make a simple idea seem more profound by complicating it with ornate, opaque, and cumbersome language. The conviction that I should be an English major came in an honors class taught by Professor Soule during my sophomore year. Here I encountered Henry James's *Portrait of a Lady*, a book so compelling yet so difficult that I read it through the night—afraid to stop. I worried I might lose the rhythm of that complex syntax, and I was enchanted and absorbed by this complex portrait of a woman, Isabel Archer, who goes off to Europe and marries a perfect beast of a man, Gilbert Osmond, but who manages to suffer and grow in wholly admirable ways. Isabel has a fine, nuanced, alluring sensibility as did James, the literary craftsman who wrote about her with such depth, subtlety, and artistry. Moreover, Isabel, like me, had ventured into new territory and sought out new experiences. Here was another fictional sister illuminating how to be a woman in modern society.

That a student could major in reading such resonant and compelling novels seemed an irresistibly indulgent pleasure. My writing was still mannered, and I was intimidated into silence by the glib and confident class discussion of my fellow honors students. But Professor Soule saw something in my papers that caused him to "get up and have a cigarette," which he said was his highest compliment, and his quiet encouragement and expression of faith in my incipient potential meant a great deal at the time.

From that course on, I never veered far from a career in English, first in the English honors program, then to Harvard for a master's degree, and on to the University of Michigan for a PhD. The honors program at Madison provided the kind of tutorial instruction and small community easily missed at large state university. It got me to take English as a discipline and myself as a student seriously. The eight students who completed English honors in my cohort were an eclectic mix of New York Jews, Wisconsin country kids, and a few others, but we developed a bond that comes through the ordeal of intensive seminars and belabored honors theses. Senior year at my apartment, we celebrated our achievement with a party, which ended with inebriated bodies scattered all over the floor.

Most of us intended to go on to graduate school. Two male honors students were awarded Danforth Fellowships; women were ineligible. I remember chafing at this regulation somewhat but basically accepting such gender inequities, even though the summer before, I had read Betty Friedan's *The Feminine Mystique* and was developing the first awakenings of a feminist consciousness. Except for the legendary Madeline Doran, a Shakespearean scholar, all my professors were male. Almost imperceptibly, I was becoming aware of the narrowing world for women that lay ahead.

I attended a meeting at which an elderly woman, one of the first female graduates from the University of Wisconsin, talked about the early days of coeducation. She said women were not allowed to enter Bascom Hall through the front door; they had to use the side entrance and sit behind a screen at the back of the room. Well, I thought, things are certainly much better now. And indeed they were. But I would continue to learn lessons about the discrimination against women, both overt and subtle, in the various alma maters I sought to make my own.

Typically trying to keep both my social life and intellectual development moving along on parallel paths, during my junior and senior year at Wisconsin I dated a young man who was completing a PhD in engineering. What would happen when we both finished? Even though I was pretty equivocal about our relationship, I agreed to try to locate with him in the same region. When he got an assistant professorship at Boston University, I accepted placement in Harvard's Master of Arts in Teaching program, even though I had no interest in high school teaching. Pursuing a course of study at Harvard would surely be a worthwhile experience.

HARVARD UNIVERSITY

The year at Harvard, however, was difficult for me. My boyfriend wanted more commitment to our relationship than I was willing to muster, and we parted ways. My sister, who was living in New Haven and whose marriage was breaking up, was uncommunicative. While Harvard had an alluring aura as *the* bastion of higher learning and academic excellence, I found it cold, impersonal, intimidating. If ever an institution was gendered "male" and made women feel unwelcome, it was Harvard. The undergraduate library, Lamont, was closed to women, as was the faculty club. Only one of my professors, Anne Ferry—the only woman in the English Department at that time—was at all encouraging or supportive. (A few years later, she went to Wellesley.) I had grave doubts about whether I should continue forever "going to school" in a world of letters so male dominated and un-nurturing. Even more discouraging was that I felt like a fish out of water in the teaching program. I experienced practice teaching at Wayland High School during the second semester as cruel exile from the University and endured a term that was both taxing and unfulfilling. My high school English teacher got her belated revenge as I struggled to keep order in an unruly classroom.

With Harvard unwelcoming and prohibitively expensive, with no ties and no clear sense of what to do, I fell back on what I could do: "Going to school" was what I knew how to do best. With no recommendation other than a friend's casual comment, "I hear that Michigan is good," I applied to the PhD program in English at the University of Michigan in Ann Arbor and was admitted with a graduate teaching assistantship.

UNIVERSITY OF MICHIGAN

Starting in the summer of 1965, my sojourn in Ann Arbor was a much happier and more fulfilling time. Unlike chilly Harvard, Michigan was a congenial school; I was drawn into a community of teaching fellows, young professors, and other graduate students. During the rocking sixties, Ann Arbor was filled with innumerable parties and good fellowship. I was more relaxed, confident, and mature than I had been just a year earlier, and I was dedicated my studies—and also to my social life.

Every English Department, I have discovered, has a dominant culture, and Michigan's was that of the tweedy, urbane, pipe-smoking male. He discreetly acknowledged a woman's sexual attractiveness, while maintaining a scholarly demeanor. Flirtation was rampant, and a young, unmarried female graduate student was likely to get more than her fair share of attention. One married colleague impulsively and passionately kissed me one evening with no by your leave. I was invited to parties where I suspected I was supposed to provide frisson for the husband, while another man was included to perform the same service for the wife. The social revolution of the sixties unglued couples and motivated people in bizarre ways.

The flirtation, presumption of male privilege, and sexism didn't stop there. I received calls late at night from one debonair professor, old enough to be my father, who thought we should go out for "coffee." Another took me to lunch and, after his double martini, grabbed my hand and said: "I can't stand the thought that you are unmarried." Later, when my official dossier was inadvertently returned to me, I learned that this professor saw nothing inappropriate in writing, "She will knock the eyes out of even the most elderly professor." Another chatted openly about how the Department had not hired a young woman professor because she was too attractive to be taken seriously, and besides she would likely get married and give up her work. Later, another older professor, who had championed my career and who had written for my dossier that I would be an excellent candidate for a position at a "good women's college," was enraged when he heard that I married shortly before finishing my dissertation. "Go buy a station wagon, live in the suburbs," he said in disgust, convinced that I had thrown over my career for marriage.

Although I was dismayed by this outburst, I was not surprised. Michigan was an unapologetic male camp. The austere chairman, Warner Rice, addressed his colleagues as "Gentleman," ignoring the one woman in the English Department. Today, I am considerably less tolerant of such blatant sexist and discriminatory behavior. Now we recognize sexual harassment for what it is. But as a young woman, I was learning about the complex gender politics of the modern world, academia especially. Men may have monopolized the power of position, but I was aware of or skilled at exercising my own power, derived from youth, attractiveness, and brains, to advance my career. My self-confidence as a literary scholar and determination to pursue English as a profession increased during my time at Michigan.

I had the good fortune to take Lyall Powers's class on William Faulkner during my first summer in Ann Arbor and became enthralled by the power of his fiction. Professor Powers became an important mentor and directed my dissertation. He had a gift for guiding his students to engage interesting questions, inspiring me to think deeply about Faulkner and to join a wonderful conversation with this gentle and supportive professor. I was intrigued by how Faulkner's works "fit together" into a grand design, the complex and multifaceted world of Yoknapawtapha County. And I was fascinated by the part-whole duality of Faulkner's world—the notion that stories or novels, while complete in themselves, took on added enrichment when seen in context of the artist's whole corpus.

A valuable clue to my nature is my life-long preoccupation with finding unity in seeming disparateness and diversity. It was a subject that I wrote about in my honors thesis, "The Unity of Joyce's *Dubliners*"; the topic of my dissertation, which looked at the "short story composite" of Joyce and Faulkner; the subject of my first book on Faulkner's craft of revising stories into longer works; and eventually, my continuing preoccupation as a college administrator trying to pull warring factions together into common cause. I'm sure this preoccupation has deep psychological routes, related in part to my attempt to compose a harmonious life made up of the disparate pieces of the self and amid dislocations and discontinuities of daily experiences.

Away from intimidating and exclusionary Harvard, I felt energized, stimulated, and confident of my abilities to do just that. Studying for comprehensive exams gave me an appreciation for the scope and breadth of the literary canon. I got satisfaction from teaching freshman composition to students who were for the most part capable and motivated. By the time I was ready to write my dissertation in 1967, though, I began to feel that Ann Arbor was a small place and that my world was narrow. Here again was that restlessness that never let me get too comfortable in one place. Again

I needed to pull up stakes and light out for a new territory. As the recipient of two fellowships, I felt flush with money, something like thirty-eight hundred dollars a year. If I were to be a serious student of English literature, it was high time that I saw England, I reasoned. So, after fulfilling my teaching obligation first semester, I set off for London in January of 1968, with only the addresses of a few friends of friends as a guide.

Before I left, I applied for a job at Wayne State University in Detroit and was offered an instructorship at a princely seventy-five hundred dollars a year. Wayne State had a "revolving door" policy in those days, hiring batches of instructors to fill the dozens of sections of freshman composition and other introductory courses. The job was a fallback option. I thought it entirely possible that, like a Jamesian heroine, I might spend years in England or Europe. Of course, I had neither the fortune nor the allure of an heiress, but still, something might come up. I always believed in life's contingencies, which might lead me down unexpected pathways. In the meantime, I had a task to complete, the writing of my dissertation, which I thought I could do perfectly well using the British Museum and London University as my bases of operation.

STUDY ABROAD

As it turned out, British libraries did not have all the materials that I needed for my research on William Faulkner and James Joyce, and I made only preliminary progress on my dissertation. But the year was consequential. I became part of a little group of Americans scholars who gathered at the British Museum each day to ask: "Did you see the news today?!" This was 1968, the year the world changed, a year of startling events: the strong showing of Eugene McCarthy in the New Hampshire primary; President Lyndon Johnson's decision not to seek reelection; the tragic assassinations of Martin Luther King and Bobby Kennedy; and the solidifying and radicalizing of opposition to the Vietnam War. The United States looked tumultuous and violent from funky but relatively placid England. When I returned to the States, I could feel the profound shift. The counterculture had become dominant, and I had missed experiencing this climactic turning point, a watershed time in American culture. I felt strangely cheated.

But life was stimulating in London. I loved it from the first moment in January when I arrived at the Earl's Court flat of English friend

Marigold. I breathed the bracing fresh air from the open windows and took in the green lawns and blooming gardens, which were still thriving in winter. London was liberating in much the same way the University of Wisconsin had been when I was eighteen. Here was a culture teeming with life and steeped in history, and I was at least for a time an ingénue without a history and connections, ready to experience the limitless possibilities of contingency and self-creation.

Responding to an ad in the *Evening Standard*, I moved into a flat on Gloucester Road in Kensington with three other young women, but those open windows, that bracing, damp fresh air, and those overcast winter days were charming for just so long. I worked hard not to be obnoxiously "American," but I could not adjust to the lack of central heating and was perpetually cold, no matter where I was, including in the library. I tried to park myself in overheated cafes for long, bone-warming lunches. A nice hot bath in the evening should have done the trick, and I did my utmost to arrange it. But the flat's answer to "hot" water was one of those curious English devices designed to heat the water as it came out of the tap. Of course, if you ran the water too fast, it would be tepid. If you ran it too slow, it would cool in the freezing tub before you got in. And heating the bathroom with a space heater seemed downright unsafe given the dangers of conjoining water and electricity. Even more distressingly, I could never get warm in bed at night. In addition to a hot water bottle, a space heater, and spare blankets, I bought an English electric blanket, the kind that goes on the bottom and that should be switched off when you get into bed. But the heat quickly dissipated into the clammy English cold, and I had to switch on the heater on again and remember to turn it off. Several mornings I woke up with scorched knees. In danger of electrocution in both bath and bed, I moved out of Gloucester Road after two months, relocating to a centrally heated flat, which I shared with another woman, in Chalk Farm, south of Hampstead. The accommodation seemed altogether luxurious by comparison. This experience was not the first time that I was made aware of how thoroughly I valued American comforts and conveniences. I wasn't raised in the aspiring middle class for nothing.

Shortly after I arrived in London, I went with my English flat mates to a "mixer" dance of London University graduates at Chelsea Town Hall. This was the tail end of an old custom; discotheques were starting to dot the landscape of swinging London, and these stuffy, old fashioned dances seemed antiquated remnants of another age, but who am I to criticize? It served me quite well. After being paraded around the floor in bemusement by some less-than-savory types, I was asked to dance by Tom, a tall, handsome, young solicitor. Not to be outdone by my mother, I not only danced but "took a chance" with this stranger and began to go out with him, a custom that has persisted for fifty years.

As our relationship grew more serious, Tom and I thought about what we might do in the fall, when my fellowship money would run out. I needed either to find work or return to the instructorship at Wayne State University. Although I was offered a position at a technical college in London, I felt the strong pull of the States. I may sound Philistine, but America was "mine own," and I missed the convenience and familiarity my culture. Most of all, I wanted to get on with my dissertation, earn my doctorate, and enter professional life. Tom was interested in at least having a look at the States, so we scraped together enough money for a bumpy, claustrophobic, and interminable flight on Icelandic Airlines to New York, then ventured a Greyhound bus trip to Detroit, where we stayed overnight in the fourth-floor apartment of my friend, Mary, on what was surely one of the hottest days of the year.

It was a testament to his tolerance and endurance that Tom did not pack up and immediately go home. He was airsick, along with dozens of other passengers, as the poorly ventilated plane circled New York. He was stunned by size of the country, the omnipresent guns packed by policeman and guards, and the extraordinary size of American cars. And he suffered the misery of heat prostration in Mary's airless, sweltering flat, kept alive only by the grace of a small fan, and, worse than that, he had yet to meet my parents.

And so unpromisingly began a sojourn in Detroit that would last seventeen years. During this time I finally finished being a student and took my place as a teacher, rising through the ranks from instructor to full professor, only to be lured into a "temporary" stint as an administrator through a circuitous route I shall detail in the next chapter.

Joanne and Tom on Belle Isle in Detroit, Michigan, in 1969

} 4 {

WAYNE STATE UNIVERSITY
AND UNC-GREENSBORO

Becoming "the Other"

Before beginning my new job at Wayne State and moving to Detroit, Tom and I flew to Wisconsin to visit my parents and pick up my possessions. Bristling with curiosity, my parents didn't know what to make of Tom, this foreigner who talked so softly and bizarrely that my father couldn't understand a word he said. My mother was relieved that his hair wasn't too long and he didn't look much like any of the Beatles, although to his discredit, he wasn't a Catholic. After the visit, we drove back to Detroit in my old car, a 1963 Valiant, with my mongrel dog, Daisy, in tow, vestiges of my graduate-student life that I had left in Wisconsin for safekeeping.

WAYNE STATE UNIVERSITY

Naively, we rented a furnished apartment for a hundred dollars a month at 1615 West Canfield Street. The building stood across the freeway maze that cut up and cut off neighborhoods adjacent to the Wayne campus and near the epicenter of the riot that had devastated the city the year before. The neighborhood was still rife with crime and violence. Our first evening in Detroit, we were too tired to unload the bicycle in the locked car, after hauling up all our new hand-me-downs from Wisconsin. In the early hours of the morning I heard the telling squeak of the car door and jumped out of bed to see the bike being hauled off. I shouted out the window, but all I got for my outrage was "the finger" from the brazen thief.

Tom and I quickly discovered that it was too dangerous in our unsafe neighborhood for us to walk with Daisy. So each morning and evening we let her loose for a time, and she ran with a pack of slum dogs, surely having a much better time than she would have at the end of a leash. Across the street was a small storefront with extraordinary traffic, probably a distributor for the immensely popular and illegal "numbers." A couple of times I saw vicious fights in the alley across the street as I peered out our windows. Yet Canfield quickly became "home" as we accustomed ourselves to the people and the routines of the neighborhood. On the corner sat Cunningham's, a drugstore that had been burned out in the riot and rebuilt with riot-style windows high up out of harm's way.

It was fascinating to see the rash and brash "Motor City" through Tom's bewildered eyes. Genteel England was never like this. Still deeply steeped in his English ways, he put on a jacket and tie when he went down to the drugstore to buy a pack of cigarettes. We chatted regularly with a genial African American man who sold newspapers on the corner, and we shared grim camaraderie with the people in our building, uniting with them in periodic revolt against the landlord over the erratic heat and, worst of all, the roach invasions that required weaponizing shoes to smash them against the wall. One evening the resident building manager did a "midnight flit," stripping whatever he could, including the door, from his apartment and absconding.

In the beginning, we were extremely short of cash, and Wayne State didn't pay its employees until a month after they began. But we found a bonanza in our cupboards: dozens of glass bottles that we could redeem. Every week we took in ten bottles, got the deposit, and bought a dollar's worth of gas—nineteen cents a gallon during the gas wars— with the money, and we subsisted off of the food stuffs that we had brought with us from Wisconsin. Finally though our diet deteriorated to odd cans of vegetables, and I had to take out a consumer loan.

Serving a university enrollment of over thirty-two thousand students, the English Department was huge, with over ninety members, and I felt anonymous my first year. One older professor, Alva Gay, was assigned to supervise my teaching. He attended a couple of my classes and wrote a report for the file, but this portly, balding professor was more fascinated by my legs than my pedagogy. Leering at me coming down the long corridors of State Hall one day, he said, "It will be a very sad day when miniskirts go out of style." Somehow during the year, I managed to write my dissertation, teach three classes each quarter, and help Tom apply for jobs. Many days I was just a few chapters ahead of the students in daunting books like *Moby Dick*. I told them that we would discuss the book in sections rather than in its entirety and prohibited discussion of later pages "in case others in the class were not there yet."

After a couple of months we realized that Tom's employment prospects on a visitors' visa were nil. Committed to staying together, we decided to marry secretly to secure a permanent visa and then to plan a formal public wedding "for my mother" in Wisconsin later. So one Saturday in November, we went down to City Hall and waited along with other couples for the judge's endorsement. We dressed up for the occasion, of course, and were bemused by the fact that some prospective brides had their hair in rollers during the ceremony, apparently primping themselves for later and worthier events.

Keeping our secret marriage strictly to ourselves, Tom and I had a proper Catholic wedding with family in Wisconsin the next summer. Afterward we moved to a rented house in Highland Park, a community of kempt, modest, lower-middle-class homes, a neighborhood that gradually succumbed to the urban blight that would devastate Detroit in the years ahead. Our marriage was (and continues to be) strong and harmonious; I found great sustenance and calm in this relationship. It provided the emotional balance I needed in my life. Tom's selfless accommodation and the abiding stability of our alliance made possible my forays into the male-dominated professional world. Relaxed, patient, secure in himself, he didn't have the driving American passion to find identity and purpose in "work," as I did. Well-educated and newly married, he wanted a good job, of course, and was now armed with a green card, but his London School of Economics law credentials did not lead to easy placement in the job market of Detroit. Eventually, after some abortive jobs and periods of unemployment, he settled for a number of years into a position with the state of Michigan that drew on his background in the law and land use.

Meanwhile, at Wayne State over the next few years, I was drawn into fellowship and society with a cohort of young colleagues in the English Department. Many were ABDs or recent PhDs, but "times they were a changing," and some became disaffected, latter-day hippies who could not, or would not, sustain the disciplined paths they had taken as graduate students. In that unsettling period of late sixties and early seventies, antiwar activism, disillusionment with government, authority, and conventional expectations, and the allure of countercultural life styles hit my generation hard in early adulthood. Some colleagues experimented with drugs and meditation. Others, following a different route, became addicted to the leisure and comforts they had been denied in graduate school and were unable to sustain the asceticism required of the scholar or invest the effort needed to finish dissertations, or to continue scholarship after the dissertation. Several dropped out of the world of academe, never able to reenter.

But another breed of academics—young, ambitious people determined to make their way in the profession—gradually reshaped the English Department into a more-dynamic place. Senior colleagues finally saw the increasingly talented younger folk not only as grist for the writing program but as scholar-teachers who could augment the reputation and strength of the department. To secure time for scholarship, I took a year off—a good idea in theory—but Tom lost his job, and I had to work part time so that we could subsist. Nonetheless, the leave provided the opportunity for sustained scholarship, netted articles accepted for publication, and advanced a book manuscript toward publication. Senior faculty started to view me as a more-serious professional. And fortuitously, they altered the revolving-door policy and converted my terminal contract into a tenure-track position. Eventually, in 1975 I was awarded tenure. With job security in hand, I settled into a stable career at Wayne State.

I taught courses ranging from remedial English composition to advanced graduate seminars. Wayne State's students were drawn from the diverse cultures of the metropolitan area, and they were diverse in age as well. Teenagers and senior citizens took my classes. But most Wayne students were young adults juggling complicated lives and demanding work schedules. Some were painfully deficient in both basic skills and critical thinking, and English 130, the remedial class into which over half the freshman class were directed by the placement test, could be a grim and labor-intensive assignment, involving hours of individual tutorials and huge numbers of papers to grade. It was yeoman's work for which I could summon liberal fervor because students were so needy, but it could be equally tedious and disheartening labor. The English Department was overwhelmed by its commitment to teaching composition, and everyone, from graduate students to full professors, contributed to the program. But the more junior you were in the department, the more composition you taught.

Given my subsequent positions at universities where the English faculty are not an enclave of writing specialists and that have institutionalized writing programs across the curriculum, I look back at the composition factory at Wayne State with mixed feelings. It employed many people, including me. Composition was our bread and butter; we tried to make it a wholesome, nutritious meal. But basic writing courses were a long way down the food chain from our cultural—and professional—specialties, upper-division and graduate courses in literature. These were mostly fun and rewarding to teach, and students generally enjoyed the reading, writing, and instruction.

My courses attracted their share of oddballs and oddities. Five police officers were enrolled in an evening class one quarter, at a time when the Detroit Police Department was subsidizing officer education. I felt very safe being escorted to my car by my armed students. One of these officers told me heatedly that if he caught one of his children with Kurt Vonnegut's *Slaughterhouse Five*, the book we were reading for class, he would burn it for its smutty language. I refrained from saying "things could always be worse," thinking of *Ulysses* or *Clockwork Orange*. Instead, I politely defended the book on its artistic merits.

"Let's have an affair," said a note from another of my students who apparently believed in the direct approach. I had no inkling that his knowing, sympathetic glances from the back of the room were less about books than romance. Other students, both men and women, developed crushes on me. As I tiptoed through the emotional minefields of their dependency, I learned just how charged student-teacher relationships could be and how laden with issues of gender and family they often were. One student wrote me several times during the semester about his father: what a bastard he was; how difficult had been his relationship with his father; how much he hated him. Later, one of my student evaluations read enigmatically: "You are my father."

I most definitely was not his father, but I did become a mother, birthing a beautiful son, William, in June 1976. Tom and I had equivocated for years about having a child, putting off the decision, but finally, after I got tenure and with the biological clock ticking, we decided to go for it. And thank goodness we did. I can't imagine our life without William; he deeply enriched our lives. The presence of a baby in the house after so many years of freedom and quiet, though, was a shock to our system, and Tom and I struggled to accommodate our baby's clearly vocalized needs. I returned to the classroom in September, after the summer at home, and acclimated myself to the dizzying act of juggling duties and schedules. I vividly remember trying to grade papers and breast feed at the same time (I don't recommend it). Fortunately, a neighbor, who took in children, provided loving care and needed relief. When he was eighteen months old, I enrolled William in Montieth Nursery School, a cooperative program used by students, faculty, and community people. The nursery, located in an old house on Wayne State's campus and adjacent to State Hall where I taught, was a great comfort to me. Many days I could see the children playing from my window. Other days I was on the grounds myself, logging my hours in the cooperative program.

Some of my students at Wayne were young mothers, with whom I shared a life of nursery school and child care as well as books and literature. And further compounding the complexities of student-teacher relationships, some of my graduate students functioned as surrogate mothers for me and my son. Among the graduate students were several older women who had taken time out to raise families. Many were exceptionally talented and articulate, and these classes, some of which transpired in my living room, were exhilarating to teach. I developed close friendships with some of these women. The many female students and several female colleagues ensured that Wayne State's English Department was not a men's club in the way Michigan's had been in the sixties. Women could and did thrive professionally among us, and the department was far better for their engagement in its classes, curriculum, and business.

At that time, Detroit had the unhappy distinction as the reigning "murder capital" of the United States. And shockingly murder intruded into our academic world; Phil Traci, Shakespearean scholar and genial colleague, was shot dead after coming home one night with an acquaintance he met at a bar. And years later, after we had moved from the city, I was stunned to learn that another colleague and good friend in English, Ken Angyal, was murdered, along with his wife, by their only son in their home. A young man in his twenties, Ken's son set the house ablaze and committed suicide. Ken and I had companionable lunches during which we often talked about books (which he avidly collected) and our families. He clearly loved his son, Thad, deeply. How can it be that that Ken, his family, his book-filled house, and all he valued were erased as if they never existed? These two murders of colleagues, horrible beyond imagining, were reminders that we faculty work in universities—the so-called Ivory Tower—but live in the world, in our communities, blighted or gentrified, downscale or upscale.

Detroit's reputation was so bad and parts of it looked so devastated—whole neighborhoods were blighted by shortsighted, destructive HUD policies and by the 1967 riot—that the city seemed uninhabitable to many people. But despite everything, it was livable. In fact, I developed great fondness for Detroit. The neighborhoods and freeways, the beautiful Detroit River and Belle Isle, and what Joyce Carol Oates calls "the beat, the beat" gave it a distinctive energy and dynamism. In the aftermath of the Detroit riot and with the liberalism of the late sixties, it seemed that Detroit could enjoy a rebirth, a "renaissance," symbolized by the mammoth structure, the Renaissance Center, which was supposed to revitalize downtown—but didn't.

In 1972 Tom and I bought at a bargain price a splendid mock-Tudor house, complete with a turret, stained-glass, leaded windows, winding staircase, and ivy-covered walls, in a lovely residential neighborhood of northwest Detroit. Our friends dubbed the place "Castle Creighton" and called us "Lord and Lady Creighton." Our move to the neighborhood paralleled that of a whole cadre of other young professionals, many of whom became our friends. For the thirteen years that we lived there, we belonged to a genuine community. We knew all the neighbors on our street, joined them in block parties, and chatted with them in casual moments; we frequently hosted dinner parties for academic colleagues. But such residential neighborhoods were islands of tranquility and beauty amid the irrepressible violence and decay of so much of Detroit. One day, that suppressed violence very nearly exploded at me, but I was saved by an automatic garage-door opener.

At the intersection of an artery street with an optional left turn, I went straight ahead, an action interpreted by the driver of the car on the right as "cutting" in. He became enraged and pursued me. When I slowed down or sped up, he did too. He followed me block after block deep into our neighborhood. As I rounded the last corner, I pressed the garage opener and sailed in, the door closing behind me. "It's lucky you're in that garage!" he shouted, lacing his fury with unrepeatable epithets. I escaped road rage this time, but I could never quite relax when walking or driving down the border streets of Livernois or Woodward Avenue. And it wasn't until we moved away that I felt the tension relax in my body. Life in Detroit involved an incessant wariness and vigilance, a sixth sense for danger.

Because of this vaguely menacing environment, I was glad to have William near me in the child-care center housed on the Wayne State campus, which was itself another island in the heart of the city's slums. While William was still in nursery school, however, the university administration decided that it was time to "get out of the child-care business" and proposed closing down Montieth Nursery. Alarmed, I became an activist of the worst kind, a single-issue politician, to defend the nursery. I spoke out in faculty forums, wrote to officials, and worked out compelling cost-benefit analyses. I was tireless and unrelenting, spurred on by a just, righteous, and self-interested cause. And in the end, the administration caved, the nursery was saved, and my child-care arrangements remained intact. But ironically, this challenge to the university led me along a circuitous path to my own administrative career.

When I spoke out in university forums, I was observed by others, including Wally Williams, the acting dean of the College of Liberal Arts, who thought that I was effective and persuasive. "Come work with me," he implored. "I need that kind of advocacy in the Dean's Office." "No," I told him emphatically. "I have no interest in administration. I'm quite happy doing what I do." I was loath to reveal how much of an anathema I felt administration was. Only drudges and drones did such work. Why would anyone want to do *that*? I loved both scholarship and teaching. The life of a tenured professor had a certain glamour and panache, and the flexibility of hours was unbeatable. But Wally wouldn't take no for an answer; he called me repeatedly—pestered me—urged me to reconsider. Finally, I too

William and Best Friend, Bennett, in front of Detroit Home

caved, agreeing to serve one year only, after which I would take my scheduled sabbatical. One year. I could stand that, I thought.

Part of the reason I capitulated to Wally's appeal was that by this time, 1982, I had achieved full professor, another professional milestone, and I saw a long stretch of sameness before me. Having reached this plateau at age forty, would I simply repeat myself for the next twenty-five years? I had been in the job for fourteen years. And, in truth, the English Department was becoming a less-comfortable and -congenial place to be. I found tiresome the rivalries over what was fashionable and what was not, who was "in" and who was "out." I was growing weary with the recondite discourse and the fractious politics that had overtaken the subject matter, discipline, and departmental life of English.

The move across the street into the administrative offices in Mackenzie Hall would free me from this little hot house and launch me into a different world, one with its own peculiar discourse and politics. It was nothing short of ridiculous that these people, the bureaucrats, thought they were Wayne State University; the real university lay across the street in the classrooms. But overnight I became "the other," one of those deluded administrators who couldn't be trusted but who still held some kind of inchoate "power" and so must be approached with caution, deference, compelling arguments, and heart-rending predictions of imminent ruin.

I was made dean of the Arts and Humanities, worked closely with the chairs of twelve or so departments, and reported to the dean of the College of Liberal Arts. While very large, Liberal Arts was but one unit within the much-larger university, which included powerful professional schools and was led by a new, tough-minded president, David Adamany. The administration was rigidly hierarchal, authoritarian, and almost entirely composed of white males. The higher the floor in Mackenzie Hall, the more powerful the administrators. I occupied an office on the second floor with the status-less undergraduate offices and advising center. Wally's office was located on the fifth floor; the provost and president, on the exalted twelfth. Years after I left Wayne, the university demolished Mackenzie Hall and the English Department moved out of State Hall. In my consciousness, though, these buildings and arrangements still exist, housing potent memories of my Wayne State experiences.

Looking on me as his discovery, Wally Williams was delighted with my work. He himself was new, acting, African American, and from an area, Nutrition Sciences, of relatively low status in the university. He thought of us as outsiders bonded together in this fortress of white males, who disparaged women and blacks. But Wally's own position was less than secure. When the search was undertaken to find a permanent dean, he was eliminated from consideration, and shortly thereafter he left Wayne State to become a dean at another institution, and too soon after that, he had an untimely death.

As dean of the Arts and Humanities, I helped to leverage the fortunes of our division by promoting unity and concert and discouraging fighting and division. My message was simple: let's work together; the whole is greater than the sum of the parts. So I spearheaded an NEH Challenge Grant application that joined the departments together in a newly formed Humanities Council and put forward ambitious goals. When we received the highly competitive grant, I reluctantly agreed to extend my administrative stint to oversee it. These efforts helped to enrich our coffers with new funds and our spirits with new energy. Still, I didn't think of myself as an "administrator," that dreaded "other." Instead, I was a faculty member on a temporary administrative assignment.

That stance was harder to maintain when I entertained taking the position of dean of Arts and Sciences at the University of North Carolina in Greensboro. Admittedly, courtship by a university or college is heady stuff; you feel that you can again "light out" to a new territory and begin a whole new life. After seventeen years, I had fully expected to live and die in Detroit. But the city had been inexorably changing. The hopefulness that had given rise to the "renaissance" in the seventies was eroding and washing away. The same liberals who had moved into our neighborhood started, one by one, to move out. Tom and I thought we were unique, but it turns out we were acting in concert with others; we became part of the accelerating exodus from Detroit. The precipitating moment for us was a break-in at our house.

We returned one Friday evening from a pizza outing to hear noises upstairs in our house. Tom shouted, "Who's there?" We could hear the intruder dashing about nosily. We learned later that the would-be thief jumped from the second story window. William, who was nine years old at the time, was shaken up by the event and experienced long-lasting trauma, which required therapy to address. Afraid now, he imagined noises in the house. Each night he insisted we check all the closets and the attic before he went to bed. He became frightened of the neighborhood, where he had freely roamed for years. Soon he wouldn't leave the block, then he was fearful just standing outside in the yard. Clearly, we needed to move somewhere else where he would feel safe. So we pulled up stakes and moved to Greensboro, North Carolina.

THE UNIVERSITY OF NORTH CAROLINA AT GREENSBORO

Adjusting to Greensboro, the town and university, was much harder than I had anticipated. For a long time, I missed my friends, Detroit, and the life that we had built for seventeen years. I have often likened my administrative career to a Faustian bargain: you sell your soul and your sense of rootedness to the Devil of ambition and are doomed to an itinerant life. I learned that being the "real" dean, unlike being the "associate" dean, was feeling the heat of the kitchen in a direct and unrelenting way. I was initially oppressed by the weight of the office, the sheer drudgery of paperwork, the wall of civil deference that separated me from faculty colleagues, and the loneliness and dreariness of being "the other."

Although people repeatedly said to Tom and me, "You're going to love Greensboro," we didn't even like it for a while. The southern heat and humidity were oppressive, and the culture was uncomfortably conservative. Used to "the beat, the beat" of Detroit, the city of Greensboro seemed too laid back, downright sleepy. "What do you think of life in Greensboro?" someone asked Tom. "It's like living in an open grave," he retorted, and I'm afraid he wasn't kidding. And his own difficulties with employment exacerbated the problem. After the straight and sometimes rude talk of Detroit, we didn't know quite what to make of the syrupy civility that characterized casual discourse. Despite its gracious exterior, Old Greensboro was not especially welcoming to outsiders, and native white southerners looked somewhat askance at us northerners.

But we lived amid newcomers and academicians recently settled in Greensboro, a regional center for many corporations and site of several colleges and universities. Over time I grew fond of Greensboro. The town had lovely residential neighborhoods, where a kind of bland, middle-class lifestyle predominated. The school and sports activities of our young child drew us into a pleasant, casual familiarity with other families, and we developed comfortable friendships with other university people.

Moreover, I faced up to the challenges and potential of the deanship. The College of Arts and Sciences was by far the largest unit within the University of North Carolina at Greensboro (UNCG), then an institution of 10,500 students. The College housed nearly half the faculty and generated more than half the student credit hours. There were also five professional schools. When I arrived, the College was divided against itself and demoralized by the increasing emphasis on the professional schools. College departments competed with each other, often acrimoniously, for diminishing resources.

Yet a relatively recent institutional statement claimed that the mission of UNCG was to "offer the finest opportunity for liberal education in the state." The university was originally Woman's College of North Carolina, the state's distinguished liberal arts college for women, and it continued to draw fine faculty in the liberal arts disciplines. It seemed obvious to me that much could be gained by energizing and building on the liberal arts. Nothing was to be gained from defeatism and squabbling among departments and programs. Basically, my message was that together we could be a powerful force within the university; divided, we were doomed to be ignored. This was the same message I had used at Wayne State. Perhaps leadership is as simple as that, convincing people that more can be gained from working together than apart.

And work together we did, building up palpable *esprit de corps* and momentum on curricular initiatives. Well-respected faculty colleagues joined me in leadership roles as associate deans. To help "center" the College, we worked to strengthen the general education curriculum and to develop new coordinated freshman seminars, faculty seminars, and a writing-across-the-curriculum program. We gave increased support for interdisciplinary programs and established a new Center for Critical Inquiry in the Liberal Arts. Buoying our spirits was the award of a highly competitive NEH grant to help support these efforts.

While we made good progress, moving ahead was not easy amid daunting bureaucratic structures. UNCG was one of sixteen campuses in the UNC system. Multiple bureaucratic layers on our own campus were overlaid by many more of the general administration of the university system and of the state personnel bureaucracy. Added to the mix were the unpredictable political maneuverings within the North Carolina State Legislature. As Woman's College, UNCG had been one of the original three campuses in the system, but this proud lineage did not secure the institution a favored position within the system. Other ambitious campuses were vying for favor, growth, and expanded missions. Without effective political clout, UNCG often lost the battle for fiscal sustenance in the legislature.

It was at UNCG that I first became aware of how indelibly institutions can be imprinted with gender characteristics. People claimed that Woman's College had been stereotypically "female" in its institutional style and way of dealing with state authorities: it was "modest," "self-sacrificing," and "civil"; it "made do" with limited resources; and it voluntarily "turned back" money even when not required. As a result, UNCG was historically underfunded. Similarly, I found the faculty excessively "civil," "modest," and "passive," at least initially. I was determined to instill a more-assertive spirit in the collective psyche, an aspiration that would later seem foolhardy when I moved to Wesleyan and encountered a faculty that had excessive amounts of these qualities.

The chancellor of our campus sought to address the problems of inadequate resources and the "inferior" image by emphasizing graduate and professional programs. Such a strategy implicitly downplayed UNCG's traditional strengths in undergraduate liberal arts education, perhaps in part because that curriculum was so clearly associated with the Woman's College. So it may well have been that my agenda as dean—strengthening the liberal arts core—was at odds with the tacit agenda of higher administrators, but that conflict was not immediately apparent.

Although UNCG had been admitting male students for over twenty years, it was still struggling to attract sufficient male applicants in the late 1980s. To help address this problem, the chancellor decided to upgrade intercollegiate athletics. Without the support of the faculty and arousing the ire of many loyal alumnae, he made a decision to move the school from Division III to Division I status in the NCAA.

Shortly thereafter the vice-chancellor for Academic Affairs, Elisabeth Zinser, launched a major planning initiative, employing a deeply problematical approach. She met confidentially with a small committee and developed a plan without any consultation whatsoever with the deans, who were allegedly in charge of our units, or the faculty at large. She eventually released a mammoth document entitled *Quo Vadimus?* (Where Are We Going). A key part of the plan, I was shocked to learn, was to de-center and dismantle the College of Arts and Sciences. Instead of the College overseeing liberal education, she proposed a university dean of Undergraduate Studies who would report to her office. Her office also would assume oversight of all interdisciplinary programs. Furthermore, while I had steadfastly opposed the professional-school ambitions of the large Department of Communication and Theatre, which wanted leave the College of Arts and Sciences, she supported this change. So, with its central functions moved to the Office of the Vice-Chancellor and with its size dramatically decreased, the College of Arts and Sciences would no longer be central or centered, and would easily revert to separate, uncoordinated departments much weakened in the competition for resources with the professional schools.

Elisabeth envisioned her office as the "center" of university education out of which all academic functions would radiate. Trained in nursing and higher-education administration, she had a kind of democratic egalitarianism: liberal is professional; professional is liberal; everyone does liberal education. But she underestimated the forces of traditionalism and resistance to radical restructuring. *Quo Vadimus?* was embarrassing both in its rhetorical excesses and in its overweening and unworkable re-engineering of institutional design. It provoked impassioned outrage and eloquent belittlement from many College faculty. Indeed, the release of *Quo Vadimus?* marked the beginning of open insurrection against the vice-chancellor.

I was put in a tough spot. I had to continue working with the vice-chancellor, who was my supervisor, but I felt deeply betrayed and angry. Elisabeth should not have surprised me and others with this plan; the absence of consultation and process was deeply troubling. Our relationship inevitably became strained. A sympathetic view of her aspiration might be that Elisabeth too envisioned the whole as greater than the sum of the parts. In some ways her approach was a caricature, a larger vision, of mine, but with less respect for the complexities of the academic terrain, particularly the liberal arts, that she so boldly re-charted. The crucial difference between our approaches to planning was that I insisted on an open and collaborative process whereas she confidently spun and veiled her "vision" before presenting it in whole cloth to a shocked, outraged community—particularly College faculty.

Amid this turmoil, everything suddenly changed. During spring break in March of 1988, it was announced that Vice-Chancellor Zinser had accepted the presidency of Gallaudet University and would be leaving before the end of the term. Suppressed jubilation overtook the campus. Her reign at Gallaudet, however, was the week that wasn't. The students at this institution for the hearing-impaired were outraged that a deaf person was not appointed president and staged an impassioned rebellion that effectively prevented the new president from taking office. We watched television news each night with fascination and sinking hearts; our vice-chancellor metamorphosed into a television personality; her new position melted away before our eyes. By the end of spring break she was back in her old office at UNCG.

So we limped along that year and the next, urging the chancellor to step in to adjudicate the conflict and clarify institutional direction, while we tried to keep momentum going on other College plans. In the spring of 1989 rumors began circulating that Elisabeth was "on the market" and finally that she had accepted another presidency. Soon thereafter *Quo Vadimus?* was relegated to the shelf. Its four hundred pages were bound in a white plastic binder, appropriately enough, for it was a white elephant, a testament to the tremendous expense in time, money, and spirit that ill-conceived institutional planning can suck out of an institution.

I have often asked myself whether institutions are well served by the itinerant academic leaders, like Elisabeth and myself, who pass through them, stir things up, and raise expectations. Typically, a new dean, provost, or president comes in with a flurry of attention and initiates a major planning process, which can generate positive energy and creative thinking about aspirations for the future. But the fiasco of *Quo Vadimus?* showed that planning without consultation and reflection can produce a discordant, unworkable product and provoke an uprising against the administration. But even without such a counterinsurgency, itinerant academic leaders often leave an institution before plans are fully implemented, disrupting institutional momentum in the process. Is hiring them just a waste of time, money, and spirit? Why not, instead of this periodic disruption, draw administrative leaders from the institution's own faculty? Such practice helps break down the old binary of "us" and "them." That was my strategy when I drew faculty colleagues into the Dean's Office to work with me. But often there's a dearth of interest or administrative aptitude among the regular faculty. And that talent and capacity for administration, once identified, can become a saleable asset in university markets, and these people too can evolve into the itinerant circuit riders of academia.

Beyond these professional challenges and questions, the useful life of an academic leader in any one institution is discrete and delimited. In conversation one day, a seasoned administrator told me that a new leader started the job with a certain amount of credit, like cards. Gradually, he or she must play those cards, diminishing the stock of good will until the credit is all used up and it's time to go. The natural cycle was about seven years, he thought. Some academic leaders stay for many productive years beyond seven (as I was to do later in my career), but sometimes their constituents feel "it's time for them to go" and may grumble in discontent or conspire to topple them in the meantime.

Philosophically, I came to see administrators as "replaceable parts" of omnivorous and enduring institutions. On darker days I surrealistically envisioned institutions as vampires feeding off of the lifeblood of people who dedicate themselves to their welfare, then indiscriminately moving on to draw blood from the next guys. On brighter days I took comfort in the enduring strength of institutions of higher learning, which are so much stronger than any individual who contributes to them at any one time. A college or university moves on resiliently after being shepherded by a good leader. A poor leader, on the other hand, can inflict a lot of harm, leave behind a lot of damage, and disrupt institutional momentum.

I had always known that administration was an insalubrious life, which is why I had resisted committing myself to it. Only after several years at UNCG did I admit to myself that I had crossed over to the "dark side"—that I had made a career shift into administration. I remember the day that I testified publicly before the bemused

College faculty that "I am an administrator," an admission that was arguably as hard to say as "I am an alcoholic." But I saw in the many parallels between my scholarly work and academic leadership that I was "reading" the institution, in much the same way I read and interpreted a novel by using the tools of literary analysis. Academic leadership, I realized, is fundamentally an interpretive task. Indeed, I have always been deeply skeptical of any academic leader who starts out with a fully formed "vision" and tries to impose it on the institution. Rather, what is needed in a new leader is the ability to *see* the college or university and appreciate both what is already there and what is incipiently possible. That you do through close "reading" and widespread consultation. Apparently, I had an appetite and aptitude for that. And I accepted my fate, however "dark."

A later epiphany, after I had moved to Wesleyan University, was realizing that institutions are rather like people. They have their own distinctive collective psyches and personality disorders. And perhaps, instead of literary analysis, administration requires another skill set, psychoanalysis. That is a subject I shall turn to in the next chapter. Suffice it to say that by the time I left UNCG, I had made my peace with myself: I was an administrator and I was ready for the next challenge.

} 5 {

WESLEYAN UNIVERSITY

"The Fascination of What's Difficult"

If I had come to embrace the role of academic leader at Greensboro, I tested that role to the limit at my next stop, Wesleyan University. My Wesleyan experience has sometimes reminded me of one of Yeats's poems: "The fascination of what's difficult / Has dried the sap out of my veins, and rent / Spontaneous joy and natural content / Out of my heart." But something valuable may get wrenched out of this struggle. Sometimes even, as Yeats wrote in another poem, a "terrible beauty" is born.[1] I shall always think of our successful administrative endeavors at Wesleyan as a "terrible beauty," but at the time, I could have used a little more "spontaneous joy."

Compared to the bustle generated by over ten thousand students and multiple spheres of activity at UNCG, Wesleyan, with under three thousand students. seemed a small, comparatively simple world unto itself. In only two days of interviewing for the Office of Vice-President for Academic Affairs and Provost, the place was sharply etched in my mind, and the word "Wesleyan" quickly took on meaning and exuded force as a collective cultural term. Of course, the Wesleyan I knew was of a particular time, 1990–1995, and it was filtered through my unique perspectives as a new administrator. My view—my interpretation—may well bear no relationship to the Wesleyan of today or that of other observers at the time.

Because the president, Bill Chace, asked candidates for the position to respond in writing to questions about the job and themselves, I have a document of my initial impressions. From the start I was both drawn to and challenged by Wesleyan; its values were my values. And although Wesleyan was in many ways an admirable place, there was something displeasing, jarring, and narcissistic about it, at least for me. To confront Wesleyan was to deal in some way with a caricature of myself and the liberal values I had wholeheartedly embraced. The university offered a powerful challenge, personal and institutional.

Founded in Middletown, Connecticut in 1831, Wesleyan University thought of itself as both an "elite" liberal arts college on par with Williams and Amherst and a "little university" on par with Brown and other private universities. Intellectual seriousness characterized Wesleyan. For the most part, faculty were committed scholars and students inquisitive learners. In the sixties, Wesleyan had been a pioneer in the enrollment of significant numbers of minority students and maintained a strong commitment to inclusion and diversity. Sometimes referred to as "diversity university," Wesleyan was nonetheless an elitist institution nowhere near as diverse socioeconomically, ethnically, and politically as Wayne State University. Leftist and liberal values reigned supreme at Wesleyan to the degree that I coined the term "totalitarian liberalism" to describe the intolerance for any views differing or divergent from those dominating the campus.

Wesleyan's liberalism was both political and educational. Its tradition of fierce individualism attracted independently minded and sometimes-eccentric and -edgy students, who contributed to Wesleyan's latter-day countercultural flavor and flair. Like me, many faculty had come of age in the sixties, and Wesleyan remained an island—some would say a little hot house—of sixties culture seemingly cut off from larger currents in post-Vietnam America.

I certainly sensed its insularity during my initial interviews. Perhaps because I had been at much-larger, more-comprehensive public universities, I was surprised by how much Wesleyan was preoccupied with itself, its internal politics, and its reputation among other elite liberal-arts institutions. Wesleyan defiantly asserted its so-called uniqueness as an institution more liberal, more individualistic, more diverse, and more committed to excellence than its closest competitors, but was anxious about how it was perceived in the college market place and by its institutional peers. Wesleyan was at once proud and boastful, insecure and apprehensive. From the first I was drawn to psychological terms and tools to comprehend "Wesleyan," a subject I shall return to later.

Both fascinated and repelled by Wesleyan, I was uncertain about whether to accept the job. A strong draw was the president, Bill Chace; I thought, yes, I would like to work with him. Unfailingly, I appreciated Bill's effervescent good humor, urbanity, wit, and intelligence. He got all-out effort from his colleagues because he gave to them so much respect, space, and support. Yet his was a troubled presidency, and initially, leadership from his office was faltering. Although Bill grew into the job over the years, he and Wesleyan got off to a rocky start and never achieved a comfortable measure of compatibility.

The previous year, the search for my position had failed, necessitating a redo and delaying the new administration's planning. More critically, President Chace's inaugural address, given in October 1989 at the beginning of his second year, enraged many faculty, who thought he was trying to make Wesleyan more like a small college and less like a "little university." They feared that he intended to emphasize teaching more at the expense of research. Wesleyan professors agreed among themselves about little else but their shared commitment to the scholar-teacher model of faculty responsibility. In other words, they believed faculty scholarship must be valued and supported because it was essential to teaching at the highest level. Threatening the importance of research, or seeming to, were "fighting words." Shortly after I accepted the position in the spring of 1990, Wesleyan was in upheaval. Student radicals were stirring up protests and unrest. This activity shockingly climaxed with the firebombing of the president's office. While no one was hurt, this episode was the nadir of the seemingly jinxed the Chace presidency. Nothing seemed to go right for Bill.

I heard about these incidents from afar, although I had just accepted the job. I was told that two charismatic, manipulative, and malevolent student leaders, one of whom was deeply disturbed, fomented unrest in the student body. Tragically, the unstable student leader was murdered the following summer in Hartford during a drug deal gone awry. The other major suspect in the firebombing, while found not guilty (a verdict that many thought wrong), was suspended for a poor academic record. By the time I arrived the next fall, students were stunned into silence by the violent outcome of events, and the campus was tense and unsettled.

Even during my initial visits to campus, I was taken back by the loud, in-your-face, New York City–style of the ordinary discourse. The manner contrasted starkly with the deferential southern civility of UNCG. Once ensconced, I was welcomed by many collegial, charming, and community-spirited individuals, but shrill and strident voices set the tone at many campus gatherings, where an atmosphere of skepticism, resistance, and wariness prevailed. The failure of civility wasn't intentionally rude, so much as reflexive and unreflective. I felt in faculty and students an almost-palpable mood of anxiety, hostility, and distrust toward the Chase administration in particular and toward "authority" in general. The strong values of individualism dovetailed with decentralization in campus governance, work patterns, and living styles. Both students and faculty were used to operating as free agents in a privileged university environment. Altogether, there was a robust sense of individual rights and privileges and a weaker ethic of responsibility and obligation.

Presiding over this uneasy community was the officers' group, which met weekly with the president. The omnipresent topic in this forum was the budget. The institution had a long history of boom and bust, with windfalls of money generating ambitious plans that were impossible to sustain over the long term. It was my misfortune to arrive in a period of bust. The institution was overextended, annual budget deficits were common, and a backlog of deferred maintenance added to budget pressure. The gist of the talk was "we're in trouble, what should we cut?" I credit myself with turning around this exercise to ask the important questions, "What do we value? What must we preserve and build?" I could not imagine presiding over a totally negative agenda. I was convinced that we needed to engage our natural constituencies, the faculty especially, in a discussion and articulation of mission and aspirations for the future, especially in light of the anger, confusion, and anxiety engendered by Bill's inaugural address. We had to move forward positively even while we devised a plan to cut the budget and achieve fiscal equilibrium.

So I was a proponent, as usual, for institutional planning. But first, jurisdictional boundaries had to be redrawn. For instance, the discussion of academic matters had to be relocated from the officers' group to the academic division. I brought into my office three terrific faculty colleagues to serve as divisional deans and gave them broad responsibilities. They served essentially as a kitchen cabinet, working collegially and collaboratively with me. With the deans' assistance I tried to build an administrative network through department chairs to the faculty, but this venture was less successful.

Chairs, for the most part, could not and would not take on an institutional role at Wesleyan. They were wary, defensive, and turf-bound. In the highly decentralized system of governance, faculty looked on the rotating departmental chair as a tedious, unwanted chore with little status, power, or influence for all the headaches it brought. As a result, departmental planning was poor, and collaborative institutional planning was nonexistent. The way to succeed, people presumed, was not through formal, organized channels of governance but through informal, circuitous routes to upper administration, especially through personal entreaties to the president. Much to his credit, Bill blocked these end runs around my office. He, like me, wanted the faculty to partner with us in envisioning, articulating, and executing a productive agenda for the university. Soon after he arrived on campus, Bill asked that a faculty chair, not the president, preside at faculty meetings. He also wanted to meet regularly with a faculty planning committee to discuss institutional problems and hammer out rational solutions. So a new committee, the Institutional Planning Advisory Committee (IPAC), emerged from what had been its relatively moribund predecessor concerned mainly with benefits issues. This would be a good start to cultivating faculty engagement and trust, I hoped.

Bill and I met regularly with IPAC to discuss drafts of the various pieces of institutional planning we commissioned and to hear faculty views. The first year, these meetings were often dominated by some of Wesleyan's most-outspoken and -irascible faculty members, who were curiously and purposely chosen by their colleagues for this service. Especially evident in our meetings were the deep divisions across the three academic divisions: Sciences, Social Sciences, and Arts and Humanities. The social sciences resented what they saw as preferential treatment of the sciences. With PhD programs, science departments seemed to others to have more than their fair share of institutional resources and to do less than their fair share of teaching and advising. Faculty in the sciences were at once deeply defensive and self-congratulatory, justifying their graduate mission in the university and feeling besieged by misunderstanding and shortsightedness among their colleagues. Two faculty members from opposing divisions carried on this debate in the committee; neither was willing to let the other have the last word in their barbed exchanges.

When not derailed by acrimonious bickering, filibustering, and grandstanding, I tried to be honest, direct, and focused in these meetings. We had spirited and seemingly productive dialogue. One of the most difficult issues, though, was budget. For a long time many members of IPAC remained in denial. The budget problems were, they proposed, concocted by the administration in order to extract acquiescence from the faculty. Or, if not entire fabrications, the fiscal problems were caused by poor management and should be solved by better management: raise more money; make better investments; cut other aspects of the institution. Don't cut the academic program, which is the core, the "nucleus," of the place. And, to be sure, improved management, fund-raising, investment management, and tightening in other areas were needed as well. But the budget deficit was of such magnitude that fiscal recovery would necessitate reductions on the academic side too. IPAC, Bill, and I carefully went over the budgets, painstakingly exploring alternatives and finding no way out of this hard truth. It seemed as if the committee, except for one implacable member, would accept the validity of the evidence and get on with the next steps. But I was naive.

IPAC's report to the faculty, after the first year of these meetings, scathingly criticized the administration for its alleged withholding of information and its distortion of budget problems. I was surprised and hurt, but I learned a lesson. It was one thing for Wesleyan faculty to hold discussions in private with the administration; it was quite another to go on record in public endorsing a position that peers viewed as one of co-optation. "They'll turn on you," I was warned, and that is essentially what happened. This excoriation was an example of how deeply resistant the Wesleyan faculty was to shared governance. Better to resist, to protest, to grandstand, to accuse, to refuse cooperation than to accept a responsible role in working out shared problems. I was especially surprised that the more-mild-mannered folk went along with the mean-spirited ones, but that was proof of deep resistance to what I hoped to accomplish: developing a genuine collaboration with faculty leadership.

Not all faculty were like these shrill complainers. On the contrary, most were not. The silent majority had opted out of the communal life of the institution and had left the ground open to the more-outrageous folk. One astute faculty member said about one of his colleagues, the most outspoken, self-centered, and childlike of them all: "He's our carnival." Indeed, I believe he acted out the insecurities, anxieties, and anger that other more-civil people felt at some level. Because he touched some subterranean chord, he was tolerated with bemusement and even fondness. But he was transparent and childlike in his impassioned dedication to his self-interest. More villainous were those folk who deliberately misrepresented for effect and who personalized their vitriolic bad temper and projected all that was wrong with the world of Wesleyan onto administrators who were motivated by "evil" or faculty who had been "co-opted."

But I should also note that during my time at Wesleyan, many strong and effective faculty members undertook significant leadership roles, and under the *Academic Plan*, major institutional improvements were effected: a new first-year program; an expanded program for writing across the curriculum; a major initiative in International Studies, including the creation of an Office of International Studies; and the launching of the Freeman Scholars Program to bring Asian students to the campus. We named faculty directors to Graduate Studies and to a new Office of Research and Sponsored Programs. Although the "noise" would sometimes drive one to despair about achieving collaboration with the faculty, in fact a great deal of faculty good citizenship manifested itself at this time.

In its second year, IPAC membership had changed to include mostly fair-minded faculty, including the chair who led his colleagues through a tough, rigorous review of the budget and emerging *University Plan*. During this year I met with each department and program in a kind of mini-review to assess the outlay of faculty resources, and by late winter, I presented to IPAC for discussion and debate a detailed plan and justification for where I proposed faculty lines and resources would be cut over a period of five years, mostly through attrition or reductions in nontenure lines. IPAC faculty chose not to take a position on the particular cuts, but they did endorse the general assumptions and budget parameters of the plan. And in an act of leadership, they tried to educate the faculty and students about the necessity of budget reduction.

We held many forums for community education, working hard to develop a collaborative and consensual process, but it was hard going. In addition to the faculty-line cuts, there were also reductions in the operating budget and in staff, and we issued new policy guidelines for teaching loads, never a popular idea. In the last months of this process, a kind of frenzied paranoia about the impending faculty cuts absorbed the campus. Wild rumors would develop like wildfires, fed by the Woodward-and-Bernstein-like investigations of the student paper, *The Argus*. I was besieged by petitions, letters, and phone calls from outraged students or faculty or alumni or community citizens who feared that their favorite program would get the axe. Rumors that Italian would be eliminated even brought out letters to the editor in *The Middletown Press*, not surprising, I suppose, in this Italian-dominated town.

Now fully imagined as the "other" by the opposition, I was subjected to a barrage of angry outbursts, misrepresentations, and abuse. I was caricatured and vilified in the student paper as the enemy of people, as if the idea of faculty cuts emerged from my sadistic nature rather than from fiscal realities. On one occasion, a member of the Advisory Committee on Tenure and Promotion said with wry self-irony after a department had come in to make an impassioned defense against a position the committee had taken: "Let's do what we do so well, let's cave in." He was right: There was a long-standing pattern of caving in at Wesleyan, and no decision was ever perceived to be final. I thought "Challenge Authority" should be Wesleyan's motto. I revised a Yogi Berra aphorism to "it ain't over *when* it's over" as the summation of the Wesleyan ethos. But then I was not acculturated by Wesleyan. I didn't cave in easily, and I found the nagging, badgering, and wheedling unseemly and unpersuasive. I could never understand the political stupidity of some of people who seemed to think that repeated insults would eventually win me or anyone over. So I held fast.

The worst kind of acting out came near the end of my last year at Wesleyan, when I received a death threat on voice mail, which said in part: "Just because you inveigled your way into tenure, you may think you are something, but you are nothing. You have done more to damage this institution than anyone else. If anyone deserves to die, you do." While the perpetrators of this call remained unidentified, I suspect they were students campaigning to "Save Bernstein," to get a permanent position for a long-standing part-time adjunct faculty. Lobbying for him had gone on for over a decade. Fortunately, nothing came of this threat (although public safety officers, surreptitiously dressed in academic regalia, surrounded me as bodyguards at commencement) and most people did not trespass into criminal incivility.

In fact, the level of disturbance was highest before the plan of reduction was released in April 1993. After that, a kind of calm and even acceptance prevailed. Clearly, there was wisdom in releasing the plan in its totality. "Cruelties should be committed all at once, as in that way each separate one is less felt," Machiavelli sagely advises.[2] Not only were the proposed cuts presented all together, but each one was accompanied by a description of the process, rationale, and timetable. I think that the reception was relatively calm, because it was difficult to fault the processes and hard to avoid the consequences of inaction. I felt that I had weathered the storm through both careful planning and sheer endurance. Our process had been quite unlike that of nearby Yale University, where the upper administration had developed a plan in private and, upon releasing it, had engendered the rage of the faculty and eventually caused the resignation of several high-level administrators, including the president and provost. Despite the resentment, pain, and turmoil, our dedication to collaboration paid off in the long run at Wesleyan.

But the ordeal did take its belated toll on me. Not many weeks later, inexplicably I had difficulty walking. I went for what turned out to be a series of medical tests, but no diagnosis of my condition was ever made, except that the symptoms were neurological. After about six weeks, they disappeared. I suppose "stress" could be blamed for this condition. As the chairman of the Board of Trustees sometimes said to me in empathy: "You are where the rubber hits the road." And that, indeed, is how it sometimes felt. It was an arduous, uphill drive to create the *University Plan* and secure its general acceptance among an often-suspicious faculty.

By the start of the fall semester in 1993, we had clearly passed through the nadir and were emerging on the other side. The *University Plan* was working: academic initiatives were underway; budgets were balanced; deferred maintenance was being addressed; admission numbers were rising; financial aid was, at least temporarily, under control; but most of all, the mood was better and the campus seemed to settle into a reluctant acceptance of the regimen applied under the *Plan*. Yet displaced anger and resentment was still looking for a target. And I was dismayed to see some of it spill over onto faculty leadership. IPAC, especially its chair, was targeted for vilification. The committee's cooperation was viewed as co-optation in some quarters, and some faculty questioned IPAC's very existence. The next year, in a mood of gleeful committee bashing, the faculty voted to abolish it.

Understandably, faculty often got frustrated when their time was absorbed in "unfulfilling" committee work; nonetheless, it was depressing to listen to some argue that they should be excused from any role in institutional governance. These faculty seemed to welcome the installation of a benevolent dictator, although they reserved the right to refuse going along with him or her. Dedicated as I was to the principle of shared governance, I saw this move as a setback, but by then intervening events transpired at the university, including Bill Chace's resignation, my service for a year as interim president, and, subsequently, my plans to leave Wesleyan.

In the spring of 1994 Bill surprised everyone, including me, by revealing his decision to accept the presidency of Emory University in Atlanta, Georgia. Subsequently, Ray Denworth, chairman of the Board of Trustees, asked me to serve as acting president. I didn't know what to think. Bill's planned departure left me feeling the deep loss of his unflagging, abiding collegiality. I was reluctant to take on a job that I thought I would hate. I was not an especially gregarious academician, after all. I didn't have the temperament for all the glad-handing required of a college president. On the other hand, I was pleased that Ray asked me to step up. I read his request as an act of confidence in and a validation of the course we had set Wesleyan on with the *University Plan*. So, after thinking over his offer for a few days, I accepted the job.

When he asked me to serve as interim president, Chairman Denworth used vivid military terms. "You had been out there with a machete," he said, "while Bill was in the tent with the radio. How would you like to take over the radio for a while?" And that, in fact, was how different the two jobs felt. Being the academic vice-president was a tough slog. As interim president, I could come up from the roadbed and survey our work. The privilege and pleasure of serving as president, I quickly realized, are the vistas it provides. Standing back, I was proud of what we had accomplished. Having gone through a difficult period of retrenching and shoring up, the university was regaining strength and poised for a brighter future. From the perspective afforded by the president's office, I appreciated Wesleyan with the new insight.

As interim president, I took every opportunity to make the transition a time of reflection and celebration. The results were tangible. The spirit of rallying around the school was refreshing and sustaining. Truthfully and sadly, there was a feeling of relief that Bill Chace was gone; he became the convenient scapegoat on whom people heaped abuse—often unfairly. But I knew that Bill had left a solid legacy; the *University Plan* had tangibly strengthened an institution that had been in disarray and deficit for some time. I was glad to have a year to enjoy the fruits of our labors.

And enjoy them I did. I was surprised at how much I liked the presidency. In part I really took satisfaction from setting the university's agenda and tone, which the president controls much more than the academic vice-president. Another pleasure of the job was exactly what I thought I would not like: interacting with the larger community. After having been enclaved among faculty all my adult life, getting out and about in public, feeling the fresh winds of the larger world, and meeting with interesting people from diverse settings energized me, especially after the bruising work of the vice-presidency. I saw how much more there was to "Wesleyan" than the campus community alone. The job of engaging the Board of Trustees, the larger world of higher education, philanthropic organizations, and local and state communities invigorated me. And most especially, I enjoyed meeting the alumni, whom I found to be invariably smart, independently minded, and interesting. Repeatedly, they credited the institution with the development of their critical thinking, the foundation of their adult lives and professional careers. That "challenge authority" acculturation had its upside.

Like other presidents, I was made acutely aware that the institution is a product of the myriad tangible and intangible contributions of people past and present as well as its accumulated history, customs, policies, and traditions. An institution is stronger and more resilient than any one individual or a single generation of individuals. Yet in spite of all of this diffused strength, a president also appreciates the fragility of the place and the humbling responsibility of looking after this deep legacy.

The presidency, I decided, was a job worthy of consideration. Despite my original misgivings, I seemed to have the temperament for it, after all. Being a *real* president seemed like the next inevitable stage of my professional career. I let my name go forward in the presidential search at Mount Holyoke College, for given the impending change in administration at Wesleyan, my future as provost was uncertain. But the more I thought about it, the more I didn't want to go back to my old job. Going forward seemed the only alternative on the road of the itinerant administrator.

Meanwhile, scores of people were urging me to throw my hat in the ring for the Wesleyan presidency, and several nominated me for the job. Because I had developed real affection for Wesleyan, I was tempted to accept the nomination, but I first talked informally and privately with Chairman Denworth to seek his advice. He told me bluntly that I would have no chance, that I was too associated with budget-cutting. They were looking for someone different, very likely a nonacademic. I was shocked by Ray's well-intentioned but brutal directness and dismayed that I was disparaged and dismissed without a hearing for doing the tough, unpopular work of budget control, which the Board itself had authorized. But then "Wesleyan" would never get high marks for its manners or civility. While affronted by this putdown, I didn't dwell on it, because soon I was being courted flatteringly by Mount Holyoke, which offered me the presidency in January 1995. Gratified by the welcoming embrace of Mount Holyoke, I knew that moving was right for both me and for Wesleyan.

As I reflect back on my Wesleyan experiences, the issue of gender stands out. I was the first woman provost and later the first and only female president at Wesleyan. The search committee was almost entirely male, and all five finalists for the permanent position were men. How was gender a factor in my experience there? If institutions take on a particular character, it is fair to say that most of them, Wesleyan prominently among them, are male-like, even though graduates call them their alma mater. This is not surprising: most colleges and universities were all-male institutions not so long ago, and they are products of a society, an educational establishment, and an intellectual heritage that have been overwhelmingly dominated by men. UNCG, on the other hand, was gendered "female," although some people fervently worked to erase this "stigma."

Wesleyan became coeducational twice—in 1872 and again in 1970. After being a early adopter of coeducation, it rather ingloriously stopped admitting women in 1909 even though its early female students did very well. In fact, all four women students in the entering class of 1876 graduated Phi Beta Kappa, and over the years, other students too excelled academically and quickly rose to leadership positions. Around the turn of the century, though, sentiment about coeducation gradually turned negative. Many male students, Board members, and alumni feared that Wesleyan—in having women students while its all-male competitors did not—would be perceived as a "namby-pamby college." Wesleyan's "pride and boast" were said to be its "masculine virility and strength." They feared that women students, whose numbers rose to 23 percent of the total student population in 1898, would change the character and sully the reputation of the school. Not only were women unfashionable; they were unprofitable. Wesleyan's enrollments decreased while those at all-male colleges like Amherst, Williams, Trinity, Dartmouth, and Yale grew. Wesleyan was thought to be victim of "terminal feminization." Something had to be done!

A vigorous anti-coeducation campaign was explicit about wanting the institution to project a more prestigious "male" image. The social ostracization and sexist belittlement that accompanied this anti-coeducation campaign could sink to cruel levels. For example, responding to an article critical of male students' campaign of ignoring women students and excluding them from campus engagement, the student body president explained, "The majority of the women in the college are not those that would be invited to social affairs under any circumstances. . . ."[3] When the Board voted to stop admitting women after the fall of 1909, the headline of the *Wesleyan Library Monthly* read, "The Barnacle is at last to be scraped from the good ship Wesleyan!"[4]

Although women were readmitted in 1970, even in the 1990s they had for the most part assimilated into the dominant culture rather than changed or challenged it. The male-dominated counterculture of the sixties lived on in the faculty culture at Wesleyan. Meetings with women faculty, reinforced by a faculty-wide survey, taught us that women experienced much higher job frustration and professional dissatisfaction than did their male colleagues. Many women were aggrieved, distrustful, and skeptical, warily looking after their own interests, pressed by personal and professional concerns. When I arrived at Wesleyan, there was undoubtedly a high level of discontent among all faculty—men and women. Although Wesleyan prided itself on its toughness and feistiness, faculty, staff, and students were surprisingly sensitive and vulnerable, and many had a knee-jerk antipathy to all authority at the same that they were longing for recognition and validation from that authority.

Not only was Wesleyan gendered male, but its governance had been a patriarchy. At least through the haze of institutional memory, Colin Campbell, the president prior to Bill Chace, was remembered as a loving "father-like" leader, who dispensed favors under an understood system of patronage. Bill was an urbane leader, sharp, ironic, and witty. An academician with credentials from prestigious institutions, he neither wished to be nor acted like the loving "father." In retaliation, "the children" acted out their rebellion and unhappiness in the campus playground.

Both as vice-president and as president, I found myself cast into the role of parental authority, although, given my gender, whether I was viewed as the "father" or "mother" wasn't always clear. I always remember an entreaty from one older male faculty member who was frustrated that I was, apparently, the final authority. He said in exasperation: "I can't help but think of you as a woman." I instinctively wanted to say in return but prudently held my tongue: "I cannot help but think of you as a child." Confusingly, I was a woman, an authority to be defied, and a "parent" whose "love" (or indulgence) was sought.

Wesleyan's male-inflected culture was congruent with the liberal values of the "free man" upon which liberal arts education is based. The ambition of individual faculty and their departments could be likened to the individualistic and entrepreneurial spirit of American culture. Faculty explored the frontiers of knowledge. They questioned authority and barriers of all kinds. They displayed the kind of pioneering and conquering spirit that shaped our nation: man over nature, mind over matter. They built careers; they created knowledge; their disciplines evolved. A dynamic freedom and individualism, generally positive forces in American culture, shaped the institutional character of Wesleyan and other liberal arts institutions.

But liberal values can flip to their illiberal counterpart in the academy, honeycombed with privilege and entitlement, when resources are tight and when continuing growth and dynamism collide with fiscal constraint and limitation. About such an institution one might say: "We were disturbed to encounter in discussions with faculty a widespread attitude characterized by blaming, finger-pointing, distrust, and abrogation of institutional responsibility. We saw evidence of allegiance focused on departments and programs; territorial protectionism; and a mentality of Balkanization which interferes with institutional loyalty and vision." What distinguishes this institution is "the long and persistent history of adversarial attitudes and ineffectual attention to university-wide problems, and the extent to which those attitudes and characteristics have become ingrained in the university's culture."[5]

I quote the language of the visiting reaccreditation team that came to Wesleyan amid our planning process. Where were the "venerable committees" with traditions of responsibility, the team asked? Admonishing the institution, the final report noted that these same complaints had been reported by a previous reaccreditation committee ten years earlier and must be corrected in ten years hence. Predictably, the report enraged the faculty, who blamed the administration for feeding the committee these critical views. In fact, the committee's opinions were formed firsthand in meetings with IPAC and department chairs. As is so typical of Wesleyan, there were no "company manners" for the visitors—the faculty openly expressed their habitual querulousness.

I said earlier that I found Wesleyan to be a caricature of myself and of the values that I held most dear. I had been a faculty member dedicated to liberal individualism, academically and politically. It was disconcerting, then, to see liberal values take on ugly forms as they sometimes did at Wesleyan. In retrospect, I think that one of the reasons I was originally drawn into administration was that it allowed me to break away from this self-centered, sometimes-narcissistic style of development. Although I hadn't particularly thought of myself as being gendered in my administrative style, my vocabulary and methodology were full of the "c" words affiliated with female gender: community, collaboration, connectedness, communication, and common responsibilities. So too did others, both men and women, use such language. Mildly chiding me about this essentialist gendering of human traits, Bill Chace said to me skeptically, "Some of the nicest women I know are men." In my defense, I'm using these gender metaphors to describe polarized aspects of institutional culture, not of human beings. One could describe this bifurcation in nongendered terms such as "individual rights" versus "communal values." In *Habits of the Heart: Individualism and Commitment in American Life*, for example, Robert Bellah notes that in drawing up the Bill of Rights, the founding fathers presumed shared communal values drawn from the Christian religion. But as Christianity atrophied and fragmented in American life, so did the national sense of communal values, and what developed was a culture out of balance, with an exaggerated sense of individual "rights."[6]

So too were many American colleges founded on a marriage of educational and religious values. Wesleyan found its genesis in the Protestantism of John Wesley, a founder of Methodism in England and North America. The school divested itself of the religious affiliation, but the "protest" remained. Moreover, the Thoreauvian and Emersonian spirit of flinty self-reliance infused this New England college. Students were given a lot of freedom. There were no degree requirements, and they liked it that way. Students had no wish to be regimented or structured in any way. They wanted the freedom to march to a different drummer. Identity politics of various sorts generated the most passion and engagement on campus. In fairness, a large number of students were engaged in community-service projects, and the vast majority of Wesleyan students were bright, articulate, open to experience, and looking for meaning. But I felt that, with more structure in the curriculum and commitment to community, we—faculty and administrators—could have better ministered to this powerful aspiration in our students.

Most faculty at Wesleyan, like faculty elsewhere in the country, preferred to let "others," meaning administrators, deal with issues of student residential life and personal development. That is exactly how I felt as a faculty member, but after seeing institutions from the perspective of the president's office, and with a son finishing high school and looking at colleges at that time, I wished that more faculty at Wesleyan and elsewhere were engaged in the whole development of the student, the whole curriculum, the whole experience of a college education. I longed to re-infuse our work with values that are not purely intellectual or narrowly political but that are also moral and philosophical in a broader sense.

The Wesleyan I knew had changed dramatically from its origins as a small Methodist men's college, and I am sure it continued to change and evolve after I left. Undoubtedly, the greater presence of women was gradually making a difference to the male-dominated culture. Perhaps I took a small step forward for womankind (and mankind!) during my time at Wesleyan. As the first woman to serve in academic and presidential leadership roles, I tried to bring about a change in the institutional culture towards greater cooperation, collaboration, consensus-building, and community. I don't kid myself about how much progress was made. Neither Rome nor Wesleyan was built in a day, and neither can they be so quickly rebuilt on a more fully satisfying human basis. But I certainly tried, and this "fascination of what's difficult" left me with a deep and abiding respect for the tough, contentious, resilient, spirited, and maddening place that Wesleyan University was.

PART II

On Being President

College Gate at Mount Holyoke College
Photograph owned by Mount Holyoke College

} 6 {

MOUNT HOLYOKE COLLEGE
A College of Her Own

When I was first nominated for the presidency of Mount Holyoke College in fall 1994, I knew little about the institution and had never even seen its campus. But that could be remedied, since I lived only about an hour away in Middletown, Connecticut. So that Thanksgiving weekend, my visiting family and I decided to drive up to South Hadley, Massachusetts, and take a look. I remember all of us were taken with the grounds and architecture of the College: its stately row of imposing Gothic brownstones fronting College Street; the surprising vistas that greeted us as we drove through the College gate into the campus; and the multiple greens edged by monumental buildings like Williston Library and Clapp Laboratory facing one another along irregular quads; and classroom buildings and whimsically picturesque brownstone dormitories interspersed among them. As we went farther into the campus, we came upon a changing landscape with more-modern buildings situated along the banks of Stony Brook, with lovely cascading waterfalls spilling over three successive dams and linking two lovely small lakes, each circumvented by inviting trails and bordered by densely forested Prospect Hill. While not of uniform design or regimented pattern, the campus bespoke harmony, charm, and peace, blending the human and the natural, the grand and the intimate, the historic and the modern. To me, it seemed to portend a commodious place, one comfortably, insistently, and uniquely its own place. I could imagine myself here, I thought. So I let my name go forward. Meanwhile, I would learn what I could about the Mount Holyoke College.

Although Mount Holyoke was impressive, venerable, and distinguished, its identity as a women's college was a vexing issue for me. I wasn't sure I'd be a good fit. My own education and experience had been completely within coeducational institutions. I wasn't sure I even approved of single-sex education in the late twentieth century. Wasn't it anachronistic in our time? Wasn't the whole aim of education to move towards the great integration and permanent equality of the sexes, not their separation, not the privileging of one over the other? I believed that Wesleyan's deficiencies grew out of its too exclusively male acculturation. Couldn't the alternative be just as narrow and distorted? Certainly as a student, I had never given serious consideration to attending a single-sex institution, for I was lured as much by the social opportunities to meet all those young men as I was by the educational opportunities. Would I feel that I had somehow sold myself short in a world of women without the validating stamp of male approval? Would the move to Mount Holyoke be an admission that I couldn't make it in the male world of power and position? Wouldn't I be proving right my sexist professor who had said that I belonged at a "good women's college"?

Yet, despite my qualms, I could feel from the start a kind of inevitability about my alliance with Mount Holyoke—as if destiny does indeed shape our ends. I felt that I understood the job, that I was up to its challenges, that I could make a positive difference. That confidence was fed both by the gratifying courtship of the search committee during early winter of 1994-1995, which clearly favored my candidacy, and by the pragmatic chair of the Board of Trustees. Barbara Rossotti systematically addressed every obstacle I could muster, including my wish to take a six-month sabbatical from Wesleyan before beginning the job.

I'm not sure why I was so confident; the job was no cinch. Mount Holyoke, despite its many strengths, had real and pressing problems and challenges. All leading indicators were negative: the budget was seriously out of balance and worsening each year; the admissions outlook was weak and worrisome; institutional morale was low; and word on the street was that Mount Holyoke was in decline. I sensed among the various constituents deep worry, unhappiness, and a kind of paralysis about what to do. Why was this college with such manifest strengths—a distinguished history, an excellent faculty, a talented and diverse student population, a concerned Board of Trustees, a supportive alumnae body, a striking campus, among many other outstanding qualities—in trouble? How could those strengths be deployed to meet its challenges? I was intrigued by these questions. I liked reading institutions, and here was a puzzling text. The consultant to the search committee said that Mount Holyoke was an institution where the whole was less than the sum of the parts. If ever there were a challenge I couldn't resist, it was that very one. From the first, I sensed the tremendous incipient potential of those parts working together as a whole.

When I accepted the position and came to campus in February 1995, the welcome in Chapin Auditorium was so warm and welcoming that I was taken aback. These people don't know me, I thought; this is the projection of their aspirations and hopes onto me. This eagerness to be upbeat, to give me the benefit of the doubt, and to welcome me was such a contrast to the skeptical, wary, aggressively critical response that was typical Wesleyan fare. Their optimism challenged and inspired me to be equal to this leap of faith.

During my pre-presidency sabbatical, as Tom and I travelled to Japan, China, Hong Kong, Australia, and New Zealand, I had time for reflection, which strengthened my conviction that Mount Holyoke was the right job for me. I could feel it energizing me, linking me to resonant female traditions and to neglected parts of myself. Whereas I usually stand back and skeptically weigh options, this time I sensed myself leaning forward in confidence, joy, and anticipation of a new venture. If readiness was all, I was prepared to embrace this new identity and challenge.

I started at Mount Holyoke in January 1996. It was an act of faith that the campus was willing to wait for me so long, almost a year from when I was first announced. Refreshed after my break, I was primed and ready to get moving. At our January retreat, I shared with the Board my initial impressions and plan of action. I promised to deliver a strategic plan in eighteen months.

The first priority was to align myself with the faculty and to cultivate their engagement in campus affairs. Many were worried about the future of the Mount Holyoke College in the face of a declining numbers of applicants and rising deficits. Some alleged that the Board had not minded the store and had been unable to say no to the expensive indulgences of the previous president, who, they thought, had been too long in office and no longer attentive to her duties.

They believed that they, not the Board, had recognized serious problems and had tried to interject a sense of urgency and crisis. They were determined that any future president would be held accountable and that secrecy, particularly about financial matters, would be at an end.

That was fine with me. I had always found openness and directness the easiest and best route to planning and accountability. From the first I saw that the faculty's wish to face up to realities was a strength to be tapped. As a candidate, I saw denial still operating on the campus. I quizzed the search committee assiduously about the financial statements it shared with me. Did the committee realize the gravity of the budget imbalance and the untenability, for example, of a 12.5 percent annual growth rate in financial aid while revenues were growing at about 4 percent per year?

Various strategies had been devised to keep the institution afloat and to mask the serious budget imbalance it faced. A so-called "tuition stabilization fund," for example, was added to the operating budget to help to pay for the shortfall in tuition revenues caused by escalating financial aid and a less-than-robust applicant pool. This was one of several ways that the College used more of its endowment income than it acknowledged upfront. Another was its use of unrestricted bequests that happen to come in each year. When I heard about that tactic, I imagined little old ladies, loyal and true Mount Holyoke alumnae, jumping into the pyre for their beloved College. It troubled me.

At my first meeting with the faculty, I received a cordial if somewhat skeptical reception to my proposal that we quickly begin a planning process. Previous planning exercises, I learned, had found their way onto the shelf. Still, I was the new president and had to be humored; the faculty was willing to give this a try and expedited the process of electing faculty representatives to the new Educational Priorities Committee (EPC). They proposed and elected a strong slate of colleagues. The students argued persuasively for representation on the committee as well, and two students joined the EPC.

It soon became a hard-working, well-respected, and tough-minded committee, which helped to build credibility with the campus community. Among ourselves, the members developed fine rapport and mutual respect, working through sometimes-difficult areas of concern and disagreement. I assumed the committee chairmanship because I knew that I could keep things moving and could generate working drafts. The committee's goal was to engage the various constituents of the College in dialogue and conversation about the strengths, weaknesses, opportunities, and challenges facing the institution. We invited individuals and groups to write directly to us, and we held innumerable meetings and forums, including discussion groups over dinner or afternoon tea at the president's house for all the faculty, in groups of about twenty, which proved to be an effective way to cultivate discussion and reflection about the College.

In these conversations, I was impressed with the deep love that faculty clearly felt for the school and with the emotional attachment that the students demonstrated for Mount Holyoke. Affection for the school, its traditions, and history was evident in the staff as well. From students and alumnae I heard recurrent testimonials about the transformative power of a Mount Holyoke education. But this love and respect for the institution were curiously conjoined with a kind of modesty and deference, even a self-deprecation, which was so unlike the aggressive self-assertiveness of Wesleyan. Not surprisingly, Mount Holyoke seemed to be gendered "female." And it was going through a crisis of self-confidence. The institution suffered from the general feeling that women's colleges were in decline following the great shift towards coeducation in the 1970s. Surveys showed that a very small number of high school graduates, fewer than 2 percent, would consider single-sex education, and many fewer would apply for admission.

With a dip in the numbers of applicants, Mount Holyoke fell out of the "top twenty" in the specious ratings of liberal arts colleges in *US News and World Report* in 1994 (only to return again the next year). The *US News* rating depressed morale on the campus, giving rise to the feelings, never far from the surface in women, of being collectively devalued, the very sentiments and perceptions that the school was dedicated to eradicating. A small number of loud voices on campus and in the alumnae body sounded the alarm about the need to go coed, while the vast majority of students, faculty, and alums were ideologically and passionately committed to the school's single-sex mission. One professor, Chris Pyle of the Department of Politics, was the prolific prophet of doomsday scenarios and dire predictions about the sinking quality and reputation of the College under its misguided and outdated single-sex mission.

Tied up with the issue of single-sex education, either explicitly or implicitly, was the fear that the College would become ever more marginalized from the mainstream of fine liberal arts colleges and take up an ideologically "feminist" agenda. The College's mission to educate women was curiously a double bind. Some feared that stressing women's education would lead the College down the road to feminist advocacy and ideology. In their view Mount Holyoke was first and foremost a liberal arts college committed to academic excellence. Only secondarily did it teach women students—a curious discounting of the College's founding and history. The curriculum must be judged by standards of excellence in the liberal arts; it shouldn't necessarily reflect or accommodate to the students' gender. Many faculty were openly skeptical of ideas such as "women's ways of knowing" and derisive of courses with a "politicized" intent. Of course, many other faculty thought all knowledge was the product of political and social processes, and in their courses they attempted to lay bare implicit assumptions about gender, race, and class.

During the previous twenty to thirty years, Mount Holyoke, like other colleges and universities, had been influenced by powerful postmodern and feminist perspectives that had been reshaping many scholarly disciplines. But despite the presence of feminist scholars on the faculty, a women's studies program, and the Five College Women's Research Center located on the campus, there was still a lot of resistance to discussing what it might mean for Mount Holyoke to embrace fully "women's education." To some faculty, feminism as a system of values and a body of knowledge was incommensurate with the traditional liberal arts. They believed that the College, as a single-sex institution, could lose its foothold in the mainstream of liberal arts education. Ironically, it sometimes seemed that women's studies in its various manifestations could thrive more readily on a coed campus, where there was less fear that it would somehow engulf the whole institution.

A similar double bind about touting the single-sex mission was apparent in the recruitment of students. Baldly put, some faculty, parents, and alumnae feared that the College, if fully feminist, would attract a disproportionate share of lesbian students—a situation that, in those days, was viewed less sanguinely than it might be now. Some faculty and alumnae parents worried that their daughters would not consider the school because it was an alleged "lesbian haven" and, besides, they wanted to be around young men. At gatherings of alumnae, one or two would invariably take me aside and ask in whispered tones about the "lesbian problem." I occasionally received a letter from dismayed parents whose daughter decided to transfer because she felt uncomfortable as a heterosexual on the campus.

This was a complicated issue, all the more so because it was difficult to talk about openly. In fact, Mount Holyoke prided itself on being inclusive and welcoming diversity of all kinds, including that of sexual orientation. No one knew with any certainty what percentage of students identified as lesbian; I doubt that it was much different than that of a coed campus. A visible and vocal minority of LBTQ students helped shape the ambience and culture of the place, in mostly positive ways, and their disproportionate representation in campus activism probably made their numbers appear larger than they really were at Mount Holyoke.

Liberal tolerance and inclusive acceptance of sexual differences were widely shared sentiments at Mount Holyoke, but some people were put off by in-your-face declarations of gay rights, and sometimes straight students felt that their boyfriends were unwelcome on campus and their heterosexuality was mocked and belittled. While it is easy to exaggerate reverse prejudice, Mount Holyoke could function like an isolated little world unto itself. The more LBTQ students claimed it as their own, the more heterosexual students needed to do the same. The best interests of the College would be served by fostering genuine diversity among the student body, yet that became harder to do as single-sex education was increasingly perceived as an anomalous choice in American higher education.

Compounding recruitment challenges was that South Hadley was perceived as a rural, isolated community, making its all-women composition seem all the more socially problematic. This characterization was categorically unfair given Mount Holyoke's robust connections to the Five College community.[1] According to marketing consultants, the College didn't appear to prospective students as an "exciting place to be," and that quality was the single most important "draw" a college could have. Indeed, Mount Holyoke had to buck all the major trends in higher education, which favored coed, preprofessional, large, urban, and public institutions.

Still, if it were too hard a sell, we *could* consider coeducation. I insisted that we would have a free and open discussion, with no sacred cows, no taboo subjects, including the single-sex mission. My attitude scared a lot of people who feared that, as an outsider with no experience in single-sex education, I was determined to coeducate the place. In truth, I had an open mind. Most of the community believed that the College's distinctiveness was integrally tied to its single-sex mission, and their devotion impressed me.

The more I got to know Mount Holyoke, the more I understood that sentiment. It was the longest-standing women's college in the world. That women should be a positive force for good in the world was an imperative embedded in the very bricks and mortar of the place. A sense of connection to those women who had come before was passed on generation to generation through rite and ritual, song and custom. "Elfing" (surprise gifts from a secret friend), milk and cookies (a 9:00 p.m. snack break), big and little sister pairings, and the laurel parade (returning alumnae in white dresses were connected by a chain of laurel to the graduating seniors) enchanted and linked successive generations of Mount Holyoke women. We also learned through market research, however, that a sense of history and tradition was one of the least-compelling motivators for prospective students. Nonetheless, a resonant history and tradition were unquestionably memorable and cherished qualities of the College for its students and graduates.

The College's warmth and friendliness were also striking. I was especially impressed with the energy, intensity, and *joie de vivre* of the students. Here were young women comfortably at home in the world of the Mount Holyoke. I could sense the blossoming, the coming to selfhood. At Mount Holyoke it was all right—indeed, it was expected—that every student would be her own person. I wouldn't have expected that women living alone on a college campus could be so happy and content, but that is the impression they daily conveyed. They felt free—had the freedom—to be themselves, sometimes to the point of utter silliness. This was most evident at Fall Convocation, a curious bacchanal of screaming high spiritedness, fueled, it must be said, by pre-event tippling and by sometimes-outrageous costuming on the part of the seniors, who wore caps and gowns in recognition of their final year at the College.

But these moments of zaniness were joyful interludes in an intellectually serious school. Students placed study, concentrated and dedicated, at the center of their lives. Faculty and administrators sometimes worried that they worked too hard. Yet student satisfaction at Mount Holyoke always ranked at or near the top in surveys that included peer institutions, especially in the area of faculty teaching. Similarly, more students—women—at our College majored in the traditionally "male" subject areas, such as the sciences, mathematics, economics, and computer sciences, and went on to enjoy distinguished careers in the sciences than in comparable coed colleges. According to the data, Mount Holyoke was by far the most internationally diverse school among its peer liberal arts colleges. This diversity enriched the learning environment and served as a ready reminder of the unfinished agenda of women's education worldwide and of the College's historic role as a leader in educating women. I thought that the College could make much more of these historic links in forging new kinds of global interconnectedness in women's education, and as the years went on, we created those networks.

All in all, I came to appreciate how deeply ingrained and how passionately affirmed the gendered identity of Mount Holyoke was among students, faculty, and alumnae. Going coed would be a gut-wrenching, highly contested, likely searing experience, to say the least. It would be easier to stick with the traditional single-sex mission. But did that make sense? Would Mount Holyoke get enough good students to apply and attend to sustain the College at a high level? We were determined to examine that question dispassionately and analytically. Our work was ably assisted by economics professor Mike Robinson, who conducted extensive econometrics studies of market research, census data, and admissions records of Mount Holyoke in comparison to other colleges that had gone coed or remained single sex. His presentations of the research at faculty meetings provoked spirited discussions of the problem.

The data supported the observation that single-sex education was not the only factor inhibiting more-robust admissions and that coeducation in itself was not likely the magic bullet that would make everything better. Nor would it be a quick fix. The College's less-than-robust applicant pools had been caused, in part, by missed opportunities in recruitment, including the neglect of traditional markets on the East Coast. With savvy marketing and admissions work, Mount Holyoke could—and should—strengthen the quality and quantity of its applicant pool. Moreover, with its single-sex mission, the College had immediate "brand recognition," a well-established and highly visible place among a small group of historic, distinguished women's colleges. That market position would be lost or muted if Mount Holyoke went coed.

After much discussion in many forums, the EPC endorsed the decision to stick with the traditional mission, the education of women, at Mount Holyoke. But clearly, that choice was provisional and contingent on our success in selling same-sex education to prospective students. We recognized that a robust applicant pool was the most-critical strategic issue that faced the college and upon which everything else depended. We must see substantial gains if we were to have any hopes of turning around the College's sinking fortunes.

I took it upon myself to learn all I could about "enrollment management," a strategy of bringing together into the same administrative unit the various parts of an institution that deal with student recruitment and retention. I was convinced it was the right approach for us and set about to restructure the administration and to hire a strong leader for a new enrollment-management division. I then had the good fortune to lure Jane Brown to the College in the fall of 1997. She did an extraordinary job of melding these various offices and functions into a coordinated unit and produced stunning results. Indeed, we exceeded our ambitious goals with record-setting numbers of applicants year after year. This success was, without a doubt, the single most important aspect of the College's impressive resurgence and growing self-confidence.

Second only to the anemic applicant pool was the College's fragile financial condition. There was roughly an eight-million-dollar deficit when I took office. Mount Holyoke's financial woes, I knew, were unquestionably predicated in large part upon its "need-blind/full-funding" admissions policy. This policy was a noble experiment undertaken by a group of prestigious liberal arts colleges and universities in the 1950s. The intention was to make colleges of high caliber accessible to all students regardless of their ability to pay and to remove the question of financial aid from the admissions decision.

The institution admitted a student based exclusively on academic merits; then the "need-blind/full-funding" aid package covered whatever that student needed to attend the college.

Initially, the Ivy League, the Seven Sisters, and other affiliated colleges and universities—the so-called Overlap Group—cooperated to assess the financial needs of student applicants. They agreed to offer the same financial aid package to a particular student who applied to multiple schools within the group so that both students and colleges could make admissions decisions independent of financial considerations. This plan worked well for a number of years, but in 1991 the U.S. Justice Department filed a complaint accusing the Overlap Group of violating the Sherman Antitrust Act "by illegally conspiring to restrain price competition on financial aid" for prospective undergraduate students. Consequently, the Ivy League signed a "consent decree" agreeing not to consult on financial aid pricing.[2] This restraint was adopted by other need-blind schools as well, although MIT did not join the decree and engaged in years of wrangling with the Justice Department.

Ironically, this legal prohibition against cooperation on admissions and financial aid had exacerbated the "marketing" of higher education and pitted colleges against one another in competitive practices. Somewhat lost in this equation was the original goal of making excellent college education affordable to all students regardless of ability to pay. The Justice Department's ruling helped launch the less-salubrious dimension of enrollment management, "financial aid packaging," which like airline-ticket pricing, used sophisticated, finely tuned econometric models that correlated "ability to pay" and "eagerness to attend" a particular school.

Also complicating the picture was the growing disparity between price and affordability. Mount Holyoke's endowment was much smaller than that of many competitors, and its participation in the league of need-blind/full-funding institutions was made at a high cost, the commitment of an ever-larger share of the annual budget to financial aid. The College fueled that trend by giving larger numbers of financial-aid packages and more generous ones than many of its peers to lure students to South Hadley. As Mount Holyoke developed a reputation for generosity, it annually attracted a larger percentage of needy students, trapping itself in a vicious cycle of fiscal attrition. This practice, however noble, was unsustainable.

Unlike many schools, Mount Holyoke generously supported international students, whom it had been admitting in increasing numbers starting in the late 1980s and early 1990s to augment the weak admission pool of domestic students. Most were high achieving but very needy students, and their admission had accelerated the College's expenditures on financial aid. By the time I assumed the presidency in 1996, Mount Holyoke was an outlier among all its peers in the Consortium on the Financing of Higher Education (COFHE), a group of distinguished private colleges and universities, in significant categories and indicators: the high percentages of tuition discounting; students on financial aid; and international students. In another critical category, Mount Holyoke had the lowest average family income of all institutions in the peer group. Its average family income was below that of the University of Massachusetts, its public-university neighbor. Mount Holyoke was in danger of losing its socio-economic diversity—but the kinds of students becoming more scarce each passing year were those hailing from upper-middle-class and wealthy families. Some recalibration of the student mix, as well as some rational restructuring of the budget, was sorely needed at Mount Holyoke College.

Mount Holyoke was not the only institution struggling with the impracticalities of need-blind/full-funding admissions. This idealistic, well-intentioned policy encouraged many platitudes and much disingenuousness in higher education. Because it's patently foolish for an institution to "blind" itself to what financial aid costs might be each year, admissions officers found ingenious ways to control costs by using wait lists, by capping the total financial aid budget, by crafting so-called preferential packaging, and, sometimes, by out and out misrepresenting their practices.

Mount Holyoke simply could no longer afford to let financial aid costs rise at a precipitous rate. I was determined to educate the community about this problem and ask for full engagement to solve it. The faculty, to their great credit, were willing to take a hard, cold look at the budget and financial aid practices, even though many were ideologically committed to the principles of liberal access that originally spawned the need-blind/full-funding policy. The Faculty Planning and Budget Committee concluded that the College's deficit was driven by a growth in financial aid, not by excessive growth in expenditures. A newly appointed Task Force on Admissions and

Financial Aid, which included the two student members on the EPC, studied the matter in detail and finally recommended that the College become "need sensitive"—a practice that considers ability to pay as one of the criteria for admissions—for the final 5 to 10 percent of the applicant pool. This was a modest adjustment of the policy, but it would make a considerable difference in the College's ability to control the budget. After much discussion in many different forums, the EPC adopted this proposal as part of its draft planning document. "Need sensitive" was an unpopular move, but at the time it seemed that the College community would grudgingly accept its adoption as necessary to stabilizing the budget. We didn't know then that the seeds of unhappiness were sprouting a protest movement.

Meanwhile, we found much common ground among all constituencies about the fundamental nature of the College's mission. Challenged by trustees, who wanted a plan so succinct that it would fit on "the back of a business card," I was determined to encapsulate the mission in a single sentence, and after successive refinements, we settled on this statement: "We reaffirm our commitment to educating a diverse, residential community of women at the highest level of academic excellence and to fostering the alliance of liberal arts education with purposeful engagement in the world." That was Mount Holyoke in a nutshell. Our plan set forth a number of goals and initiatives to realize that mission more fully.

Over the summer of 1996, I worked with the EPC to develop an incomplete working draft that identified and advanced a number of areas of emphasis: women's education; the sciences; international contexts; the environment; writing, speaking, and argumentation; and leadership and advocacy. (All these themes would resonate during my presidency and beyond.) We held several forums to discuss the document and released a complete draft in February 1997. In general, the response was encouragingly positive. We continued to receive constructive criticism and to meet with faculty and student groups, who helped to refine the draft further. By early April, the EPC was ready to send to the printer the third public draft of the document. We were satisfied that the process had been open and inclusive, iterative and interactive, and that *The Plan for Mount Holyoke 2003* connected to the core ideas and generative energies of the institution, and to the views of its various communities. It was a sober look at the challenges Mount Holyoke faced. At the same time the document was a statement of aspirations outlining ambitious goals for the next six years that would revitalize the College.

But the process was abruptly derailed. We in the administration and on the EPC had underestimated the discontent brewing among a small group of students who decided to take matters into their own hands.

} 7 {

THE TROUBLES

"This Is Your True Inauguration"

I knew something was amiss when I heard chanting outside the house and the doorbell began ringing repeatedly. It was 10 p.m. on a Sunday evening in April 1997, and the planning process was winding to a conclusion. I was upstairs, already dressed for bed, and feeling somewhat under the weather. Tom answered the door. A group of students demanded that I come out to meet them. He explained that I was not available. Undeterred, they demanded that I see them immediately. Finally, after it became clear that Tom was an immovable guardian of the door, they insisted that I should meet them at 5 a.m. the next morning. "You got to be joking," he said in his unflappably British manner. Finally, after they grudgingly accepted that I would meet with them at a later hour the next morning, they handed him a list of eleven "demands."

And so began what I think of as "The Troubles," a surreal time when normal business was suspended and we struggled to find a way to minister to and contain the swirling events and passions that shook our campus. The Troubles lasted two weeks—a short time, really, although the tumult seemed interminable. This period looms larger than it probably should in my remembrance of things past. From enough distance it could be seen as a predictable student uprising in the spring, which was not uncommon on many campuses and often viewed with tolerant bemusement for the unrestrained exuberance and idealism of the young. But this tumult seemed more substantive than the typical spring restlessness at the time, and it still does as I try retrospectively to make some sense of the events. In subsequent years, students tended to mythologize this period of the College's history and the heroic students who led the fight. I want to document for the record my different view of what transpired.

The incipient student movement had been organized by a small group of self-identified student leaders freshly trained in how to stage a protest in workshops from more-experienced protest organizers at nearby University of Massachusetts (UMass), which had recently endured a protracted period of student takeovers. Following a handbook on coalition building they got at UMass, the protest leaders put together the list of eleven demands, which combined various concerns in one document. The six self-appointed leaders cared most about the preservation of need-blind admissions; the creation of two cultural spaces—one for lesbian, bisexual, and transgender students and the other for Asian American students; and the formation of an Asian American studies program. The coalition brought together odd bedfellows, including a group of conservative students alarmed that changes in the chaplaincy would weaken religious life on campus and who, with encouragement from the incumbents, lobbied for the retention of the people holding temporary positions in the chaplaincy. Support for the arts, use of the credit card for tuition payments, and other demands were apparently added in an attempt to recruit support for the movement from special interest groups in the student community.

Although it was annoying to be confronted with demands in such a belligerent way so late in the process, the planning was meant to be inclusive and iterative. Students across the campus had been engaged throughout the process, but clearly some did not feel included and wanted their voices heard *now*. So I thought we should listen. A group of administrative colleagues and I met with the students in good faith for several hours on Monday as well as the following Tuesday morning. We were eager to find a path to rapprochement. Maybe faulty communication was at the heart of the conflict. Many of the eleven demands were already met in *The Plan for Mount Holyoke 2003*. On others, we saw room for accommodation and further thinking. The one bedrock issue, which could not be compromised, however, was the necessity to stem the cost of need-blind admissions. It had huge fiscal implications; the financial viability of the College depended on it. But we could try harder to educate students about the budget realities Mount Holyoke faced.

It was frustrating and difficult to talk with the six self-appointed negotiators because they aired their demands and parsed everything we said with volleys of accusation, suspicion, and hostility. We were unable to speak without setting them off. They didn't want to hear, for example, that budgets were finite, that the College needed its faculty to develop the academic program, or that a committee was examining the issue of cultural spaces. They wanted what they wanted, *now*.

The discussions were tough going, but after hours went by we seemed to have made progress on many of the issues. My colleagues, the students, and I set up a time for further conversation later in the week. Soon thereafter, however, we learned that this attempt at rapprochement was a sham; the student negotiators' real goal was to stir things up and engender wider support by casting us, particularly me as the president, in a highly unsympathetic light. Immediately following our Tuesday-morning discussions, they went to a prearranged rally on the steps of the student center, during which they reported our conversation in blatantly distorted and inflammatory ways. Standing at the edge of the crowd, I was flabbergasted and outraged by their misrepresentation, mocking, and belittlement of me. One of the painful lessons of leadership is that you sometimes get blamed for things you never said, or did, or thought. This was such a time.

Some of the students engaged in the protest genuinely didn't hear or understand our perspective. They were deeply committed to their own interpretation and caught up in their own passions. Others though, a couple of the organizers in particular, knew very well that they were manipulating the situation. That was their strategy. Their handbook on how to stage a protest proposed identifying a "target" and using tactics such as name-calling and harassment to weaken the opponent. I was that target. Affixing labels to and casting me as the enemy or the "other," they maligned me and my leadership: I was an outsider to Mount Holyoke; I was trying to change its fundamental nature; I was racist, homophobic, and classist; I didn't respect the students and their sexual, religious, and ethnic diversity; and I wanted to recruit an entirely different student body made up of wealthy students, who would inexorably change the campus culture. So students like themselves, from impoverished or modest means, would be excluded in the future. My intentions were a desecration of the equalitarian ideals of Mary Lyon, the College's founder. I had to be resisted, the leaders exhorted, and students had to stand up for the values of Mount Holyoke, now endangered by my presidency.

This call to defend the values of the institution had its appeal. Even those who were moderate in their views were drawn to the sheer excitement, novelty, and carnival of it, at least initially. Joining the fray showed that they were neither an apathetic nor a docile generation. They were brave women willing to defy authority and put their bodies on the line out of love for the College.

I sent the student negotiators a note saying how disappointed I was with their distortion of our conversations at the public rally and stating that I would not meet with them as we had planned. Instead, I would schedule meetings to hear a broad range of student voices. On Wednesday, we sent all students a copy of the negotiators' demands and preliminary administrative responses and invited everyone to scheduled meetings to discuss them. On Thursday, I held my open office hour out in the hallways of Mary Lyon Hall to accommodate the dozens of students who showed up, including a large contingent organized by the protest leaders. Some students were genuinely upset and distraught over specific issues or more generally about what they feared was happening to the College. But others were more disingenuous.

What became memorialized was an exchange with an African American student who asked what would happen to individuals like her under the new policy of need-sensitive admission. I responded that smart students like her were likely to be very attractive to the College and, moreover, another of our goals was to increase the numbers of minority students. At this point and throughout the session, one of the student protest leaders kept popping up while most students were sitting on the floor and offered an ongoing commentary on what was said. "Did you hear that? That was racist! Can you believe that?" she said, expounding on my gross inadequacies for leadership of this college. All in all, that encounter was not a successful example of rapprochement. Passions and rhetoric were running too high, and the manipulation of the situation was too obvious for anything productive and positive to emerge.

A group of students moved from Mary Lyon Hall to the Office of Admission, and later in the day, they demanded that I meet them there and that I apologize to the student whom I had hurt with my "racist" remark. Outraged by the accusation, exhausted and disillusioned by such manipulative and confrontational gatherings, I went home. Meanwhile, the conclave over at the Office of Admission gathered adherents and about seventy-five to a hundred students, including both men and women from UMass and possibly other area colleges, occupied the building first as a sit-in. Later, about midnight, they took over the workspaces and encamped for the evening.

But at first I was unaware of the takeover. About 10:30 p.m., I had taken a sleeping pill, unplugged the phone, locked the doors, and gone to bed while, outside the house students, chanted abusive slogans, rang the doorbell, and incessantly called on the phone. This invasion of my private space was new and unsettling. But if this were to be the new realities of my world, I would find a way to get some sleep.

Later that night, however, lights flashing outside the windows and persistent banging on the door made clear that these were not demonstrating students but public safety officers trying to arouse me. They informed me that students had taken over the Office of Admission. They wanted guidance on how to handle this new circumstance. Within a short period of time, public safety officers, deans, other administrative colleagues, and concerned faculty gathered at my house to talk over the situation, which was delicate and dangerous. How would we keep it from escalating further? That was the end of sleep. We talked into the early hours of the morning.

Views ranged widely as we swung from one scenario to another. Clearly, a takeover that prevented the functioning of a key administrative building was stepping over the line of peaceful protest. Some believed we should eject the students from the building, with force if necessary, and others, that we should wait out the action and not provoke violent confrontation. Others, such as myself, favored a middle course that communicated to students the serious consequences of occupying the building. We were all aware of how easily the situation could escalate. We did not want the police involved. With the Kent State tragedy seared in our memories, we knew how easily these kinds of situations could get out of hand with lethal consequences.

We decided on a cautious step-by-step approach. At 5 a.m., the dean of the College and the director of Public Safety explained to students that they were in violation of College policy and would suffer consequences if they did not leave. At 8 a.m., the ombudsperson and I went over the building, asked students to leave so that admissions work could resume, and warned them that they risked punitive action. Some students left; others stayed put. We also met with the leaders for about two hours in hostile and unproductive conversation.

Later that morning, I called the provost at UMass to find out what she had learned from the recent takeovers, since the actions at Mount Holyoke were so clearly modeled on the university's protests. She said that their major regret was not sealing off occupied buildings. Students could go back to their rooms, shower, rest, and come back—refreshed—and other students could replenish their ranks. Another mistake was negotiating with students who were illegally occupying a building; that sends the wrong message about the efficacy of such action. I was determined to follow her advice and not duplicate the university's mistakes.

In "sealing off the building," we used both public safety officers and buildings-and-grounds personnel "dressed up" to look official with orange armbands and yokes. Enlisting every able-bodied employee we could, we staged an impressive show of force, encircling the building with police tape and then positioning guards. We also agreed among ourselves that this was all a show; we would not prevent anyone from leaving or entering the building. Nonetheless, the establishment of this perimeter had the intimidating effect we wanted: to make the students feel that they were isolated, that they were illegal intruders in the space they occupied, and that fresh recruits or replacements would be kept out.

Their isolation, however, was more psychological than real. Many persons—deans, chaplains, public safety officers, food service workers, and faculty—entered their space and interacted with them, and the students in the building used their cell phones to coordinate their actions and to keep in regular communication with their friends across the campus and in the world. Until we turned off computers and phones, they used admissions telecommunications equipment like command central, calling news organizations across the country and encouraging their coverage. Unquestionably, some of the leaders were intoxicated with their fifteen minutes of fame. While national coverage was minimal, the local television and press responded readily to their invitations to cover the event. For days television trucks took up residence on the street outside the office.

As the day wore on, a contingent of students remained in the admissions office, blocking access to the building and preventing employees from doing their work. Meanwhile, in keeping with our attempt to broaden the dialogue, that afternoon we held one of the meetings scheduled for the campus community. It was led by the chief financial officer. At 3 p.m., the dean of the College delivered to the occupying students a letter stating that if they did not leave the building by 4 p.m., they would be suspended. At that hour many students left, but their demonstration was not over. A group of them recklessly strung themselves across busy Highway 116, which traverses the campus. It was a hair-raising moment that I watched from my office window. Not only was their action dangerous, but it was also likely to draw the South Hadley police onto the scene, something we tried earnestly to avoid. Clearly, some students hoped to provoke an arrest that would play well before the television cameras. Others were exhausted, tired, reckless, unthinking, and zombie-like. Luckily, other students and faculty were as alarmed as I was. They persuaded the students to get off of the road, and another crisis was narrowly averted.

Twelve students remained in the building after the 4 p.m. deadline. In the early evening, I received a message from three of them, who asked to serve as representatives of the group occupying the building. After a lengthy discussion with these three, we reached an agreement that the threat of sanctions would be lifted if students left the building by 10 p.m. and if discussions would resume in good faith. I received a call shortly before 10:00 that evening from the student occupiers: "Would it be all right if we stayed a few minutes longer, we haven't finished vacuuming yet." Of course, I said, charmed and encouraged by this return to order, civility, and respectful tidiness.

So, it seemed, we had worked our way through a difficult situation. It was painful and exhausting, but we hadn't overplayed or underplayed our hand. We lived through a takeover, and no one was hurt. Without resorting to force, we set clear limits. Peaceful protest was fine. Illegal disruption would trigger serious sanctions. We would not negotiate with students occupying a building. But we would continue talking to any and all students who wanted to converse with us.

Although we had a moment to catch our breath, we knew very well that The Troubles weren't over. We had agreed to return to the negotiating table with a group of students who had amply demonstrated that they weren't interested in conversation and compromise. Moreover, the campus was rife with tensions. Spirited discussions of the issues animated classrooms and residence halls. The student body was fractured by dueling allegiances; roommates sometimes found themselves on opposite sides. Most students were not supportive of the takeover and the incivility of the protest leaders, even though many of them were sympathetic to some of the grievances. Some students were becoming increasingly vocal in their opposition to the tactics of these students. A petition, signed by hundreds of students, urged the broadening of the dialogue. The two students on the planning committee were worried about the illegitimacy of the protesting students' mandate to dictate the directions of the planning process.

Nonetheless, we met with the six self-appointed leaders for well over four hours on Saturday. Our goal was to get them to agree that others had to be drawn into the dialogue. Our negotiations continued the unrelenting pattern. One student in particular was doggedly humorless and deadpan, focused solely on her goals; negotiating with her was like dealing with an automaton. Others were more volatile and provocative: one student, a theatre arts major, sometimes staged impressive, tearful performances. Admittedly, they were as tired and as frustrated with us as we were with them. The students wanted to keep talking into Saturday night. I had other plans, a guest coming from out of town. The students were sarcastic about how little I valued them and the issues they raised. Why would I not cancel plans and continue talking? By the time I did get away, it was late, and we went off to a restaurant for dinner. Very hungry but also tied up in knots from the accumulated frustrations and tensions of the week, I was unable to eat, talk, or switch into a convivial mood. Rather, I felt like a prisoner of war, out on a short parole, doomed to return for torture by my sullen captors.

We met again on Sunday, for another three hours. This time the students were uncharacteristically amiable and cooperative. We hoped that they had a change of heart and were going to try reaching some resolution, but we were suspicious. Something was fishy. They readily agreed to a meeting on Tuesday, which would include other student leaders and faculty. On Monday we issued a progress report to the campus community documenting the administration's accommodation to students' concerns on several issues. In addition we held another forum on the financial condition of the College.

But, at 2:30 Monday afternoon, the student protesters held another rally at the College gate, and at 3 p.m., a group of roughly fifty students took over Mary Lyon Hall, ordering employees to leave the building or be forced to remain inside indefinitely. Mary Lyon houses many administrative offices, including my own. My office, of course, was their destination; symbolically it represented the seat of power. And they seized it. My staff was incensed and scared but also protective of their turf and things. Laurie, small, quiet, reserved, and very professional, said as she departed, "If you touch my baby's pictures, I'll kill you."

We told the students both orally and in writing that they were in clear violation of the Social Honor Code. If they did not remove themselves from the workspace by 5 p.m., they would be suspended. At five, about twenty-five students left the building; twenty-three remained. The building was sealed off with police tape and once again public safety officers and others took up their posts. Shortly thereafter, the dean of the College delivered the students a suspension notice. The students, however, were determined to encamp for the evening, and they did. Some of the leaders were still high on power and attention, playing up to the media, hanging out the windows, and delivering impromptu speeches. A few staff and faculty tried to talk with the students and encourage them to leave the building, but this bunch was a group of die-hards who had committed themselves to grandstanding, regardless of consequences.

The next morning, students blocked all doors and prevented employees from entering the building. The Offices of the Registrar, Dean of Faculty, Dean of the College, and the President, among others, hastily set up temporary quarters elsewhere on campus and attempted to carry on with their duties. Meanwhile, sentiment was shifting ever more strongly against the student occupiers and their disruptive tactics, and community sympathy was developing for me as the target of their attacks. I received literally hundreds of emails, letters, and notes as well as gifts of food from students who deplored what was happening and who wanted to express their support. I was touched and heartened by their thoughtful and insightful messages, and their insistence on fair play and open debate. Ironically, the protest movement became counterproductive, mobilizing support for me and the institutional agenda I had articulated and initiated.

We continued to assert that we would not negotiate with students occupying a building, but we would talk with elected student leaders and others, and we would hold the meeting we had scheduled. The students in Mary Lyon Hall could choose to participate if they would leave the building, but they were unwilling to do so. (They did try to enter the discussion through intermediaries and cell phones.) We held an all-day meeting on Tuesday with key administrators, members of the EPC, student leaders, and other faculty and staff. We worked step-by-step through the various issues that had been raised and arrived at as much common ground as we could identify. It was a tough, productive discussion, with all parties fully committed to acting in principled and responsible ways. On many issues, all that was necessary was to clarify or modify language. The draft planning document had been refined through the give-and-take of the highly iterative planning process. It was becoming increasingly reflective of the values and wishes of the collective community. On some issues, there was room for accommodation and compromise.

The need to move from need-blind to need-sensitive admission, however, remained the hottest and most-difficult issue. Students and faculty who had studied the numbers understood and supported the proposed modifications, but with great reluctance. On another vexing issue, that of cultural space, I moved off my previous position—that this matter continue to be studied in committee. With the urging of my colleagues, I agreed that the administration would guarantee the establishment of two cultural spaces, one for lesbian, bisexual, and transgender students, and the other for Asian American students. This was a significant change of position, and I did so with misgivings. Although the protesting students, still holed up in Mary Lyon Hall, were not a part of this discussion, they could consider this change a "victory" for the tactics of protest—circumventing the usual planning processes and meeting the "demand" for immediate action on this matter.

Also, I seriously questioned the wisdom of the move. I was not convinced that the best interests of Mount Holyoke were served in encouraging separate spaces. Our goal, as far as I was concerned, was to be an inclusive and diverse community, not a collection of discrete and physically isolated communities. But other community members had a different philosophy. A persuasive advocate for cultural space was Beverly Daniel Tatum, professor of psychology (and later to become president of Spelman College), who had just written what was to become a very influential book, *Why Are All the Black Kids Sitting Together in the Cafeteria* (1997). Her theory was that college students were still in a developmental stage and that affirming a separate ethnic identity was for some young people a necessary prelude to joining an inclusive community. Supporting that process would result, she believed, in the building of the kind of diverse community we valued. Moreover, at an earlier time (and also with the stimulus of protest movements) the campus had already gone down the road of endorsing cultural space for some groups, including for African and African American, Latina, and Native American students. Given that reality, it was hard to argue that other groups should not have separate spaces too. But I had to ask the cynical question: where did it stop? With a student body as diverse as ours, many advocacy groups could be formed, many separate spaces could be imagined, and we could balkanize our campus.

Still, Asian American and LGBT groups were full participants in our campus at this particular moment in the College's history, and they craved commensurate recognition at Mount Holyoke. I capitulated, concluding that this was an institutional matter that transcended my personal views. I yielded to the collective wisdom and values of the larger community.

After working our way through issues and arriving at a shared common document, I called the campus community together in the amphitheater at 4 p.m. that afternoon. Representatives from all of the constituent units–student leaders, faculty who had been part of the deliberations, members of the EPC, members of the administration—appeared together on the stage, visually and vocally presenting our accord and united front. Student leaders were impressively responsible and articulate, taking the lead in the event. In the question and answer session, the African American student whom I had allegedly insulted with a racist remark again raised that issue. I sincerely apologized for creating that perception and for the hurt she felt. I also insisted that I intended no racist sentiment in what I had said earlier. It seemed to strike the right note; many people later commented on the effectiveness of this moment of rapprochement and connection.

All in all, the community meeting served as a kind of cathartic climax to the craziness that had swirled around us and reasserted leadership of elected bodies and College administrators. Later, the students barricaded in Mary Lyon Hall came out of the building. All twenty-three appealed their suspensions, which were later reduced to social probation. This penalty was, in effect, a warning: if they engaged in such disruptive activity again, they would be suspended. If they met and sustained the standards of good citizenship expected by the College, all reference to social probation would be expunged upon their graduation.

I sent a letter to all members of the community expressing my sorrow at the way the events of the past couple of weeks had "strained the social fabric of our community." Although we reached a turning point, the anger and passions were far from over. Monday evening we held an open forum for the community. Many of the protesting students were seething with rage and mistrust and continued their angry diatribes. I tried to respond with reason and calm. The self-appointed leader of the student protestors still singled me out for insulting and sarcastic invective. But she never knew when to stop. She wound herself up in rhetorical flourish and let fly, becoming increasingly outrageous and disrespectful. Others in the gathering were more appalled than impressed by this venomous display, and it too helped to swing sentiment against the protesters and move us towards the restoration of order, decorum, and normality. Besides, it was getting very close to the end of the semester, and it was time to buckle down and get some work done.

No longer locked out of our workplaces, we promptly resumed our schedule to issue the *Plan* before the upcoming faculty and Board meetings, although the document was now modified by the deliberations over the past two weeks. Yet one snafu was that the document was rushed to the printer before a meeting with the EPC, so there was no opportunity for committee members to discuss and approve the recent changes. The committee was understandably upset by this oversight and determined to keep its integrity intact. This glitch was another example of the difficulties with developing a document that kept all constituents on same page. After much discussion, we decided to indicate in a note the textual changes that reflected administrative intention rather than committee consensus.

The Plan for Mount Holyoke 2003 was distributed to the campus in time for discussion at the faculty meeting the next week. At this meeting I took the opportunity to reflect on the events that had rocked the campus. Even then, I knew that not only were we dealing with some of the most-perplexing issues in higher education, but we were caught up in a cultural and generational drama of considerable consequence: playing out age-old and prototypical human conflicts in our own version of Jerusalem, or Beirut, or Kabul. I was determined to work through my anger and fatigue and try to see dimensions of this larger human drama and its sometimes-painful lessons. Here's part of what I said:

> It was certainly a stressful, difficult time. . . . I think we are grappling in our little microcosmic world with significant issues that have been at the center of human conflict across time. There are matters of communication and miscommunication writ large and small; some are heavily freighted with issues of honor, trust, idealism, integrity, power, gender identity, ethnicity, race, class, religion. We are experiencing age-old generational differences in perspectives. We're grappling with how principles and practices get wedded in the imperfect world. Laid bare are essential questions about how Colleges should function and what is the role of constituencies—students, faculty, staff, and administration within them. We are struggling with the anxiety of change. We are seeing how passions can be manipulated and stirred up, how painfully we cannot hear or understand each other, how interpretations of the "other" can be frozen into a malign shape which locks out human connection and civil discourse and leads to desperate actions.
>
> Since our community quite literally draws from the multiple cultures of American society and the world, since we are experiencing significant institutional self-assessment and change, and since most of our students are going through the major passage into adulthood, it is not surprising that the conflicts of the world and of the human heart are in our midst. Our College community is a grand experiment in building a more perfect society and, although we do well most of the time, sometimes we veer off from perfection rather abruptly. Yet these cracks in

social order, dislocations, this coming to the surface of tensions, are opportunities to grow, to learn, to educate and that's what I hope we will do. This is all too raw to synthesize well, but in an inchoate way I've learned a lot already and I see much good coming out of what has been a perfectly rotten and brutalizing experience....

"This is your true inauguration," says Lisa Workmeister-Rozas, and I think she is right. But part of that inauguration was dismay at the profound shakeup to our communal life that these events caused. Many students signed a petition deploring the way they felt silenced by the tensions in the student community, because of a charged atmosphere of accusation and intimidation.

And indeed, at the heart of the recent troubles . . . are the painful failures of human connection with the group of protesting students. I am deeply distressed about that failure. We must arrive at some rapprochement and mutual understanding. We are far from there yet. I am concerned that within the protesters are disproportionally students from groups that feel marginalized and that I—as the emblem of Mount Holyoke—am seen as not caring about them and the pain and grievances they have. I do care. I am determined to build an inclusive community where these student voices will be heard and honored. I believe that this movement identified areas of legitimate student concern. . . . But I deplore the degeneration of dialogue into name calling, accusation, misrepresentation, and coercive tactics. . . .

We tried to turn the language of demands and negotiation into productive discussion, tried to defuse the escalating desperation of students, since, in fact, many of the issues were still in process and not fixed in stone. Our conversations were not easy, but it seemed possible that we could find common ground, that we could clarify language and intent and make progress in thinking through issues, and find accommodations and compromise.

I know some people think we went too far in accommodating to students' wishes; others think we did too little. The irony of the situation was that we had tremendous common ground with the students in the first place if only we could talk about it at a level of mutual trust and understanding. What is powerful about Mount Holyoke and strong about our *Plan* is that we have such a strong consensus about essential things. . . .

The document you have before you has changed and evolved and risen up out of all of you, out of students, faculty, staff, and alumnae. It synthesizes literally hundreds of voices. . . . Everyone does not buy into everything, but we have a plan borne out of collaboration and compromise, realism and aspiration, which will move us significantly along and help to secure and build the essential Mount Holyoke for years to come. That's our accomplishment and however painful it has been to get there, it will be worth the effort: of that I am sure. . . .

I knew how critical it was symbolically that the faculty formally endorse the *Plan*, and I was pleased that they chose to do so and that the endorsement passed unanimously (with a handful of abstentions) along with a recommendation to the Board of Trustees that it support the document. By the time of the Board meeting on May 9–10, the protesters had dwindled to a small number of students (five or so), who held vigil outside the meeting room. The Board called them in and heard them out, but the Trustees, too, like the faculty as a whole, didn't think the protesters had much of a case to make against the planning process and the document that resulted. Later, with enthusiasm and gratitude for the hard work it represented, the Board unanimously endorsed the *Plan*.

From start to finish, the process of putting together the *Plan* had taken fifteen months. It was a demanding, exhausting, and, in its final weeks, exasperating process, but I was proud of the results. For the document was a concise and honest assessment of the tough realities faced by the College and laid out bold aspirations for the future. Rising up from the constituents of the College, borne out of compromise and consultation, the *Plan* had a ring of authenticity, pragmatism, and aspiration, and it proved to be a strong foundation upon which to move the College forward. It was the key to an undeniable turn around in the fortunes of Mount Holyoke in the years ahead.

During the commencement ceremony that year, one of the graduating protest leaders slipped a Hawaiian lei over my head as I handed her a diploma. Later, at a reception following the ceremony, she said to me: "I thought you needed a lei." I laughed, delighted to see that the deadly, humorless mood of the protest was behind her and that her cheeky insouciance was still intact. I knew this was a peace offering, a sign that she was ready to move on. And after graduation she and I chatted on occasion about her future plans. She would be all right.

As I look back on it, I see that the planning process had, in effect, been an initiatory rite of my presidency: it tested me and the community with stresses and strains of adjustment on both sides. But even the protest movement served to advance the authority and agenda of my presidency. By the end of the upheaval, many students had decided to throw their support to me. This spring challenge had indeed been my "true inauguration," marking the transition to a different presidency and new style of leadership.

The former president, a horsewoman and an orator of high rhetoric, had a certain glamour and mystique about her. I was more down-to-earth; I had less pizzazz; I was less given to rhetorical flourish. She had sometimes intervened benevolently and personally when individuals made special pleas to her. Repudiating the cult of the individual, I embraced and advocated the power of shared governance at Mount Holyoke. I wanted the organizational and jurisdictional structures of the College to function independently of the president. I did not allow end runs around administrative officers. Students dissatisfied with their financial aid packages, for example, learned that I would not overturn what those officers had decided. In effect, I wanted to be neither parent nor judge, but part of a self-governing community.

I learned through the student takeovers, however, that there was a significant symbolic dimension to my role as president. Like it or not, I represented Mount Holyoke College to the world and our students. It was incumbent on me to learn to be more comfortable in that role and to embrace it with more expansiveness and flexibility. Students craved a connection to me both as a person and figurehead, and apparently I had seemed remote, untouchable, and unknowable to some of them. An editorial in the student newspaper had complained that students wanted a "symbol not a CEO." When I first read this, I thought how ridiculous. If ever an institution needed to stop basking in comforting myths about itself and squarely face realities, it was Mount Holyoke. Yet I learned that my approach was indeed too CEO-like for some. Especially because I was an outsider,

Joanne, Tom, Will, and Maisie on Mount Holyoke Campus

they feared that my no-nonsense "managerial" approach might ruin or alter the essential character of the place. I had to recite and embody the verities of Mount Holyoke.

Indeed, while the College was adjusting to me, I was adjusting to it and honing an ever-greater appreciation of the power of its shared ideas, its distinguished history, its commitment to intellectual and moral seriousness, its modest but assured sense of destiny and purpose. As I learned more, I became more passionate in my advocacy of the College and connected more effectively with alumnae audiences. But it was harder for me to strike the right note with students.

As time went on, I found ways to build connections to our students. Of course, one president for twenty-two hundred students makes it hard to know them personally, and in the presidency one is buffered by an invisible barrier of deference. But through teaching classes and meeting informally with students as much as possible in their own settings, I made some progress. I thoroughly enjoyed their *esprit*, and I took great pride in their achievements. Getting a dog, Maisie, was perhaps the most-effective humanizing link. Daily walks around the campus with Tom and Maisie were a low-key way to see and be seen. These constitutionals gave students some assurance that the president was in residence at the College, and they gave the president a good excuse to poke around and keep tabs on what was happening around the campus (and to exercise as well). With all passion spent, I had settled in as president. For the foreseeable future, Mount Holyoke and I would live together and get on with the agenda we had taken such pains to develop.

} 8 {

ALUMNAE

"The College Gave Me Voice"

A new college president learns quickly that she or he isn't dealing just with the campus community but also with a vast, dispersed community of graduates. At Mount Holyoke in my time they were over thirty thousand strong, most of whom were loyal and supportive. Individually and collectively, our alumnae represented an invaluable asset, resource, and cheering section. They made up a significant portion of the Board of Trustees and populated innumerable committees and support groups that were tremendously helpful to the College, particularly in recruiting new students and raising money. Many alumnae functioned almost like paid staff in the degree of their responsibility. They formed hundreds of clubs that spanned the country and the world. They gave generously of their time and money to the College. Over 40 percent contributed to the annual fund every year, and during our first fund-raising campaign, an astonishing 81 percent contributed. Mount Holyoke College could not have sustained itself without this unpaid, loyal, enthusiastic, and generous support group.

I found the alumnae a warm, welcoming community of interesting women. Many were adventurous, accomplished, and professionally successful. Others had more- traditional lives. Nearly all carried an ingrained sense of connection to one another and to the College. I envied their rootedness to the powerful ideals of Mount Holyoke, and the longer I was affiliated with the College, the more I felt a kindred "sisterhood" with them. Alumnae turned out in significant numbers for on- and off-campus events, bringing an infectious energy with them. At a large event in Washington, D.C., early in my presidency, where the atmosphere was palpably electric, my sister, Judy, commented: "I've never seen anything like it." They were deeply interested in what was happening at the College and eager to hear good news. They were not an arrogant group. A kind of modesty or understatement was deeply engrained in the Mount Holyoke ethos. Although many were financially well off (and many were not), most displayed little ostentation. One of the men on the Board of Trustees said there was something of the "girl scout" about Mount Holyoke women. They tended to be earnest, solid, engaged women, pillars of their communities. Even with a wide range of generations and experiences, all valued their education, were serious minded, and felt the College to be part of their ongoing identity. The few misanthropes were the exception. Most were upbeat and thoughtful, whatever their political persuasion. Active in clubs, or admissions, or development work, many kept in touch with friends through the College. At the College we, in turn, stepped up our efforts to keep in touch with them. An important goal spelled out in *The Plan for Mount Holyoke 2003* was to foster the engagement of alumnae in the life and work of Mount Holyoke.

Shortly after I was named president, I was asked by an alumna trustee what I thought of an independent alumnae association. I said I could "live with it." It was not what she really wanted to hear. If I were designing a college from scratch, I would prefer to have all the players, including the alumnae association, seated at the same table and setting the agenda together. Still, Mount Holyoke had a proud, long-standing, and independent alumnae association as well as a troubled history of strained relations between the administration of the College and leaders of the association. At that time the relationship was working, and I didn't want to rock the boat. The Alumnae Association of Mount Holyoke College was a vital organization that contributed in multiple ways to the welfare of the College and its alumnae. Despite its status, the independence of the Association was a bit of an illusion. While it was a 501c3 organization with its own agenda and staffing, it was highly interdependent in function. The headquarters resided in College space, was serviced by College equipment and staff, and drew its money not from a dues structure or independent endowment but from the College itself. How that funding worked, however, was a matter articulated in historical agreements and, as it turned out, in continuing misunderstandings over budgeting issues.

In 1970 when the Association had ceased to be a fund-raising arm of the College, an agreement was drawn up between the two organizations. The Association's view of this agreement was that it retained "ownership" of funds raised in the name of the "alumnae fund," that it had first dibs on money in the fund, and that it "gifted over" the remainder to the College each year. But the College's view of this agreement was different. It contended that money given to, held by, and spent by the College belonged to it. The Association didn't gift over any money at the end of the year; indeed, it never touched these funds at all. Rather, the Association submitted its budget and was funded by the College.

This difference of interpretation of an agreement written in 1970 and modified in 1981 lay dormant for the most part. The two previous presidents of the College had danced around the issue, not wanting to tackle it directly. Nor did I. In actual practice, the "ownership" of the funds mattered little, so long as the two organizations functioned cooperatively, and they did so most of the time. Of course, there were irritants in the relationship. The Association set its own budget independent of the College's processes, assumptions, and timetable. When its expenses rose precipitously, we were powerless to address the cause. So too were we hampered by the lateness of their budget process. Another irritation was how painfully obvious it was that funds could be saved through the sharing of personnel and resources in several functions.

Despite the sometimes-cumbersome terms, we lived with this arrangement until the president of the Alumnae Association decided to pick a fight. She became upset that newly mandated accounting procedures displayed the "alumnae fund" in financial statements as revenue of the College and reckoned with the expenses of the Association "just like a department of the College." She demanded that this presentation be altered and that the College affirm the Association's ownership of the alumnae fund. After extensive discussions in the Board of Trustee's Audit Committee, auditors representing both sides agreed that the College properly represented the alumnae fund as College revenues. Still not satisfied with their conclusion, however, the Alumnae Association president insisted that the College attest in writing that the Alumnae Association of Mount Holyoke

College owned the alumnae fund. Despite consultation with lawyers and many hours of conversation at many levels, no resolution was in sight. The Board of Trustees then proposed using mediation to settle the dispute.

Negotiating teams of three persons on each side met intensively to resolve the sticking points, arriving at a "Statement of Principles," which was to form the basis of a new agreement. At the heart of document was a generous scheme whereby Mount Holyoke would hold separately thirty million of its resources in a quasi-endowment that would, within certain parameters, provide a permanent source of funding to the Association, and the Association, in turn, would relinquish any claims to ownership of the alumnae fund.

At its meeting in October 2000, the Board of Trustees discussed this matter at length and unanimously endorsed the "Statement of Principles." The Trustees expressed concern, however, with the time, energy, and money being consumed in this dispute. They advocated a timely resolution and passed a separate measure stating that if an agreement in accord with the "Statement of Principles" had not been arrived at by a certain date, the College would terminate the previous agreement between the College and the Association.

But the Association's team kept delaying the process. Finally, instead of signing, it substantially rewrote the agreement, inserting ownership issues and insisting on a termination clause that required mutual agreement. Exasperated by these demands, the College's team formally withdrew from the mediation process and shortly thereafter sent a letter withdrawing the College, after a year of transition, from the 1970/1981 agreement with the Association. Almost simultaneously with this letter, we sent another to all alumnae. Signed by both the chair of the Board and me, it explained the College's action, regretting the failure of negotiations, announcing that the disputed term "alumnae fund" would be retired, declaring that hereafter Mount Holyoke College would raise annual-support monies under the generic "annual fund," and expressing hope that the College and the Association would arrive at new understandings under these terms.

These actions surprised and enraged the Alumnae Association president, team, and board. At the meeting of our Board of Trustees in May 2001, the new president of the Association, in a private meeting with the chair and me, expressed her anger and hurt at this outcome. She declared what she had learned in the civil rights movement: "Power is not voluntarily relinquished. It must be seized." And that was what we had done—seized power! She recognized a power play when she saw one.

Obviously, we didn't see it that way. We had acted in good faith, spending countless hours and dollars in lawyer and mediator fees to arrive at an agreement both sides could accept. Still, I remember thinking as she said her accusation, perhaps she was right. Perhaps "being nice" was a doomed process from the beginning, and the College needed to use its superior clout to resolve this dispute. Some Board members had long ago come to that conclusion. The trouble with a power play, of course, is that it provokes a like response, and that indeed happened with the Association.

The Alumnae Association didn't have a legal leg to stand on. The College was perfectly within its rights to withdraw from the 1970/1981 agreement, which either party could do at any time. Since we would no longer use the disputed term "alumnae fund," the Association could make no claim to any money we would raise in the future. This was a clever move on the College's part but one that enraged the Association team. Their power was political, not legal, and they attempted to arouse the troops, the Mount Holyoke alumnae. Quick off the mark, the Association used its email list to send scathing, rambling messages to alumnae. The heated communications battle continued through several rounds, causing consternation in the alumnae ranks. A flurry of emails from alumnae began to arrive at the College. We received hundreds of emails and letters, some supportive, some critical, but most expressing distress about and distaste for this unseemly public skirmish. The College put up a Q&A on its website, responding to frequently asked questions about the dispute; the Association retorted with its own.

The Association cast the dispute in simple but distorted terms. The College was trying to stifle its independent voice, the Association claimed. It couldn't have that autonomous voice without "independent" funding. Insisting that was not the case, we recognized the Mount Holyoke Alumnae Association as a 501c3 organization; we had no control over the *Alumnae Quarterly*, the publishing arm of the Association. We neither intended nor wanted to silence the assertive, free voices of our former students. We didn't question the Association's right to spend its money as it wished. What we did dispute was the belief that the Association had an unfettered call on the College's alumnae fund.

At the reunions held a few weeks after the public disclosure of the dispute, the matter was very much in the air. Although the Association president and I had agreed to preserve decorum at the reunions and sent alumnae a note saying that the two of us would be talking and didn't want this matter to consume their time together, the Association still incited the protest by passing out to returning alumnae ribbons that said, "The College gave me voice." It did, indeed, and it seemed to me that the Association was trying to channel those voices into a single party line. This staged protest was not particularly successful, although it did cast a pall over the reunion festivities.

It was hard to understand the passion of some of these women about the alumnae-fund proprietorship. Why did they care so much? The person who started it all, the president of the Association, had grown up during the civil rights era. She believed that an important role of the Association was to watch over the College. Should the College try to do something not to the liking of its alumnae, they could, through the Association, rise up and prevent it.

I found this watchdog model distasteful because it assumed an adversarial relationship between the College and its graduates. In fact, our interests were deeply aligned. We all cared about the welfare of the College and its graduates. My own preference was to empower our graduates by making alumnae relations an integral part of the running of the College. My perspective as an administrator always was to reinforce a sense of collective responsibility for the welfare of the whole.

For some within the Association (although not personally for its president at this time), the issue requiring the most vigilance was coeducation. A wrathful Alumnae Association could make life miserable for any president who tried to lead the College in that direction. But on the fundamental matter of money lying at the heart of this dispute, they were wrong. The Association did not "own" the annual contributions of all alumnae to the College. Indeed, many alumnae balked at the idea that the Association should have a first and privileged "cut" of the money donated in good faith to the College, for they had not given their money to the Association.

While the hard reality of money fueled the conflict, the passions had deep symbolic and psychological roots. Sometimes, the Association complained revealingly that it did not want to be treated like a "child" put on an "allowance" from the College. It wanted autonomy and complained that its work was not valued and respected by the College. Running an "independent" association was for some staff and volunteers proof of adulthood and agency. Especially for older generations of alumnae, this volunteer work had real substance and meaning. In some cases it was their only work outside the home. These women were proud of their ability to run competently a complex organization. A force to be reckoned with, they could use their political clout to make their views heard and matter. They didn't want themselves or the Association diminished by a College take-over or by receiving an allowance.

The successor in the presidency of the Alumnae Association, a graduate of the class of 1976, was, like her predecessor, a successful professional with a demanding job. She had a difficult role to play, she inherited the dispute and an organization in disarray, and she carried on the fight with determination. But fundamentally, she was animated by an upbeat nature. She wanted her legacy to be a positive one, and she hoped to enjoy her time as president of the Association. We both concluded that our best interests were served by trying to work together. And, bit by bit, we picked up the pieces and carried on. Together, we met with the president and vice-president of the Mellon Foundation, and they help us sort out the issues. With the assistance of colleagues and with a great deal of patience, she and I put together an interim agreement by the end of summer 2001 and worked over the next semester to rebuild our relationship on a new foundation. Although this issue had consumed an enormous amount of time, energy, and money, and the College, and I as president, had endured a lot of abuse, it seemed that future presidents would not have to deal with this unnecessary, draining battle. The problem of the alumnae fund was another mess that my administration had cleaned up, and I took satisfaction in that. But I was assuming more closure than there was in fact.

I took a sabbatical in winter term 2002 while Bev Tatum took over my presidential duties on an interim basis. It was under her watch that the College and Alumnae Association drew up a ten-year agreement that included a set of shared core principles, the retirement of the term "alumnae fund," the clarification that the "annual fund" was owned and managed by the College, the provision of office space and computer support to the Association, and the establishment of a rather-complex funding formula, which generously guaranteed the Association a minimum 4 percent annual increase of the operating budget. This agreement bought a certain amount of peace, and both sides tried to make it work.

Some subsequent Alumnae Association leaders did much to build bridges with the College and to help overcome the bad old days of the public blow up. But others retained more-separatist notions. They believed the Association was doing significant work in service of the College (and it was), but the problem was that its initiatives were not always coordinated with ours and its emphasis was not necessarily our emphasis. In order to accomplish tasks, we were forced to set up parallel and duplicate systems. Within the context of the recession, the inefficiency and lack of opportunity to plan strategically in alumnae relations was especially evident in our redundant, uncoordinated activities and functions. Mount Holyoke spent far more money than any competitor school by a long shot to fund the Alumnae Association and College-based alumnae outreach.

While we were embroiled in these matters, my staff and I consulted with colleagues at other colleges and universities about their experiences with college and alumni/ae relations. We learned that other institutions too were working their way through complex historical relationships with their associations. Some, notably Georgetown, had undergone painful and public legal battles over funding issues. Others had suffered through tensions every bit as stinging as ours and conflicts sometimes more painful than the ones we went through to clarify funding arrangements. At a few institutions such as the University of Michigan, the alumni associations were truly separate, autonomous organizations with dues and an independent endowment. At other institutions like Wesleyan, they were totally absorbed in the institution, usually housed in the development office. At still others such as Mount Holyoke, they were hybrids with some vestiges of independence. At no other college or university but Mount Holyoke had an alumnae organization claimed to "own" the annual fund, although Wellesley College observed a gentlewomen's agreement that didn't bear too much scrutiny.

In a Darwinian way, this relationship between universities or colleges and their alumni/ae associations adapted to the peculiarities or contingencies of each institution. Vestiges of old ways that were no longer harmonious with new realities—along with the predictable resisters to change, usually the old guard—persisted in and around their institutions. Alumnae organizations had started off primarily as social clubs, and on one level, they still fulfilled that role. But the needs of graduates and colleges were radically changing. No longer did alumnae simply want convivial connections with fellow graduates; they expected valuable services from the institution: career placement assistance; access to data bases of employment information; travel opportunities; and continuing education. Colleges, in turn, needed their alumnae population to assist in increasingly sophisticated marketing, in admissions and fundraising, and in building vital links between the curriculum and the world of work. Email and the web were making possible much-more-frequent information sharing and interactivity. All this interdependence made for a much greater need to think of the alumnae function as a key and integral part of the college itself. It made sense to be as smart, savvy, and strategic about this critical part of the enterprise as about any other important function in the College

Although the new agreement did not solve the underlying disjuncture of separate administrative structures, the Alumnae Association of Mount Holyoke College continued to do much good, and the alumnae continued to be a great strength of the College. Mount Holyoke quite literally could not survive without the alumnae's abiding support both through the Association and directly with the College. They were (and are) an extraordinary group of women, who did the College proud. I felt my life deeply enriched by getting to know many of them during my presidency. It was tremendously meaningful for me to join them in "sisterhood" when I got a Mount Holyoke degree, an honorary doctorate of humane letters, in my final year as president.

} 9 {

IN THE LIMELIGHT

"It's Like Having Your Medals Stripped in Public"

Just as I was recovering from the dispute with the Alumnae Association, I received an urgent message to call Joe Ellis, professor of history at Mount Holyoke. Two months earlier, in April 2001, I had accompanied Joe to the New York dinner celebrating nominees for the Pulitzer Prize and was delighted when he won for his book, *Founding Brothers: The Revolutionary Generation* (2001). The campus was still jubilant about his success, which brought honor not only upon him but the College. A large banner congratulating Professor Ellis still hung from the College gate.

While taking a brief break at an off-campus meeting, I called Joe, who said I should know that the *Boston Globe* was pursuing a story about his past, including his Vietnam War experience. The paper had got many things wrong, he explained, but he couldn't talk about it. He wanted me to know he was "an honorable man," and he hoped I could stand by him. He was going to have to take the heat on this episode. He said he told Kevin McCaffrey, our news director, all about it, and Kevin had drafted a possible statement for me to go public with.

I was surprised and questioned Joe further. What was the *Globe* saying? How did the story get started? Why was the paper pillorying him? He answered me vaguely: it said he hadn't been to Vietnam and made other wrong allegations about his past. He implied that students had talked with the press. I was puzzled by this. If students or others had concerns, why bring them to the newspaper and not to the College itself? Why was this issue coming up now? But Joe didn't know or wouldn't say, and when I hung up, I had more questions than answers. I immediately called Kevin, who said that Joe had assured him the allegations about his fabricated Vietnam service were false. Kevin said he would draft a press release for me. He advised that we should "stand by the guy," just as we had stood with him when he was being honored.

Later, on the ride back to campus, I puzzled over this perplexing development with my colleague Charlie. Why did it matter what some professor did or didn't do over thirty years ago? What made his newsworthy now? We recalled the vexed and troubled period of the Vietnam War, when it seemed there was no way for members of our generation to play it right—the war damaged all within its orbit: those who went to Vietnam, those who fled the draft, and those who protested the War. No one emerged unscathed. Even to think about that time was troubling and unsettling.

It seemed inconceivable that Joe, who taught a course on the Vietnam War and who occasionally alluded to his time in Vietnam and apparently discussed his combat experiences in his classroom, had made up this service. Why wouldn't he address these allegations directly? Why did he say he couldn't talk? I conjectured that perhaps he was an undercover agent. This wasn't as crazy as it might seem at first: I had another colleague, a professor at Wayne State University, who had worked for the CIA under a fabricated name and identity when he was younger. Perhaps Joe too was pressed into this kind of service. It wasn't at all unlikely given his education and intelligence. Even so, what difference did it make now? Why bother to dig into the past? What purpose did it serve? How was this newsworthy? I thought it was a probably a case of overzealous investigative journalism. But did I ever seriously underestimate the interest and turmoil it would engender.

Joe had been an outstanding College citizen for almost thirty years. He was our most-honored and -feted scholar and a popular teacher. He had served the College as dean of the faculty for ten years. He had even been acting president. Winner of the National Book Award for *American Sphinx: The Character of Thomas Jefferson* (1996) along with his recent Pulitzer Prize for *Founding Brothers*, he was a great asset to Mount Holyoke College. If he insisted he had been wrongly accused, I was willing to give him the benefit of the doubt. I was committed to the presumption of innocence until proven guilty. A few months earlier, hadn't the *Globe* retracted a story about two murders at Dartmouth that suggested a love triangle when, in fact, the accused turned out to be two young men unconnected to the victims?[1] I thought perhaps the same would happen in this instance but not without first seriously invading Joe's privacy and causing a lot of upset.

While Kevin tried to dissuade the *Globe* from publishing this story and had a feeling of dread about it, I underestimated the press' and the public's interest in the issue. I quickly learned that Professor Ellis wasn't some obscure college professor cloistered in the ivory tower. As a best-selling historian, he had become a public figure whose private life was open to scrutiny by anyone. And then I was completely caught unaware by Joe's subsequent admission of guilt.

The *Globe* story—long and detailed—came out on Monday, June 18, 2001. It immediately became a big story that generated considerable national interest and struck a nerve in the public psyche. Joe's case reopened the old wounds from the troubled Vietnam period, enraging Vietnam veterans, hundreds of whom wrote me scathing emails and letters demanding that he be fired. The *Globe* revelations upset and depressed many faculty, staff, and students in the campus community, several of whom were besieged by reporters and received calls for comment. Early summer was usually a slow news time, but this was a hot story that dominated the news cycle for days.

Reeling from the story and still operating under the presumption that this was all a terrible mistake, I issued a short—and regrettable—statement that Professor Ellis was a well-respected professor and that I didn't know what purpose the pursuit of this story served the *Globe*. Hours later I received a surprising call from Joe, who said he was going to issue a public statement admitting that the central allegation was true—that he had misrepresented his Vietnam service. In his next breath, he railed against the *Globe*, slamming the many errors in the story regarding his military service, his high school experiences, and his civil rights record, labeling their representation as downright libelous. He had considered suing the paper but was advised to cut off the matter. So he was going to end the uproar with a public admission.

I was shocked and blindsided by his turnabout. Making matters worse, his belated public admission appeared in the *Globe* on the same day as my earlier statement saying "I don't know what purpose is served" by this inquiry. This jarring juxtaposition was not only embarrassing to me, but, not surprisingly, it provoked wrath about my evidently lax ethical standards regarding the veracity of professors. Of course, Joe's admission, grudging and qualified as it was, fundamentally changed my perspective. I was now obligated to set in motion a College process to understand his admission and its implications for his standing at Mount Holyoke, and I had to issue a clarification to the press, but before I could do anything, it was imperative that I talk with Joe and learn more about this situation.

I arranged to visit him at his house. Kevin accompanied me, and Chris, Joe's friend and colleague, was there, as was Joe's wife, Ellen. Clearly, Joe and Ellen felt under siege. They had disconnected their landline and were holed up in their house. They believed I should continue to stand by him. I replied that Joe's admission of guilt had cast the situation in a whole new light and that I would now need to initiate an appropriate College investigation.

The *Globe* published my subsequent letter essentially retracting my previous statement about the press' interest and asserting that the College would investigate Joe's false claims about his military service. How the College would do that was not at all clear. My colleagues and I poured through faculty legislation; the procedures for a situation of this kind were not self-evident. Later in the week I travelled to Wisconsin to celebrate my mother's and son's birthdays. But my family saw little of me. Most of my time was consumed with Joe's case. I consulted with colleagues, answered press queries, and reeled from the firestorm of newspaper coverage and from the angry and alarmed responses that swirled around me and the College. My email was deluged with messages. Kevin was flooded with the calls to the College, some of which he thought I should respond to directly. My colleagues called to express their worry about the deteriorating situation. My unfortunate remark prior to Joe's confession was played and replayed by jeering commentators. I got dragged into the mire, while my colleagues at Mount Holyoke fretted about the damage to the reputation of both the College and me.

I was angry and alarmed about being personally dragged into the center of this controversy and by the vehement partisanship of some newspaper editorialists and television commentators, but I was determined not to act rashly. No matter how hard some reporters pressed, I couldn't say what I would do and what the College procedure would be until I had the opportunity to consult with appropriate faculty colleagues. I sent a letter to the Mount Holyoke community saying that "like them I was shocked by the *Boston Globe's* allegations against Joe Ellis and surprised and saddened when he admitted subsequently that the most serious of them, fabricating service in Vietnam, was true" and that we now needed "time to work out appropriate process; time to consult, reflect, and arrive at some understanding and perspective." On June 27, I met with the dean of faculty and Faculty Advisory Committee for Appointment, Reappointments, and Promotions, which, after reviewing the matter, decided that it had proper jurisdiction and would take up the case. Shortly thereafter, I clarified for the campus community and for the press how the College would handle the matter. Although still reluctant to let go of the story, the press, for the most part, backed off while the confidential deliberations of the committee were in place and under way.

The Faculty Advisory Committee was a well-respected group of full professors, five in number, elected by their peers, who were convened by the dean of faculty, a voting member of the committee. The president was an ex officio member who attended all meetings. We quickly laid out the ground rules: our deliberations were confidential; the dean would speak for the committee; everyone else would be mum. Intelligent and fair-minded, members of Faculty Advisory Committee came into the deliberations with a range of responses towards the matter and the differences among them helped to develop nuanced perspectives on the case. For some, the *Globe's* allegation flew in the face of everything they had known about Joe as a colleague and friend. Others were less surprised, less sympathetic, and more ready to judge his actions harshly.

At the heart of the matter, of course, was the puzzling, enigmatic, dominating personality of Joe, who was invited to meet with the Committee to make a statement and to answer questions. During his time as dean of faculty, Joe had addressed cases of faculty misconduct, and he had clear ideas about how his own case should be handled. In other words, it was hard for him not to attempt to engineer his own trial and punishment. He wanted a quick admission, sanction, resolution, and restoration. But he also knew it was necessary to subject himself to the committee's and president's procedures and judgment, and when he appeared before us, he was deferential, articulate, collegial, and open. He brought his class notes for his Vietnam course, and he clarified when and how he had first let stand and then confirmed the false assumption about his service in Vietnam. He defended the integrity of the course, his other courses, and his scholarship. He noted his service and devotion to Mount Holyoke College. And he castigated himself for his "stupid" misstep, offered conjecture about the psychological causes (rooted in his relationship with his parents), and said he was seeking counseling. Clearly, it was hard for him to make this appearance, and he faced it bravely.

While he repudiated his alleged service in Vietnam, Joe also related in vivid language his experiences teaching history at the U.S. Military Academy (West Point) as a source of insight about the war. After listening to him, I wondered why he ever felt the need to fabricate a Vietnam experience when his time at West Point, 1969-1972, placed him on the "inside" of a significant military institution, the army, at the same time that it was consumed by controversy about the Mai Lai massacre and other aspects of the war. Surely, in some ways this was a privileged vantage point on the war, one certainly safer than commanding a platoon of infantry in combat in Vietnam. Even as he talked, I found myself wondering about the veracity of these accounts. Were they true? Were they embellished? Joe Ellis was a natural-born storyteller. Could he distinguish between what happened and his own coloration of it?

In addition to Joe's testimony, the Committee also studied his class notes and looked at his entire file of student evaluations. It also solicited responses from members of the community, urging faculty from the History Department and students from his last three years of teaching, in particular, to comment. The record of teaching, as evidenced both by student evaluations and also by the many thoughtful letters and emails sent to the committee, was exceptional. Joe was a beloved teacher, who had profoundly and positively impacted hundreds of students across three decades. Confronted with the admission by Professor Ellis that he had lied about his service in the Vietnam War, most students who wrote to the Committee struggled—many eloquently and insightfully—with the issues involved but nonetheless came down on the side of compassion. Nearly all defended his value to them and to the College.

The committee also reviewed many letters from faculty, staff, and alumnae, and they saw samples of the nearly twelve hundred letters and emails the dean of faculty and I received from people outside the institution, largely Vietnam veterans who harshly condemned Joe and often demanded his firing. Faculty had more-complex responses. Many thoughtfully worked through the issues. Most believed that Joe had made a serious mistake that reflected dishonor on himself and the College, and that he should apologize, receive sanctions, and seek counseling. There was disagreement, however, on what should follow for Joe. Many thought he should be restored to his place in the community after a time away. Some opined the only honorable choice was for him to resign. A few felt he should be fired.

Those most upset, understandably, were colleagues in the History Department. They were not only shaken by the controversy swirling around him but felt drawn into and sullied by it. And they claimed his misrepresentation reflected badly on all of them and on the discipline and profession of history. Regrettably, the incident opened old wounds long festering in the department. Joe's relationship with some of his colleagues had been highly problematic in normal times. Now it seemed impossible. Some colleagues wanted nothing more to do with him after all the fire he drew on them and the College.

While Professor Ellis had misrepresented himself as a Vietnam veteran in his course on the Vietnam War, these lies, it appears, were utterly gratuitous to the course, which was excellent in form, design, and content and, as one student put it, "about Vietnam[,] not about Professor Ellis." Nothing came forward to cast doubt Ellis's scholarship. A few colleagues in the field wrote to say that they always knew he was a flawed historian because of his misreading of the Sally Hemmings–Thomas Jefferson liaison. But that was a matter of legitimate scholarly dispute. Other historians defended his scholarship. Overall, Ellis's reputation as a scrupulous historian remained intact. And his personnel file documented an exemplary career from his undergraduate days onward.

After intensive investigation, the faculty committee arrived at its recommendation and submitted a confidential report to me detailing their findings. Agreeing substantially with their account and recommendation, I wrote Joe a letter outlining my disposition of the matter and attaching the committee's decision. The sanction stipulated his stepping down from his endowed chair, suspension for a year without pay, and issuing a sincere apology to me and others, including Vietnam veterans, who had been hurt by his falsehood and initial deception.

Joe wasn't happy with my letter, the committee's report, or the terms. Indeed, he considered the committee's report downright libelous, and he was very anxious about possible leaks of the document to the press. He tried to negotiate the terms I had laid down; he felt the year away should be a "leave," not a "suspension." He strongly balked at the idea of stepping down from his endowed chair. "It's like being stripped of your medals in public," he said. He seriously considered resignation. "You'll be hearing from my lawyer," he sometimes threatened when our conversations broke down. And I consulted a lawyer as well, but I kept insisting that we weren't engaged in a labor negotiation and that I thought we would be more successful talking directly rather than through lawyers. That proved to be correct. Joe really did want this matter resolved and to come back to the College.

I was especially concerned about his continuing defensiveness and casting blame onto others. In a meeting with him at my house on Friday, August 1, 2001 (for which I still have notes), he said that my letter and the advisory committee's report were "castration. . . . No sensible and rational person would accept such terms." I said that I wanted him to apologize for having misled Kevin and me, and to issue a full, sincere public apology to others he had deceived, let down, or hurt as well. He said he would apologize to me for the trouble he had caused, but he would not apologize for misleading me because he had not. There was "some truth" to his presentation of himself in class. When I pressed him, he said he had possibly misled Kevin, but not me. I said in exasperation that "you told me there are things back there I can't talk about, and that I should talk with Kevin. When I talked with Kevin, he told me you said that your 'Vietnam record was expunged.'"

Then, Joe blurted out: "It's true. It was expunged. There are things I can't talk about." He went on cryptically to reveal one shocking part of what he had allegedly done while in Vietnam, something I feel professionally compelled to continue to hold in confidence. I was, to say the least, flabbergasted by this revelation. "What am I supposed to do with that!?" I asked him. "You are to do nothing with it," he said. "You can't talk about it. I've made my public statement and that is what you're dealing with." I argued that he had put me in an impossible situation, giving me a different story in private now from what he had said earlier in public, while insisting he wasn't misleading me.

I didn't believe Joe had really been to Vietnam; it seemed a desperate eleventh hour lie. But I wasn't absolutely sure, and I'm still not. Maybe he was that secret agent, after all. This information certainly was a bombshell, an unexploded one, since Joe wrapped this disclosure in all-too-convenient confidentiality. Alternatively, sincere and self-justifying, Joe was simply not a reliable narrator of his own life. It was hard to decipher where the facts stopped and the coloration began. He seemed locked intractably in a defensive construction of reality, unwilling or unable to see the way that he was personally responsible for the messy situation in which he had put the College, his colleagues, and his family and friends. Rather, from his point of view, a vendetta against him was fueled by the press' venomous muckraking and his colleagues' jealousy. He could not execute a sincere apology either publicly or privately, although he made another attempt. Many of his colleagues were as annoyed by his second public statement as they were by the first.

While Joe would obviously have much to continue dealing with, I did my best to bring closure to this controversy at the College. After finally securing Joe's agreement to the terms and conditions of my letter, I prepared a statement to be shared first with the Mount Holyoke community and later with the public. Joe tried to dictate what I said, as did his lawyer. Indeed, I was counseled by lawyers on both sides about what I could or should not disclose, but I tried to be as clear and forthcoming as possible. Released on August 17, 2001, my letter reads in its entirety:

> Dear Members of the Mount Holyoke Community:
> I write to inform you of the College's disposition of the disclosure, first published in *The Boston Globe* on June 18, that Professor Joseph J. Ellis had falsely claimed military service in Vietnam, a charge he subsequently confirmed in a phone call to me and in a statement published on June 19 in *The Globe*. On June 27, the College's Faculty Advisory Committee on Appointments, Reappointments, and Promotions assumed responsibility for an inquiry into the matter.

In an intensive series of meetings, including a session with Professor Ellis, the Advisory Committee reviewed and considered, among other documents and information: his syllabus and file of lecture and discussion notes for his Vietnam course that he freely shared with the Committee, student evaluations from his entire career at the College, and solicited and unsolicited letters and email messages from his students and colleagues as well as from other members of the Mount Holyoke community and the public. The Advisory Committee has submitted its confidential report and recommendations to me. I thank the Committee for the care, intellectual rigor, and thoughtfulness with which it conducted its inquiry, and I now share with you, the Mount Holyoke community, the final resolution of this painful and difficult matter.

First, as President of the College, I strongly rebuke Professor Ellis for his lie about his military experience in his course entitled "The Vietnam War and American Culture" as well as with colleagues and others. Perpetuated over many years, his lie about himself clearly violates the ethics of our profession and the integrity we expect of all members of our community. Even though his fabrication appears to have been an aside in an otherwise responsible, intellectually challenging course that immersed students in a crucial chapter of U.S. history, it was a particularly egregious failing in a teacher of history. Misleading students is wrong and nothing can excuse it. Professor Ellis illegitimately appropriated an authority that was not his and abused his students' trust. His misrepresentation damaged collegial relations within the College and hurt the Mount Holyoke community and others outside it.

Second, Professor Ellis will be suspended for one year without pay. In addition, he has voluntarily stepped down from his endowed chair until such time as the Trustees may wish to reinstate it. The year away should give him and the College time for reflection and repair. This sanction is consistent with our honor code for students and its emphasis on education, reflection, and ultimately restoration to an honorable place in our community. Professor Ellis has accepted the College's censure and sanctions. He has apologized to me personally and has expanded his earlier public apology. His statement will be posted, along with this letter, on the Mount Holyoke Web site.

This is a very difficult matter for Professor Ellis and for all of us who know and admire him as teacher, colleague, and friend. He made a terrible mistake. We cannot condone it. Moreover, we deplore the disrespect Professor Ellis's lie has shown to Vietnam veterans, and, on behalf of all of us at the College, I apologize for any pain his misrepresentation has caused them and their families.

While the College must censure Professor Ellis for his serious failing and the damage it has done, yet, we also must acknowledge his twenty-nine years of truly distinguished teaching, scholarship, and service to the College. One cannot review his record without being impressed with the power and effectiveness of his teaching, the substance and grace of his writing, and the way his administrative contributions have, in countless ways, been woven into the fabric of the College. The Advisory Committee and I believe that Mount Holyoke College can unequivocally condemn Professor Ellis's lie and impose significant sanctions, at the same time that it can accept his apology and make room for his return and future service to the College.

I earnestly hope that Professor Ellis and the Mount Holyoke community will find educational and restorative benefit in this painful experience.

Sincerely,

Joanne V. Creighton

I, along with several others of my colleagues, made ourselves available to the press for interviews. I talked, I believe, to ten or so news outlets including the *New York Times, Washington Post*, the *Los Angeles Times*, and the Associated Press. Our goal was to get the news out clearly and all at once. Fortunately, the letter and judgment were well received on and off campus alike. This resolution even evoked a supportive editorial in the *New York Times* and favorable commentary in other major news outlets.[2] Most surprising was that Vietnam veterans, for the most part, were satisfied with the College's decision, and a number of them graciously wrote to say so. Although some veterans had threatened to demonstrate on our campus if Ellis were not dismissed, most were satisfied that his unethical behavior was treated seriously and sanctions were imposed. They had expected much less from me and the College. The veterans also appreciated that we replied to everyone who wrote us. Many apparently didn't expect our polite and forthcoming responses to their sometimes intemperate messages, and scores wrote back more civilly themselves to say so.

I learned a lot about the ongoing angst of the troubled Vietnam era in U.S. history, and my heart went out to the many veterans who were obviously still suffering from the war. I understood, too, why the Ellis matter struck such a deep nerve in them. They had served in a conflict that, for years, had brought them no glory. It was the war that America lost, that divided a nation, that had used up soldiers and released them broken, lost, ignored, and vaguely disgraced. But in more recent times, particularly beginning in the 1980s, there had been growing appreciation for the sacrifice and heroism that their service often entailed. And now Ellis was, it seemed, falsely horning in on and "stealing" their belated recognition. In fact, a recent book on the subject exposed a surprisingly large number of pretenders who were now claiming "stolen valor."[3] A number of these pretenders or poachers were college professors. One case, which unfolded at the University of Oklahoma, was resolved only months before the Ellis story broke. It, unlike Joe's, was not big news, but then the professor in question was not a Pulitzer Prize winner.

The irony was that Joe was well aware of this book and sympathetic to the issues it raised. A further irony is that he, perhaps more than most others of our generation, appreciated the complexities of this war and the valor, casualties, and angst of these soldiers. His Vietnam course was rich and nuanced; he fully accorded veterans their due. He empathized with them and felt guilty, he said, about his luck at evading their fate. He created a persona that joined them in their brotherhood as combat veterans. Imitation is the sincerest form of flattery. Even if Joe didn't quite take full responsibility for his misrepresentation, he nonetheless got his share of Vietnam angst, after all, but not of the kind he was bargaining for, when he created a soldier persona, which was called out by the *Globe*.

A further irony is that students at a politically liberal women's college are probably the least likely of any group of people to be impressed with wartime experience and exploits. They didn't need such proofs of Joe's or anyone's manhood. I think they might admire the bravery of the draft resisters and the antiwar protestors more than the courage of the combat soldiers. In other words, Joe's misrepresentation was a gratuitous self-indulgence intended to bolster his male authority, his privilege, his reputation. And worst of all—it was completely unnecessary. Students were already sufficiently wowed by Professor Ellis.

Although Joe genuinely loved the College and cared about its welfare, he was a rather anomalous presence on an all-women's campus. He had come directly from West Point, all-male at that time, 1972, and was an outspoken advocate for coeducation, although not as vociferously as some of his colleagues. But he rumbled on about it behind the scenes, wrote me periodic diatribes about how the College's excellence was being threatened, and how male professors were increasingly marginalized by feminist ideologues and ever-more-dominant lesbian culture. The only way to stop this trend was to go coed, he argued. Furthermore, he was contemptuous of some of the newer directions in historical scholarship that stressed the importance of race, class, and gender. He himself, he wryly liked to note, focused on dead white men. Joe personally found brotherhood or refuge on campus with a small group of like-minded, aging white, male professors. Their "faculty club" was the male locker room, he said. He also was a member of a crusty all-male club of long vintage in the town and enjoyed this exclusive brotherhood too.

Many of his female colleagues found him much less charming than many students did. Joe was one of the "old boys," predictable in his male attitudes and tiresome in his swaggering arrogance. I was pleased to have drawn Joe into a more-active public role. He liked representing the College; I liked having him do so. He enjoyed offering me advice, serving as a kind of self-appointed adviser without portfolio—occasionally submitting unsolicited, confidential, handwritten missives about the issues of the day. And I always found his interpretations interesting and insightful, even though I often didn't agree with them. We got together occasionally for lunch or other social gatherings. He had a large circle of friends, and he and Ellen threw good parties. Passionate, intelligent, articulate, amusing, and opinionated, Joe was always a lively presence. Throughout the difficult situation that he and I found ourselves in, we maintained a level of warmth and connection. Joe tried to manipulate me at the end, to be sure, but that was Joe. I was equally tenacious in the battle of wills. If being disciplined by a women president added to his humiliation, Joe accepted it with manly grace.

Although Joe and I worked through our strained relationship, he and his colleagues in the History Department could not resolve their differences. The tensions roiled on well after the matter was officially "settled." His colleagues were upset by the turmoil Joe brought on the department and remained angry with him for being insufficiently repentant with them. He, in turn, felt that they were using this incident as an excuse to get back at him and to settle old scores. Joe needed to reach out and reestablish a harmonious connection with them, but in his abortive efforts to do so, he found colleagues enormously prickly and affronted. Some relationships were so soured that rapprochement was perhaps hopeless. I was frustrated and impatient with them all.

The History Department was just one of many dysfunctional departments I had seen over my career, with colleagues harboring grievances and carping on one another. I always found it ironic that these faculty had so carefully chosen one another through the tenure process. It was a marriage gone bad, and the partners were tied to each other for life. Henry Kissinger had apparently said that departmental politics are so nasty because the stakes are so low. But he got it wrong. In fact, even though the issues are often trivial, the stakes are high, because departmental affairs are rife with *ad hominem* internecine battles played out over a professional lifetime.

Joe, for all his professional success, was not the least bit impervious to the barbs of these departmental battles. And then, as he himself so vividly said, he had given his colleagues a loaded gun to point at him. After a couple of meetings with the dean of faculty and me to air their distress, the history faculty reluctantly faced the fact that Joe was coming back after his suspension. Many didn't want to interact with him, and he felt the same way. He decided that he would have a "separation" but not a "divorce." He would teach and do his work, but not participate in departmental business, and that was just fine with his colleagues.

I have puzzled over the way that Joe's strengths and weaknesses stemmed from the same core personality. His ego, his dominating presence, filled up any room he entered. In this, he seems to me a prototypical American male hero—full of life and, in some ways, more vulnerable because of it. Joe reminded me of Bill Clinton and fictional characters such as Fitzgerald's Jay Gatsby or Faulkner's Thomas Sutpen. These self-made men rise from obscure origins to positions of power and adulation. They are intelligent, crafty, and charismatic; they are supremely self-centered and self-confident. Remarkably, they impose themselves on reality—they shape reality to fit their dreams. And they can point to the tangible monuments to their success: a presidency, a mansion, a Pulitzer Prize. But in single-mindedly pursuing their dream, they incur certain moral lapses along the way. "Can't repeat the past?" Gatsby cries out. "Why of course you can!"[4]

In a way Joe Ellis and Thomas Sutpen were saying the same thing. Joe wrote himself into that history. In so doing he, like his American hero counterparts, slipped inexorably outside the bounds of acceptable behavior. "You see, I had a design in my mind. Whether it was a good or a bad design is beside the point; the question is, Where did I make the mistake in it?" asks Sutpen.[5] But he can't see that mistake, his own moral failure. Nor can Clinton, or Gatsby, or Ellis. It is easier for these men to see themselves as victims and their demise as imposed from some external, malevolent force rather than coming from within themselves. This pattern of moral blindness is peculiarly American, perhaps because of the high stock we place in these self-made men. They are our heroes—they demonstrate the truth of the American dream: You *can* go from rags to riches, from obscurity to fame. In America, everything is possible. These heroes are glorified, unless and until their clay feet are exposed, and then too they are fodder for voyeurs who can't get enough of their disgrace. They are our carnival; their tawdry drama is acted out on the public stage.

Later in the year, it was revealed that well-known historians William Ambrose and Doris Kearns Goodwin had plagiarized passages in their published books.[6] These failings were linked in some people's minds to Joe's lie about his Vietnam experience, although the cases were quite different. Ambrose's and Goodwin's failings compromised their scholarship, whereas Joe's methods as a historian remained unsullied. Plagiarism in scholarship seems to me a more reprehensible sin than lying about one's personal experience to students, although both are bad and both serve to discredit historians in the public eye. All three historians had become public personalities, who endured the highs and lows of being in the public spotlight. Such "star" status is not accorded to most academics, and it is probably just as well. The popular acclaim feeds the ego at the expense, perhaps, of good judgment and moral discretion.

Reprehensible as Joe's lie about himself was, I believe we all rewrite the past to some extent. Locked in our heads and our subjective view of experience, we all tell ourselves and others stories about our past. We cast and recast our memories into self-confirming interpretations—self-revelations even—that we keep refining as we change and grow in perspective. And that is certainly what I am doing in this memoir. What actually happened becomes murkier as it is entwined with the dominant narrative of our lives. Undoubtedly, most of us don't create experiences out of whole cloth, and most of us don't have the truth of our stories checked by an investigative newspaper reporter. Although Joe's scholarship stood up under this intense public scrutiny, I had always wondered, when I read his engaging and readable texts, about his ability to recreate scenes, to draw lines of conjecture around certain bald facts. For there's a lot of art in historical writing, a lot of creative imagination, the same kind that could be employed to embellish a life.

When I first heard about the Ellis matter, my initial response was to question the newspaper's interest in this subject. That response got me into a lot of trouble, and I learned to be more circumspect about what I say to the press. Yet as I think about these events with the advantage of distance, I return again to my original response. Wasn't the flap over this issue a massive overreaction to one man's lie about his experience? Why did it matter to a national audience what Joe Ellis did or didn't do thirty years before? His lie was, indeed, a personal failing, more than likely rooted in psychological causes, and it was relevant to Mount Holyoke College because the lie had entered the classroom and abrogated the trust between teacher and student. But, in actual fact, little damage was done to his students. More destruction was brought to collegial relationships at Mount Holyoke, especially in the History Department, and to veterans for whom this story reawakened old traumas. The person most damaged by Joe's lie, however, was Joe himself. His suffering was more than commensurate with the crime; he had to endure the public humiliation that ensued. With a kind of poetic justice befitting a prototypical American tragedy, he fell from an exalted position to one of deep humiliation by his own hand. Joe himself had provoked this story by telling a newspaper reporter about his so-called Vietnam experience, while the reporter was doing a story about Joe's forthcoming book. This reporter became suspicious and checked out the facts. Although Joe suspected that one of his colleagues gave the *Globe* his class lists, that bit of the story is unverified. What is known is that Joe himself tipped off the reporter.

Less than a month after the formal conclusion of the College's handling of this matter, the horrific events of September 11, 2001, and their aftermath enveloped the nation. Joe's story was totally eclipsed. It was a reality check on what was a matter of genuine public interest.

Tom and Will

} 10 {

IN THE GROOVE

Orchestrating Shared Governance

Nothing later was to match the *sturm und drang* of the three challenges in my early presidency: the student takeovers, the alumnae association brouhaha, and the Joe Ellis scandal. There were shaky moments and missteps in the handling of each, to be sure, but I righted myself and, through these ordeals—which tested process and principle, toughness and ability to withstand public scrutiny—my presidency was ultimately strengthened, and with that, I had a good run for over fourteen years.

During that time I was frequently asked, "How do you handle work/life balance?" "What balance?" I sometimes flippantly responded. All-consuming "work" does indeed take over life, or perhaps "simulate" life for a college president. But my better answer to the question is "A supportive family." Our close and harmonious little family of husband Tom, son Will, and dog Maisie provided an island of peace and sanity amid the incessant demands and challenges of the job.

Each time we moved, William amenably adjusted to the new community. He made fast friends, fit right into the neighborhood, soccer league, and middle school when we moved to Greensboro, North Carolina, then thrived academically and athletically (as a championship swimmer) at Middletown High School in Connecticut, a school that reminded me of the nurturing small-town public high school I had experienced thirty years earlier. His undergraduate days at Duke University coincided with our first years in South Hadley, so he did not reside with us in president's house. But he was frequently home, always in close communication, and always with us in spirit.

Meanwhile, Tom was the man on the spot who generously adapted to each move and took over much of the management of our private life. He shopped, cooked, paid bills, and ran errands, and performed his consulting work and read extensively. He accompanied me on many trips, during which we managed to squeeze in some private time. We travelled annually to London, took family vacations, went with Maisie on thousands of walks, watched hundreds of films, and drank tens of thousands of cups of tea. ("A nice cup of tea" is an indispensable ritual as well as the first line of defense in meeting any of life's challenges.) Tom deliberately kept a low public profile as the "president's spouse"—a label decidedly *not* his cup of tea, even though people invariably found him charming when he did venture out into the College community. He selectively came to dinners or events, but otherwise kept inviolate his separate life. He was unfailingly empathetic when I regaled him day-by-day with the highs and lows of being in the president's chair. Although we lived on the edge of campus, our island of privacy was respected (broken only during the student protests).

"If you want a friend, get a dog," said one seasoned male trustee early in my presidency, and we did. Maisie, our beagle best friend, was deeply loyal and loving to her family, and she became First Dog on campus, although, private and quirky, she was shy and uncomfortable with her celebrity. Meanwhile, in addition to warmly cordial relations with many faculty, staff, trustees, alumnae, and other presidents, I developed a few close friendships with colleagues as well, grateful to occasionally break through the isolating wall of deference insulating a college president. I remembered nostalgically the history-laden, cherished friendships we left behind on the itinerant path to a college presidency, and in post-presidency it has been a pleasure to see long-lost friends and to piece life back together again.

Sustained by a supportive family, I found a lot of satisfaction in my work, which was really my avocation. I am proud of Mount Holyoke College's dramatic revitalization during my tenure: its successive classes of strong students and years of record-setting applications for admission; the progressive strengthening of the academic program with the hiring of over ninety tenure-track faculty; and the creation of new interdisciplinary programs and three highly successful, generously supported new centers. These three undertakings—the Weissman Center for Leadership and the Liberal Arts, the McCulloch Center for Global Initiatives, and the Miller Worley Center for the Environment—instantiated key components of the College's mission. Undergirding our success was the elimination of the eight-million-dollar structural debt, restoration of fiscal equilibrium and a more robust endowment through careful financial management and successful fund-raising, which generated over $450 million in gifts. The College also added 150,000 square feet of new or renovated space in one of the most-significant building periods in the College's history.

Although the campus of Mount Holyoke has always been exceptionally beautiful, it was in need of refurbishing and revitalization when I arrived. Our landscape consultant remarked, quite tellingly, that the campus seemed dark and lonely. When I first walked around, I asked, "Where are the people?" There seemed to be a dearth of inviting spaces for people to relax, mingle, and hang out in. My first temporary fix for that problem was to scatter dozens of Adirondack chairs around the lawns. Later, in the cavalcade of landscape and building projects we undertook, the College attempted both to lighten up the built environment—painting trim lighter colors and opening enclosed structures to embrace the surrounding landscape—and to animate and connect the campus through the creation of both indoor and outdoor communal spaces. Central to this effort were a science center, Kendade Hall, which pulled together disparate buildings and disciplines around a new connector building with a dramatic atrium; a significantly improved Blanchard Campus Center, which opened up and out to the sky and landscape and immediately became the hub for student life; and several other projects that were models of felicitous renovation and refurbishing. Among the latter were a more-vitalized music building, art museum, library, admissions office, and fitness center.

The only totally new construction was a residence hall. Pleasingly anchoring the southwest corner of the campus, it was a building at once venerable and "hip." It blended respect for architectural tradition with a modern "wow" factor in its glassy opening out to the brook and dale at the rear of the building. I loved the planning of every last detail of this building, from its massive footprint to its bathroom fixtures, all so harmoniously melded together. Mary Lyon commented famously that "stone and bricks and mortar speak a language which vibrates through my very soul."[1] I knew exactly what she meant. The tangibility of bricks and mortar was so satisfying, so unlike the seemingly ephemeral nature of much of the daily work of an administrator. Watching the structure go up was deeply moving to me, and I was greatly surprised that in a final tribute, this building was named for me.

More important than improvements to buildings and grounds was the restoration of the institutional confidence during my tenure. An unmistakable sense of buoyancy, optimism, and energy supplanted the widespread malaise and anxiety that had greeted me when I arrived at Mount Holyoke. For well over a decade we were a highly functioning institution that brought its constituents together in common cause around shared educational and institutional goals. Let me isolate key components of that transformation.

Most fundamental to raising spirits, I believe, was the motivating force of planning. I explained earlier how I led a comprehensive planning process during my first fifteen months in office, which produced *The Plan for Mount Holyoke 2003*. As the College systematically met its planning goals, success built upon success, spawning additional plans across many dimensions of the institution and leading to a second comprehensive institutional plan, *The Plan for Mount Holyoke 2010*, the completion of which coincided with my stepping down as president after nearly fifteen years of service. This systematic planning helped to create a can-do attitude on campus, displacing the sense of helplessness and inertia that had gripped the place when I started.

Leadership was also essential. As president, I "orchestrated" shared governance. By that, I mean that I placed myself clearly at the center of planning, which I saw as an educational process, an opportunity "to read" the institution. I sought to reflect, to take stock, and assess, and then to develop a plan, a blueprint for action. My approach was inductive and respectful: I led with questions and listened carefully. I chose to be the drafter of the planning document, because it helped me to gain a nuanced understanding of the motivating core of the institution, and, not incidentally, I was able to control, shape, and move along the planning process. To my mind the president can be likened to an orchestra conductor, drawing the constituents' voices together to make beautiful music. I was determined to make planning aspirational and positive. Even while retrenching the budget, I tried to keep the focus on the big picture and higher purposes of the

College. People get mired in their own parochial view and problems; they need to be energized by the larger view. Only after articulating shared values and aspirations did we try to address the problems and challenges that inhibited or prevented their realization.

In addressing them I was, as one trustee described, "fearlessly candid." There were no sacred cows, no forbidden subjects. We could talk about the dreaded taboo, coeducation, as well as the escalating expenses of a policy of need-blind admission, the less-than-robust applicant pool, and the fiscal disequilibrium threatening the financial stability of the College. Everything was on the table.

Furthermore, I'm a great believer in drafts. I assumed the presidency in January 1996, and by August, we sent out to all campus constituents a first draft of the plan. This speed and lack of caution shocked Barbara Rossotti, our Board chair. "You did what?" She feared I would be discredited before I got my feet firmly on the ground. But on the contrary, drafts allow you to test out ideas without boxing yourself into the corner. ("What? You don't like this idea? That's okay; it's only a draft. How would you reframe the issue?") Drafts help you to implement and oversee iterative, interactive processes, to stake out territory, and to get people used to ideas and invested in shaping the document. In both planning processes during my presidency, we shared three public drafts before the final document was drawn up. The final plans were unanimously approved by both the faculty and the Board of Trustees—no small feat. The documents had been had been shaped, refined, and vetted by an extraordinary number of contributors. It is fair to say that the final plans were owned by the constituents of the College, and indeed they took ownership of the implementation.

The ultimate objective of the planning process, in my view, was to reaffirm the mission and draw energy and direction from it. If you get the mission right, it resonates with authenticity and inspires loyalty and good work from its constituents. It becomes the engine that drives the institution forward. In this fact, I'm reminded of Jim Collins's book about corporate strategy, *Good to Great*, which builds on Isaiah Berlin's famous essay dividing the world into hedgehogs and foxes: "The fox knows many things but the hedgehog knows one big thing." Collins champions the hedgehog corporation. "Its One Big Thing," says Collins, "is a confluence of what it is deeply passionate about, what it can be best in the world at, and what drives its economic engine."[2] A merely good fox corporation, in contrast, darts around in cunning fashion, devising complex strategies for sneak attacks on the hedgehog.

So too, a great college's strength is to be found in knowing One Big Thing. Its distinctive mission at its hedgehogian best is a synthesis of what constituents are deeply passionate about, what the institution excels at, and what compels broad support. I applied Collins's approach to my administration of Mount Holyoke, tapping into the passion, energy, and support in the faculty, staff, students, and graduates who loved this venerable institution of higher learning and who wished to see it thrive in the twenty-first century.

The mission-centeredness of the liberal arts college was what most impressed me when I moved from public to private education, and Mount Holyoke had a particularly impassioned sense of its mission. That we could, with some effort, weld all the essential elements of Mount Holyoke together into a single sentence warmed my English-professor soul. That mission—with its twin foci on academic excellence and moral purposefulness, with its dual emphasis on diversity and community, and with its passionate commitment to the liberal arts and to residential women's education—was our touchstone, the foundation of our ambitious goals. To get everyone on the same page—quite literally—we widely distributed a one-page synopsis of the plan. I tirelessly talked about the planning agenda, giving it a high priority and profile, making it matter to everyone, and seeking to draw them all in. I knew I had succeeded in this goal when the students' tongue-in-cheek Junior Show in 1997 spoofed about the terrible panic that beset the college community when the *Plan* was lost.

While the sense of mission was strong and motivating, the market was comparatively weak for the kind of education Mount Holyoke was offering. We were cheered by the gains in our applicant pool, but they were hard won. We were fighting all the dominant trends in higher education, which favored and rewarded large, urban, professional, nonresidential, and especially coed education. Added to that was the persistent financial need of a large segment of our applicant pool, particularly international students. Yet through the efforts of a savvy admissions and college-relations team, we bucked the trends and met our annual goals very well during the years of my presidency. But there were days of doubt. I frequently mused that we shouldn't have to work so hard to sell an education so good, so powerful, so right. Still, spirits and confidence were high about how we were doing. We could suspend, at least for a time, the question always hanging over a women's college: Can we survive with this mission? Indeed, our tactic was to embrace that mission.

Shared governance was essential for success. So many people contributed to the resurgence of Mount Holyoke. I assembled an extraordinarily talented group of senior administrators, who helped to carry our agenda out from Mary Lyon Hall into the precincts of the college. Staff across the institution, always loyal and dedicated, responded positively to being drawn into a collective enterprise. Senior officers, who had a great deal of independence to run their own shops, at the same time came together as a team, a kitchen cabinet. Together with me, they oversaw all aspects of institutional operations. I modeled and encouraged candor and openness with this group, as I did with all cohorts, and they responded in kind. All major institutional decisions came before the senior staff for discussion and review. In the senior-staff conference room, territorial advocacy was left at the door; our shared goal was what was wisest and best for the institution as a whole. We engaged in high-spirited but unfailingly collegial and respectful discussions, developing through our give-and-take nuanced understandings and decisions. We knew at the time that our joyful *esprit de corps* was special and rare; that the good old days were "now." Indeed, we noted just that fact at a celebratory dinner marking the completion of my tenth year in office. That good fellowship continued for over four more years.

While building a good senior team is essential to orchestrating governance, even more critical is calibrating the relationships with the Board of Trustees and the faculty. A president's success in large part will rise or fall on how skillfully he or she relates to and handles them. The Janus-faced college president stands between the Board and the faculty, is a member of both, is accountable to both, must speak the language of both, must be able to translate one to the other, and must help to facilitate communication and shared work, while serving as the executive leader who sets a clear agenda and keeps the focus on it for the institution.[3]

Board members bring much-needed, larger world perspectives to what can be a relatively insular college campus. Trustees can enrich a college in multiple ways: intellectual, reputational, political, social, and monetary. They are typically generous with their time, energy, and money, and they are essential to the very existence of our colleges. But, in truth, a board of trustees is a curious entity. It is a body of unpaid volunteers; many have no experience in the administration of higher education. They come to the campus typically three or four times a year and are vested with considerable authority and responsibility for the welfare of the institution. The board is the "boss" of the president, but most trustees have no in-depth understanding of the president's job or of the guilds of professionals who make up the complex academic culture, nor do trustees have the time to learn all they need to know. Part of the president's job is to help educate the board and to ensure that important institutional information is synthesized and organized in such a way that the board can exercise strategic oversight of the president and of the institution. Of course, trustees will use their own professional judgment honed from other contexts as well, offering often-valuable perspectives. This job of educating trustees is always a work-in-progress. Typically some trustees are cycling off and new members are coming onto the board, so its composition and dynamics keep changing from year to year.

Just as the president must try to explain the institution to the board, he or she must also try to explain the board to the campus—to the students and staff and especially to the faculty. The president is the most important interface between the on-campus and off-campus constituencies, elucidating issues, negotiating between sides, and reconciling what can sometimes seem like two different cultures—that of academia and of business—for many trustees, in my experience, work in corporate America. What is valuable about this interface and educational for the president is that much is to be learned from both perspectives.

Faculty members have a great wealth of knowledge to impart to students and hold deep commitments to academic standards, but they can be naive about how their institution resides in a competitive world. Likewise many trustees have highly developed business acumen, but they can be impatient and unrealistic about how to get things done in an academic environment. The trick is to draw from the strengths of trustees and faculty, while not being deterred by their limitations. In this environment of shared governance, a critical issue is jurisdictional boundaries. Who is responsible for what? In truth, as president, I tried to maintain strict boundaries with the Board of Trustees and blur them with the faculty, although I also labored to unite both in the common cause of shaping and pursuing the priorities of Mount Holyoke.

Having long been a faculty member before joining the administration, I advocated that in governing the College, we were all in this enterprise together, with the faculty playing a central role. Shared governance with the faculty is more than ideal; it is essential. The faculty has legislative power and responsibility for the curriculum and academic appointments. Their expertise is fundamental to any academic planning and valuable in most administrative arenas. The president ignores or underestimates the faculty's role at her peril. They can and do topple presidencies, quite frequently in fact.

From my first moment on the Mount Holyoke campus and throughout my tenure, I worked to build trust with the faculty and to make them full-fledged partners in advancing the College. In this process, I was blessed to work for twelve years with Dean of Faculty Don O'Shea. A terrific administrator, he was beloved by the faculty for his unfailing intelligence and humor, and for his support of their work. With a critical and discerning eye in his oversight of new hires, he continued to build a strong faculty of scholar-teachers during my presidency.

In addition to the intellectual energy of a strong faculty, I was impressed repeatedly by their fundamental civility and willingness to pitch in, an attitude so unlike other more cantankerous and resistant faculty I had sometimes encountered. Most were committed to the collective welfare of the institution, not just to their own career enhancement. Despite the interminable haggling over some issues, I could count on most faculty to face facts constructively and try to contribute to a rational solution. After their initial hesitancy, they responded positively to my calls for collaborative leadership. They knew better than many faculties do that their fate was a shared one and that their welfare was contingent upon that of the institution as a whole. They also recognized that Mount Holyoke College was about advancing not only intellectual goals but also developmental education, preparing young women for lives of service and leadership. Mary Lyon's imperative—"Go forward; attempt great things; accomplish great things"—infused the culture at Mount Holyoke.

Indeed, acculturated as I had been within large, secular universities, I was impressed with this unabashed idealism.

Moreover, faculty were eager to work across disciplinary lines, perhaps more so than faculty at larger institutions who might find themselves enclaved within a department. A spirit of innovation spawned a richly interdisciplinary curriculum. Overarching interdisciplinary themes became areas of emphasis in our plans: leadership and public-interest advocacy; environmental responsibility, stewardship, and literacy; global education; science education. These ideas were showcased in new centers that became centerpieces of institutional renewal at Mount Holyoke.

Complementing a strong faculty was a dedicated Board of Trustees made up of many talented, intelligent, and accomplished people, who brought a wealth of experience and a range of perspectives to the institution. I've always been impressed with the time, energy, and, in many cases, money that individuals on nonprofit boards give to their institutions, and certainly Mount Holyoke was no exception. Many of the trustees at Mount Holyoke were deeply loyal alumnae; the smaller numbers of men were often fathers or husbands of Mount Holyoke women.

The central Board member, of course, is the chair, who sets the tone and agenda and who works closely with the president. I felt great simpatico with Chair Barbara Rossotti, who so determinedly lured me to Mount Holyoke. I instinctively knew that Barbara, smart, sensitive, and supportive as well as pragmatic and iron-willed, would be a wonderful partner in institutional governance. And indeed she was. Although she had been a member of the Board before I arrived, she was deeply dissatisfied with its functioning. Given the negatives I noticed as a candidate—a budget out of balance, weak admissions outlook, low morale, sense of institutional drift, and faculty mobilization against the president—I could well understand her discomfort. She said to me, "I'm going to take the Board to the woodshed," and so she did. Even before I took office, she held a retreat to begin the process of self-assessment. Trustees took a survey to measure the Board's sense of its own effectiveness against an AGB (Association of Government Boards) template. They gave themselves failing grades in both form and substance and committed themselves to renewal. When I took office in January 1996, the Board began a systematic process of turning itself around. Influenced by the work and advice of consultants Richard P. Chait and Barbara E. Taylor, who came to campus, we developed a dashboard of leading indicators to help direct the Board's focus on strategic oversight of the institution.[4] The Board strengthened its committees, its use of time, and its oversight of the president.

Under the wise leadership of Barbara Rossotti, and then of Ellie Claus, the next chair, the Board year-by-year became progressively stronger and more strategic. We worked together to make jurisdictional areas of responsibility for faculty, Board, and administration clear and functional. While I led the process of institutional planning and implementation, the Board engaged with us at a high level in an oversight role. It brainstormed with us, reviewed and critiqued drafts of the plans, and ultimately approved them. It interacted with faculty and students in various ways but did not micromanage campus matters. The committees of the Board worked closely with the senior staff, and in fact, the trustees and senior staff developed a strong sense of partnership and camaraderie. When the Board had greater expertise in specific areas such as asset management, capital planning, and fund-raising, it took a stronger role; when it had less knowledge on an issue such as academic programming, it received and reviewed the recommendations of the president and dean of faculty, which had been developed in close cooperation with the faculty.

Altogether, the Board, senior staff, and I enjoyed a productive relationship. Trustees were a terrific band of colleagues unfailingly supportive and ready to engage in major institution building. They stuck with me through the lows—the student sit-ins of spring 1997, the Joe Ellis scandal that landed us in the national press in the summer of 2001, and the painful dispute with the Alumnae Association that erupted about the same time. And they were present for the highs as we moved forward ever more confidently out of disunity, disarray, and fiscal disequilibrium into collective purpose, balanced budgets, record-high numbers of applicants and fund-raising totals, an ever-stronger faculty and student body, vital new academic centers, beautiful new indoor and outdoor spaces, and increased national and international presence. As president of Mount Holyoke, I couldn't have asked for a more-productive, -diligent, -dedicated Board of Trustees, which effected far-reaching positive institutional change in the College.

Fund-raising, of course, was extremely important in that institutional resurgence, and the Board's leadership there was absolutely critical. For the most part, Mount Holyoke's Board was not made up of high rollers who gave multimillion-dollar gifts to the College. On the whole, trustee gifts had been not particularly impressive during the previous administration, nor was the Board closely involved in fund-raising. Rather, the former president, along with the chief development officer, had played the dominant role. As is typical of everything during my administration, collaboration characterized the fund-raising effort we put in place. I said to Charlie Haight, when I hired him as the head of development, that I wanted to "go fast" in moving fund-raising forward for the institution, and he assured me that he would do just that. He set up an exemplary on-campus operation and partnered effectively with the Board's Development Committee, which, in turn, designed a plan for a broadly based fund-raising effort. Within a very short period of time, a campaign steering committee was established and vast networks of volunteers fanned out into the precincts. *The Plan for Mount Holyoke 2003* provided the blueprint for the campaign's case statement, which articulated a coherent strategy and clear, effective tactics. Trustees stepped up impressively to contribute and play a leadership role. We were buoyed by institutional momentum and the booming economy at the turn of the millennium. Even when hit with the traumatic 9/11 attacks and all its collateral emotional and economic damage, our campaign recovered and steamed along to a triumphant conclusion.

It is said that a president is mainly a fund-raiser, and the presumption is that this is a distasteful duty. I would say that a more appropriate term is "friend raiser" and that this is a surprisingly enjoyable responsibility. What's not to like about being welcomed into the world of the privileged, enjoying their homes, their haunts, and their company? My sister joked that Tom and I were the "honorary rich," and that indeed was true. It was a chance to visit worlds radically different from that of academia. Potential major donors were almost invariably accomplished, worldly, and interesting people, who wanted to make a difference through wise and enlightened philanthropy. Most were already predisposed to support Mount Holyoke College and help it realize its potential.

My role was to make the perfect match between the donors' inclinations and the College's needs. Advocacy is the essence of the president's job and that was a skill I had been developing from the inauspicious start of my administrative career as a child-care advocate. When you love the College and are excited about your plans to make it even better, as I was, cheerleading is a very natural role to play. I developed a deep affection and respect for the several major donors I got to know well during my tenure at Mount Holyoke. It was much more a privilege than duty to keep in touch with them. Indeed, my life was enriched by knowing them.

We were enjoying the splendid success of the campaign—which exceeded its original $200 million goal by raising $257 million—and we were contemplating a second campaign, when Leslie Anne Miller began her term as Board chair. In early summer of 2004, she invited me to her Philadelphia home to start our relationship off on a friendly basis. As we sat down for a chat over cups of tea that morning, she said that her highest priority was to find the right time for me to leave the presidency. I was shocked and nonplussed. A timely and graceful exit is something you have to think about, of course, but that thought was not on my mind at that particular juncture in the full flush of the success of our various efforts. Nor was it easy to imagine stepping away from a job that I loved and a life that was to a large extent defined by the job.

Still, after I had some months to think about it, I understood the importance of an orderly succession plan. At a respectful and leisurely pace, Leslie brought together a small group of trustees for periodic confidential conversations with me about transition planning. They were a supportive group, who wanted the best for both Mount Holyoke and me. After exploring alternatives we decided that I would finish in 2010, as *The Plan for Mount Holyoke 2010* wrapped up. Under this scenario, we could begin a new fund-raising campaign under my leadership, and at the midpoint, I could take a valedictory "victory lap" celebrating my presidency and step down. After that, the College could complete the campaign under the leadership of the new president, taking advantage of the excitement of her arrival to generate renewed energy for the final push of the campaign. This plan seemed sensible but remained under wraps for a long time, given that it was developed six years in advance of my departure.

Witty and energetic, Leslie took charge of meetings more forcefully than her predecessors. She proposed a Board retreat that was facilitated by consultant Richard P. Chait, who was bursting with his new ideas. He proposed that boards of trustees should be more engaged in institutional planning and leadership rather than just performing an oversight role. A merely "strategic" board receives, reviews, and approves or disapproves the recommendations of the president. A "generative" board, he argued, is an organ with a higher calling and could serve the institution more fully. At times, this board could "co-pilot" with the president: "Like copilots of commercial aircraft who typically take turns flying . . . trustees and executives can take turns initiating generative deliberations; one can lead and the other respond."[5] Under the generative model, the jurisdictional responsibilities of the administration and board are somewhat permeable and flexible, with the board playing a more active part in institutional planning than it had traditionally.

This idea that Trustees should have a more "generative" role was music to the ears of some members of our Board. They also liked the idea of more retreat-like meetings, which cut through established meeting formats, grappled with larger challenges facing the institution, and set a Board "action agenda." Out of this momentum a retreat of the Board and senior staff was planned for January 2008. We invited two other recently retired college presidents, Nancy Vickers of Bryn Mawr and Nancy Dye of Oberlin. Dye had been the chair of the reaccreditation visiting committee that had come to the campus the previous fall.

The Board urged us to focus attention on long-term issues and to speak frankly about the challenges facing the institution. So the two former presidents and I laid out in stark terms the challenges facing women's and liberal arts colleges at this point in their history. Our kind of school, as stated earlier in the chapter, was rowing upstream against all the trends in higher education. We faced severe and interrelated admissions and financial challenges. We could continue as we were for a while, but not forever. The College needed more revenue generation than we could project under the current model. For the longer term some mission change or expansion might well be contemplated—not necessarily the bugaboo of coeducation—but, less radically, perhaps the development of new revenue-generating programs. With two-and-a-half years of *The Plan for Mount Holyoke 2010* remaining, it was early to initiate a new, all-inclusive planning process, but it was not too soon to do preplanning and brainstorming. We could begin those discussions in advance of the next president and next phase of planning. It was a particularly propitious moment to do that work because the College had never been stronger or more highly functioning. Its strength and health were attested to by a glowing accreditation report. We had the time and space to engage in careful deliberation rather than darting hither and thither to manage crisis.

We in the senior administration were long used to the fact that even though the College was getting stronger, the challenges of the educational environment were also intensifying. But many trustees were shaken by this presentation of the unvarnished truth, and it brought out a high degree of anxiety about the sustainability of the institution. That reality, coupled with my announcement the following spring that I would be stepping down in 2010 and followed by the deepening recession in 2009, put the Board in a state of near panic. The trustees wanted to "do" something about this "crisis" and do it now.

Being so restive, they began to second-guess the administration and to want more reports, more meetings, more control. Trustees highly placed in investment banking and related businesses, who felt the full brunt of the financial collapse in their professional lives as the Great Recession set in during 2008, brought their sense of alarm and urgency to our boardroom. They seemed impatient with the measured, systematic, decentralized way we approached budget cutting in the College and urged us to take a more-corporate-like, top-down draconian approach. "Never waste a crisis," they chanted, wanting to see more-radical restructuring and workforce reduction.

The problem with top-down restructuring, though, is that it doesn't work in academia. Using our own well-honed methods, we adjusted to the shock of reduced resources, trimmed expenditures, kept essential services intact, minimized layoffs, maintained a high degree of cooperation and good will in our community and, in sum, weathered the economic downturn quite well, arguably much better than the financial sector. I believed Mount Holyoke was a model of fiscal discipline and responsibility during the recession and that heavy-handed measures would have been unwise and destructive.

After the meeting unveiling my plan to step down, the Board had a particularly long executive session, after which Leslie dropped by my house and essentially said, "We've listened to you all these years, but we will exercise our authority more overtly in the transition."

Later I learned that she had engaged a consulting firm, established a transition committee of the Board, and moved ahead quickly to develop transition plans. An outside consultant came to campus to interview the senior staff and me. Shortly thereafter, I received a formal letter from Leslie explaining that the Board had completed its "work plan" and set up a September retreat, during which we were to "consolidate data" regarding "central issues facing the College." Clearly the Board was now in charge.

I found this situation unsettling. In my view, under ideal circumstances the president and senior staff manage the institution with the Board one step removed—receiving, reviewing, and suggesting, but not directly managing or micromanaging. But, as a transition nears, the Board may well feel the need—as it did in these circumstances at Mount Holyoke—to take back some of the authority it has delegated to the president and spend more time educating itself about the challenges of the institution, as it sorts through what kind of new president it wants. This can be good, although the value added by these extra meetings is sometimes questionable. In my experience, trustees love to grapple with big issues. But no matter how many briefing papers they read, they cannot know the institution well enough to "take over" the job of setting institutional direction from the top down, although they might think they can. The president and the senior administration may feel compelled, as we did, to play a backstopping role, trying to interject greater judiciousness and collaboration and to avoid conflicting messages from the leadership of the institution.

So I don't agree with the blurring of boundaries between president and board that Richard Chait advocates in *Governance as Leadership.* I say, be careful what you wish for. Copiloting in higher education can be confusing and downright counterproductive. A board has plenty of consequential, engaging work to do without confusing its role with that of the president. That said, a transition, of course, necessitates dual leadership and dual messaging to some degree. In our case, the Board's anxiety about the future translated into getting the presidential search process going very early, and so too did the search committee move along with great dispatch, making its selection in the early fall 2009. The new president was announced in October, eight months before she was to take office. She became a

Joanne and the New Residence Hall
Photograph owned by Mount Holyoke College

frequent visitor to the campus and at off-campus events. It was awkward and confusing, to say the least, to have two presidents and a Board of Trustees all leading the institution at the same time.

While it was an unsettling transitional period, momentum on *The Plan for Mount Holyoke 2010* was not interrupted, nor was fundraising for the campaign. In the end, everything came out just fine. With all passion spent, with a new leader selected, with time running out on my presidency, I did a valedictory tour, meeting with warmly supportive alumnae groups in various cities. The Board and senior administration put together a splendid celebration of my presidency. Leslie was more than gracious and generous. She had been a strong chair and an unfailingly supportive partner during her six years in the job, and the two of us completed our terms together.

I felt a sense of completion and accomplishment from my years in the presidency and a deep fondness for Mount Holyoke and its abiding *esprit de corps*. At the farewell reception, I was gratified by the accolades, delighted to receive an honorary degree from the College, and totally surprised and touched to have the new residence hall named after me. In my remarks that evening, I said:

> We are bounded together by shared values, history, and tradition and by our collective commitment to make the legacy we inherited even stronger. It is so satisfying to be part of something bigger than oneself and to contribute to strengthening an institution that has such a positive effect on the world. So, I hope we can see today as a celebration not of me but of the College, of its intrinsic value, and of how it has blossomed so impressively with the engagement and support of all of you.

Indeed, that sense of common bonds and communal effort was the most-impressive and -fulfilling dimension of being part of this very special institution.

} 11 {

HAVERFORD COLLEGE

Play It Again

I had a sabbatical the year following my exit from the Mount Holyoke presidency, during which I began to adjust to the post-presidency and new routine of life in Amherst, a congenial place to live quite apart from Mount Holyoke. Here was a chance to start anew. Did I have a personal life outside the presidential role that had "simulated" life and for so long? I tried my hand at "making house," going to exercise classes, cultivating a deck garden, learning how to fix things (after having been infantilized by all the services that accompany a college presidency), returning to literary scholarship, doing some academic consulting, and, most radically of all, enjoying an open schedule. With a three-year appointment as a Five College professor, I was looking forward to a return to teaching at the University of Massachusetts that fall.

But in early August, I received a surprising call about Haverford College: Would I consider serving as interim president? At first, I thought no. We were just settling in; I couldn't disrupt our lives once again. But after a series of increasingly serious conversations, I agreed to take the position. It was an opportunity to get "to read" another fine institution "up close and personal." The commitment was limited to one year. We would not have to move house but merely take personal items, our dog, Maisie, and ourselves. Furthermore, I had to admit to myself that I was floundering a bit in the vacuum of post-presidency. Here was an opportunity to serve as president again and do so at a very fine institution as a coda to my professional career. It was too good to pass up. As usual, Tom was wonderfully accommodating, and we decided to trek off to the Philadelphia area.

It was a great rush. I arrived at Haverford in September 2011 and stayed at the campus center just as the former president was packing up at the president's house and the new students were arriving for the new academic year. I had much to learn very quickly. The institution was reeling from the disruption of an abruptly terminated presidency and from significant tensions and factions within the faculty and with the Board of Managers. Frayed nerves and a collective sense of disarray and anxiety prevailed. The College needed someone calm, steady, and experienced to take charge, cool things down, and refocus campus energy to constructive ends.

One fractious issue was whether the incumbent provost should continue in that office. She had been embroiled in a conflict with the president; many on the Board of Managers wanted her out; faculty lined up in camps for and against her; and she was determined to stand her ground. During the Board's telephonic conference to confirm my hiring, some five minutes were devoted to ratifying my appointment and almost three hours to discussing what to do about the provost. This instance was the first of many examples I would observe of Haverfordians' heroic efforts to operate under consensus: the thoughtful, laborious, tedious, and respectful way that its constituents strove, always valiantly and sometimes fruitlessly, to achieve accord. The Board's practice of consensus was the secular adaptation of the traditional Quaker process of seeking unity through the Spirit. I came away impressed with the carefully reasoned positions of the Board of Managers, with their respect for one another and patience in hearing out every nuance of concern from every last holdout, but, admittedly, their practice also strained *my* patience and left me somewhat incredulous that so many people were willing to invest so much time in this way.

I thought the provost should continue with the final year of her appointment. After protracted discussion, the Board finally concurred. Consequently, the responsibility of sorting out the aftermath of disruption shifted from the Board to me. I also inherited the awkwardness and complications accompanying the ongoing presence of the previous president on campus, and his not entirely welcomed placement into a tenured position in the Biology Department. But step by step the provost and I worked through issues and developed a good working relationship. By the end of the year, she had made plans to move on to another college. I also brokered rapprochement between the Biology Department and the former president, who was unfailingly cordial, and by the end of the academic year, he too had taken another job. Within a year it seemed that Haverford College could put all the turmoil engendered by this leadership crisis behind it and refocus on its educational mission and its normal functions.

My arrival on campus coincided with "Customs Week," an orientation program for first-year students run by upperclassmen and -women. Customs Week was designed both to inform freshmen about what they needed to know and to draw them into a sense of community through zany activities and probing discussions about Haverford's customs and values. Central to those values was the Honor Code, through which Haverford students committed themselves to a shared code of conduct based on personal integrity and respect for others and on a student-run judicial system overseen by an Honor Council. Students also played a major role in overseeing dorm life, and they had a highly developed governance system, which included twice-yearly plenary sessions in which the entire student body came together to consider proposed resolutions and to reaffirm the Honor Code.

The biannual plenary was a spectacle. Accustomed to long hours of deliberation, students arrived sometimes in pajamas, with blankets, food, and stacks of homework. Others sold food or set up tables for other causes. Meanwhile, other students splayed themselves around on the bleachers and gym floor. Some, completely comfortable in their Haverfordian geekiness, played chess or computer games. Others read books, did homework, chatted, or roamed around, paying intermittent attention to the elaborate governance processes playing out in the front of the big space, tuning in when students lined up in support of or opposition to resolutions or made impromptu speeches to the assembled group. All had their cell phones at the ready, and most were in use much of the time. Here was democratic self-governance in action in the messy, noisy arena of high-spirited, multitasking young people.

Through such ritualized customs painstakingly and lovingly passed on to the next generation, students created a self-actualizing culture. And in the process, they made Haverford and its values their own. They held the institution to a high standard. Typically (and refreshingly, from my point of view), they did not make "demands" on the administration but displayed a remarkable degree of reasonableness and maturity in addressing matters of concern and coming up with shared solutions and accommodations.

They were tough and uncompromising in their peer review of Honor Council cases, on which they spent an inordinate amount of time. I was repeatedly impressed with their impeccable logic and moral idealism, but in a couple of cases I thought the sanctions were too severe and disproportionate to the offense, and I lessened them, although not without provoking some criticism. In this, as in so many things, Haverford students took their responsibility and authority very seriously and resented (albeit politely) the presumption of a higher authority. I did worry that peer adjudication was inappropriate for grievances that might, in fact, be serious crimes, such as sexual assault. While no new sexual-assault cases were brought forward during my tenure, an old one was still brewing, complexly intertwined as it was with a lawsuit and countersuit.

Yet for the most part, the self-administered Honor Code worked. And in this valorization of individual conscience over higher authority, students reaffirmed the very essence of the Haverford's ethos, eloquently articulated by President Isaac Sharpless in 1888—and so often quoted:

> For your consciences and your judgments we have not sought to bind; and see you to it that no other institution, no political party, no social circle, no religious organization, no pet ambitions put such chains on you as would tempt you to sacrifice one iota of the moral freedom of your consciences or the intellectual freedom of your judgments.[1]

Indeed, Haverford, more than any other institution I have known, was unabashedly value-laden. Its dual emphases on intellectual and moral freedom, its often-cited Honor Code, its persistent ethical questioning, its pervasive civility and respect for the views of others, its conscious choice to remain a relatively small community of self-governing individuals, even its moment of silence at the beginning of meetings—these were fundamental to the Quaker rootedness of the College, which inflected the institution in a distinctive way and set it apart.

Despite Haverford's historical origins, there were very few practicing Quakers in the community. But Haverford was literally "owned" by the Quaker-affiliated Corporation of Haverford College. The Corporation held legal title to the College's assets and elected some members of its Board of Managers. The Corporation was made up of approximately two hundred persons who were active members of the Religious Society of Friends or fellow travelers such as alumni or past members of the Board. The Corporation convened once annually, and its Advisory Committee met approximately four times a year with the president of the College.

Reminiscent for me of the historical bond between Mount Holyoke College and its Alumnae Association, Haverford College and the Corporation of Haverford College politely coexisted in this relationship, which it seemed wise to honor in its current form and not to probe too deeply. I concluded it was my job to keep the Corporation apprised of what was happening at the College and to draw its members into the same conversations, albeit highly synoptic ones, about issues that I had with campus constituents. The Corporation for the most part was supportive and proud of the College and stayed out of its business, outside gently pressuring the institution to increase its support for Quaker elements, including helping to subsidize a Quaker affairs office, although in the recent past, a source of tension had been the process of selecting members of the Board of Managers. The College had successfully pushed for a greater number of Managers who could be unaffiliated with the Society of Friends.

The Board of Managers had a small number of practicing Quakers or Quaker sympathizers who often were involved in education and humanistic enterprises. Meanwhile, a considerably larger number of Managers were highly successful, often wealthy professional people, many from the financial sector. This striking difference in backgrounds and perspectives accounted for some curious swings in Board discussions, but a fundamental civility and respect reigned in our meetings. The College had gone coeducational in 1980, and the Board and its alumni population were male dominated, but its chair was a woman, Catherine Koshland. An academic herself (vice-provost at the University California, Berkley) and a major donor, she was well respected for her understanding of academic culture in general and Haverford in particular. She and vice-chair Chris Norton were helpful and supportive to me but did not micromanage the

College. They were seemingly relieved to let me get on with the job of administering Haverford, while they turned their attention to the search for a new president.

At first, conversations with the Board of Managers were consumed with the recent crisis of leadership at the College, but as this matter shifted onto my shoulders, they began to ask how the crisis happened and how such developments could be avoided in the future? The Board chided itself for ignoring to the matter until concerned parties began communicating their distress through back channels. The lack of a regular, structured presidential evaluation was one of many instances of Quaker culture that privileged trust and informality over the practices of formal governance. Determined to start over with my presidency, the Board, in consultation with me, put together a plan for a more-regularized presidential evaluation, a process akin to what had existed at Mount Holyoke, which Haverford's Board assiduously followed during my tenure there.

At a retreat in late September 2011, the Board turned its attention to larger issues facing the institution. Because Haverford seemed to me very insular, with all of the students and about sixty percent of the faculty living on campus, I thought it would be helpful to try to contextualize the College's position within higher education. To this end, I reviewed the history of the liberal arts college from its origins in the nineteenth century, when it had been in the vanguard of the spread of educational opportunity in the United States, to its current rarified position in the now vastly-expanded educational landscape of the twenty-first century. Of the over eighteen million students in the United States now enrolled, only about fifty thousand attended small liberal arts colleges. The dominant trends in higher education were towards large, public, urban institutions, many with adult learners and with nonresidential, online, career-prep options. So Haverford was deliberately defying the trends and embraced its distinctiveness as a small, private, bucolic, and community-oriented liberal arts college dedicated to the intellectual and moral education of young people.

Drawing on my experience at two public universities and two liberal arts colleges, I argued that Haverford had an advantageous position in the marketplace. Indeed, my presidency at Mount Holyoke allowed me to see Haverford's advantages in sharp relief. It shared many strengths with Mount Holyoke: academic excellence in the liberal arts; strong teachers/scholars/mentors; an effective learning environment; a beautiful campus; and a powerful, value-laden mission. But Haverford enjoyed a reputation higher than Mount Holyoke's as one of the very best colleges in the country, an esteemed position stoked by its top-ten ranking on the ever-spurious and -maddening but highly influential *US News and World Report* college rankings. It also amassed a more-robust applicant pool and could be highly selective in the constitution of its student body. In addition, while Mount Holyoke struggled with the perception that it was located in the country away from fashionable urban buzz, Haverford boasted an advantageous location: its campus was bucolic but its location was urban, with the city of Philadelphia and other affiliated institutions resting on its doorstep. And most consequentially, Haverford was coed; it did not have Mount Holyoke's challenge of selling single-sex education, although its Bi-College partner, Bryn Mawr College, certainly did.

So Haverford had the luxury to be what it quintessentially was. But it needed to continue building its academic programs, to address some pressing facility needs, to update its administrative systems, and, most critically, to manage and grow its inadequate financial resources, which had been devastated in the 2008–2009 recession. The administrative systems at Haverford were surprisingly underdeveloped. The College had evolved imperfectly from its origins as a much smaller place of informal understandings and Quaker handshakes. The institution was woefully behind in terms of technological infrastructure. Many administrative operations simply weren't formalized but rather overseen by administrators with a lot of unchecked discretion and authority. Some enterprises, such as the bookstore and summer programs, for example, were run casually, almost like mom-and-pop operations.

The most consequential effect of this lack of accountability and professionalism, however, was the way the College's investments had been handled—not by disciplined asset allocation but by a committee made up largely of alumni from the finance industry. In the past the alumni apparently did not adhere to rational, structured practices of asset allocation but sometimes played favorites among investment options, without giving sufficient attention to conflicts of interest or illiquidity. When the stock market was booming in the early 2000s, the market value of Haverford's endowment soared;

when the recession hit, it tanked, and illiquidity necessitated selling assets for substantial loss. Overall, the value of the endowment declined 39 percent in the Great Recession, one of the worst performances among Haverford's peers. And while a major revamping and strengthening of endowment management were undertaken before I came to campus, the endowment did not rebound as robustly as it did at some institutions.

As a result, the value of Haverford's endowment, already modest in comparison to that of its peers before the recession, was afterwards a fraction of its competitors'. This was arguably a game-changing loss, making it unlikely that Haverford could sustain over the long haul its competition with wealthier institutions such as Amherst, Williams, Swarthmore, and others. Nor could it so easily act like a leading college in its spending practices, although it tried. Many people inside and outside the College saw its generous commitment to financial aid as an embodiment of the institution's ethical values. Not only was it a need-blind/full-funding institution, the Board of Managers, in the heady flush of pre-recession days, had recently implemented the policy of *no loans*, an admirable but extremely expensive decision resulting in a dramatic rise in the annual costs of financial aid.

As had been my practice at Mount Holyoke, I developed with the senior staff a draft list of goals for the year and shared it with all constituencies: the Board, the faculty, student and staff groups, and the Corporation. The object was to get everyone on the same page. The key goal I called "recentering," by which I meant using the transition to take stock, to draw strength from shared values, to put the house in order, and to move forward. And closely allied with that process was open communication with all campus constituents about challenges and opportunities facing the institution.

In the beginning, my outreach to the faculty was initially met with some skepticism; the factionalism that had plagued the community was slow to die. The faculty met as a body once a month, but their exercise of Quaker self-governance was much less impressive than the students' practice. The agenda was filled with many procedural matters and small items that allowed little opportunity to address larger issues facing the College. Governing through consensus consumed an inordinate amount of time in communal wordsmithing or listening to the harangues of disaffected individuals. Many items died on the floor in irresolution, leaving the faculty deadlocked in unhappy frustration. One faculty member sardonically explained, "At about 5:30 pm at most faculty meetings, I just wanted to slit my own throat and be done with it."

A number of faculty seemed to assume that the Board had all the power and responsibility. So, like children to a parent, they expected the Board to meet their demands and solve institutional problems, and when it didn't, they railed against it. Always an advocate for shared governance, I kept insisting that their and the Board's interests were aligned—that faculty had an important role to play and needed to partner with the Board to address issues facing the institution. I used every opportunity to draw in the faculty. For instance, I shared the same materials with both groups and designed the next Board meeting to include opportunities for both social and formal board-faculty interaction.

The hard pill for the faculty to swallow, as it was for the Board, was that the Great Recession had dealt a significant blow to the College's resources. Plans that may have been feasible before the downturn were now much more difficult to carry out. Many faculty believed the Board must fulfill the commitment it had made years before to expand the faculty by twenty-seven lines, even though the recession had devastated resources and the presidency had changed over twice since then and was still in transition. A glum resentment of the "other," the Board, prevailed. Faculty felt overstretched by the multiple pressures of teaching, research, and service, especially since the requirement that all students do a senior thesis involved a great deal of faculty time.

Faculty were indeed stretched by multiple demands, yet the hard fact remained that expansion had to await the resources to implement it. So I encouraged the faculty to set aside harping on the loss and casting blame, to come together as a body, and to strategize about how best to position the College for success in the future. I also thought it good to remember that the faculty's "hardship" was a relative thing; it was a distinct privilege to be affiliated with such a fine institution and to have such excellent students. This reinterpretation of reality as a glass half-full did gradually gain traction. Overall, the year was a successful transition from angst and disarray at the beginning to a calmer, more-optimistic recentering on the central purposes of the institution at the end.

I felt I had done my job. People seemed pleased with my efforts, and I was getting ready to start closing out my interim appointment, when I got a call from the chair of the Board asking me to stay on a second year because the preferred presidential candidate, Daniel Weiss, was unable to start for another twelve months. Although the continuance involved postponing my Five College Professorship once again, I agreed to do it. I met the president-elect, Daniel Weiss, and we agreed that we would work together to make the transition as seamless as possible to insure that the year was not a lull in institutional development but a positive step forward. He proposed that we have a "model transition" by crafting a two-year planning process, with me leading the first year and he the second, and this is exactly what we did. The arrangement worked remarkably well. He handled his president-in-waiting status with tact and discretion, keeping a low profile on campus and concentrating on getting to know the off-campus community, while I handled campus business and designed and rolled out the planning process.

I couldn't have done this without first securing the services of Kim Benston, professor of English, who agreed, after considerable arm-twisting, to serve as interim provost. (To my pleasure, he has subsequently become president.) His leadership and collegiality were splendid in every way, and he carried more than his fair share of the work of launching the planning process and, in subsequent years, of implementing the plan. We were ably aided by Jesse Lytle, new chief of staff, whom I recruited from Mount Holyoke, and he too did yeoman work in the planning process.

Kim, Jesse, and I joined in the process with a newly formed faculty committee that picked up where a previous planning report, *Blueprint for Academic Enrichment,* had left off. The former document grew out of earlier departmental planning and was largely a compendium of requests for new faculty positions. The new planning effort took a more College-wide perspective on issues, concentrating on potential growth in mutually enriching linkages across the disciplines and in emerging new interdisciplinary areas of interest. In addition to new faculty lines, the plan identified critical campus spaces that needed renovation to support the academic program and envisioned ways to build on strengths and improve the educational experience for students. We made good progress on institutional planning over the year, essentially following the playbook that I had developed through my experience twice leading planning exercises at Mount Holyoke. And in the next year, Dan Weiss and colleagues expanded this work in productive ways and presented the Board and community a complete draft by its April meeting in 2013.

Altogether my experience at Haverford was a positive one: I felt valued and valuable. It was a pleasure to see this fine institution right itself, gather its considerable strength, and look forward to a productive future. I left the presidency with an appreciation of the fundamental simplicity and power of Haverford College, which so unapologetically embraced and affirmed its historical mission as a consensual community devoted to academic excellence and to intellectual and moral freedom.

As I explained earlier, I was drawn to gender metaphors when I described the institutional character of Wesleyan and Mount Holyoke because each culture had characteristics stereotypically associated with male or female. But such metaphors didn't seem apt for Haverford. Despite its long male-only history, it "androgynously" valued both the individual and the community, freedom and responsibility, critical inquiry and basic civility. It had comfortably assimilated women students, starting in 1980. And predating that watershed was its long-standing "Bi-Co" relationship with Bryn Mawr College.

Haverford Board members of longer vintage had fond memories of the time when Haverford and Bryn Mawr were coordinate male and female colleges with a great deal of interaction. That connection continued into the present day in a number of ways, of course, but the gender imbalance of students was sometimes an awkwardness or impediment. In truth, several members of the Board were perplexed by what they saw as Bryn Mawr's "recalcitrance" in its commitment to an "antiquated" model of single-sex education. This devotion, they believed, was holding the institution back and lowering its status and reputation, and also potentially inhibiting efforts to build ventures between the two colleges. Indeed, like Mount Holyoke, Bryn Mawr College faced the steep challenge of selling the single-sex mission to high school girls, who in overwhelming numbers were predisposed to reject that option. Its applicant pool was less robust than Haverford's. The common view at Haverford was that Bryn Mawr had previously been the more-rigorous and -prestigious school but that the quality of its students and the measure of its prestige had fallen in recent decades while those of Haverford had risen. So, in their minds, it was Bryn Mawr's dogged adherence to the single sex-mission and Haverford's embrace of coeducation that made all the difference in their recent fortunes.

Of course, Bryn Mawr folks viewed this matter differently. Just like Mount Holyoke, the institution was full of passionate believers in the power of the single-sex mission. The institution fulsomely embraced women's education worldwide with a growing population of international students, who gave their campus a more cosmopolitan flavor than Haverford's more-homogeneous American-dominated student body.

From the vantage point of Haverford, where male and female students coexisted in a comfortable friendship and cohabitation, the rationale for women's colleges seemed less compelling than it did when I was at Mount Holyoke. It was a welcome reprieve not to deal with the marketing challenges of the women's college. Indeed, heretically, I sometimes thought that it would have been easier on all institutions of higher learning—and certainly their presidents and marketing directors—if the Supreme Court had not made in its rulings on gender equity an exception for women's colleges and if these institutions had been forced to coeducate. But that august body had not, and so the weighty responsibility for deciding to remain single sex or go coed was squarely in the hands of each institution—a subject I will return to in the conclusion as I sum up my education as a woman college president.

} 12 {

REFLECTIONS OF A WOMAN
COLLEGE PRESIDENT

My life journey took me a long way culturally from the backcountry society of northern Wisconsin where I grew up. Leaving necessitated deracination, for once you pull up that old tap root, you can't put it down again, and you can't go home again either. From the first grade on, lured onward by the mind-expanding world of school, I could never get enough, so that even now, many decades later, I'm still in school. Academia became my *alma mater*, other mother, formative and demanding, and ultimately irresistible and fulfilling. I was shaped by this *mater* and her values for better or worse. Sometimes I was acutely conscious of the discordance of some of the presumptions of this world with those of my real mother. But I made my choice and weaned myself away from her views, and only in retrospect, do I see how much I underestimated Mother and the life-sustaining values of her universe, how much I learned from her and other mothers and sisters, and how much I left behind in throwing in my lot with the world of the modern university.

Still, there was no room for me to grow under my mother's thumb in northern Wisconsin. What's a young woman with a keen interest in books and learning to do? Go to school, of course. "Home" became the university or college where I was living at the time as an undergraduate and masters or PhD student. Then as a professor moving up through the ranks and as an administrator who took on progressively greater responsibility as dean, provost, and president, and now, in full cycle, I am back again in the classroom. I served three years as an itinerant Five College professor, teaching successively at the University of Massachusetts, Amherst College, Hampshire College, and then back to Mount Holyoke. I've been affiliated with eleven universities or colleges as student, professor, or administrator.

This educational odyssey took me from public, comprehensive, large universities to private, elite, ever-smaller liberal arts colleges. Along the way I developed great respect for the value, variety, and genius of American universities and colleges, and I saw education from various perspectives at institutions that differed radically from each other in some respects but that also shared some fundamental similarities and purposes, the most central ones being that they were dynamic repositories, laboratories, and transmitters of the scientific, cultural, and humanistic heritage of our society. They were full of energy generated by smart, interesting, creative people, and their central purpose was giving students a transformational education that opened up possibilities for personal and professional enrichment.

The value of colleges and universities is inestimable. Where would American society be without them? What could be more important than advancing knowledge and passing on to successive generations the accumulated learning and wisdom of humankind? American colleges and universities are respected the world over. Yet in this country these institutions are often taken for granted and sometimes disparaged, mocked, and misunderstood. Displaying a disheartening degree of anti-intellectualism, some Americans see them as potentially dangerous and subversive and fear their uprooting of traditional values and old certainties. That was certainly Mother's worst fear and suspicion when I went off to the University of Wisconsin. Colleges and universities are at times caricatured as "ivory tower" retreats from the "real" world—wasteful resorts where privileged professors and spoiled students indulge in abstruse, arcane, and irrelevant studies. But for me, it is the so-called "real" world—with its crass commercialism and shallow celebrity culture; its simplistic, jingoistic, reactionary views; its "fake news," "alternative facts," disparagement of science and reasoned discourse—that is limited and limiting. Young people need to be liberated from the confines of a parochial and meretricious world view and opened up to the life of the mind and the world of books and learning that may well reveal rewarding paths to personal fulfillment and the greater good.

It was my good luck to move from public comprehensive universities to private liberal arts colleges. These colleges were deeply consonant with my own liberal arts background and academic values. They were also altogether simpler, more knowable, more manageable, and more suitable to my talents than large, complex universities. The liberal arts college is blissfully free from the endless bureaucratic layers and approval processes that complicate and inhibit initiatives and aspirations in a state system, such as the sixteen-campus University of North Carolina. At a private college the president is overseen by a board, and that's that! Except for the critical fact that the faculty is another critical player in institutional governance.

Given my small-town background, small colleges in some ways duplicated for me the self-contained community of my childhood, but with an important difference. These later communities were schools, my preferred environment. And they were held together not by the traditional and conservative values my mother espoused but by what seemed to me the more enlightened values of secular humanism, liberal learning, and liberal thought.

The three private colleges I was affiliated with shared some fundamental qualities: high standards of academic excellence; a lively intellectual atmosphere and learning environment, where serious scholar-teachers attentively mentored smart idealistic students; and a robust faith in the efficacy of a liberal arts education and the qualities of mind, judgment, and discernment that it engendered. All three—Wesleyan, Mount Holyoke, and Haverford—were pioneering institutions founded in the early nineteenth century and emerging out of Christian missionary evangelicalism, be it Methodism for Wesleyan (1831), Quakerism for Haverford (1833), or a nondenominational early feminism as was the case for Mount Holyoke (1837). From the start, they saw their mission as both the intellectual and moral development of young people. All eventually dropped a religious affiliation and couched their values in terms of secular humanism, although Haverford retained deep connections to Quakerism in its campus ethos and governance practices, and through its anomalous ownership by The Corporation of Haverford College.

Honoring their historical traditions, Haverford and Mount Holyoke continued to be small colleges with cogent missions focused on the intellectual and ethical development of young people. Both institutions were grounded in their identity—Haverford as a Quaker-rooted community and Mount Holyoke as a pioneer and champion of women's higher education. Both enjoyed a robust culture and achieved a sense of wholeness unique to those institutions. In contrast, Wesleyan, larger and more diverse, did indeed evince a "little university" rather than small-college vibe and express a more-capacious and -conflicted sense of mission. The science faculty were protective of their graduate programs, and the social science faculty, with their undergraduate-only role and their greater teaching burdens, resented the disparity. Some on the Wesleyan Board and in the alumni population nostalgically clung to the small-college, fraternity-centered model of an earlier time. And vestiges of the fraternity system of that era and its athletic culture still persisted into the present. The liberalism of sixties brought in cohorts of black and other minority students, who pressed forward their wishes and needs, and in 1970 coeducation brought with it not only women but a doubling of the institution's size. The Freeman Asian Scholars program, begun the 1990s, contributed to an increasing presence of international students. In recent decades Wesleyan developed an independent-minded, cosmopolitan, and edgy student culture.

So, quite unlike the more-coherent and -cogent Haverford or Mount Holyoke, several "Wesleyans" competed and sometimes collided with one another, giving the University a restless and, at times, contentious energy. I admired that energy but learned how hard it made the effective administration of a university or college affairs. Haverford, in contrast, was considerably smaller, eleven hundred students to Wesleyan's nearly three thousand. But Haverford was perhaps too small. It seemed a more-homogenous and more insular institution, less refreshed by the larger world stimulations. And Mount Holyoke, with about twenty-two hundred students, was strikingly different from the other two in look and feel, mainly because its student body was all women but also because, of the three, its student population was noticeably the most racially and ethnically diverse. A high proportion of its students, perhaps one-third, were women of color from the developing world or were American students of color. Haverford and Mount Holyoke boasted a strong sense of community; Wesleyan emphasized individualism. With no degree requirements and no required thesis (as at Haverford), Wesleyan students had a lot of freedom "to do their own thing," reflecting the powerful cultural legacy of the counterculture of the 1960s and early 1970s.

Although Wesleyan, Mount Holyoke, and Haverford had much in common, each liberal arts college was a unique community defined by its own history, values, and purpose. I became an avid "reader" of each place and culture. The more I read the institution, the stronger my conviction that the key to leadership was to appreciate and connect to the motivating core ideals and the sense of purpose implicit in the history and culture of each institution. In all three cases, my leadership was about respecting what had been achieved at these institutions and about valuing the people who were already there. My goal was always to draw from them core ideals and aspirations for future growth and success.

The central challenge of academic leadership in all three institutions, it seemed to me, was always the same—to make shared governance work. However terrific liberal arts colleges were for students, some faculty seemed less content than they might be when you consider their daily privileges: working on a beautiful campus; teaching intelligent, engaged, and eager students; pursuing their own scholarly interests; enjoying a flexible schedule; and interacting with colleagues in a largely self-governed community. Despite these advantages—gifts even—these little communities had some "small town" liabilities and "family" dynamics as well. Some faculty were absorbed by tensions and personal antipathies within their departments; others seemed childlike toward the "parent"—the dean, provost, president, or trustees—who could dispense or withhold "love" to rivalrous siblings. In my experience faculty, perpetually "in school," could lock themselves into a syndrome of constantly seeking approval and reward from authority figures in their community.

Some faculty groused about all they work they performed, but most seemed to appreciate being part of a liberal arts college. To be sure, they did have demanding jobs. Like university faculty, they were expected to be scholar-teachers excelling at both research and teaching but fulfilling both without the perks and accommodations that a large university might provide to facilitate that complex work. They were pulled back and forth between the contemplative life of research—the obligation that many preferred—and the daily and more-pressing demands of teaching and mentoring students. And, on top of that, they were expected to be good citizens of the college and to participate in its governance. Although "service" was recognized as the third leg of their faculty stool of responsibility, it was often disparaged and devalued as a time-waster.

Despite their skepticism, an institution of higher learning needed the participation of faculty deeply familiar with the shape and new directions of knowledge in any dialogue intended to chart a wise and ambitious course for the future. At all the institutions where I served in a leadership role, a number of faculty did step up in impressive ways to engage in institutional planning and to lead important initiatives. I believe that many found, as I did, a lot of fulfillment and satisfaction in working together with others on projects that advanced the college. It was "communal" work in every sense. So much of professorial labor, in contrast, is solitary. Cooperation on a university project could be a refreshing and rewarding endeavor, offering a chance to be part of something larger than the academic self and to feel the energy of being part of or contributing to a functioning, participatory community.

As president, I saw my key role as "orchestrating" shared governance. I tried to keep the faculty and the board engaged and in alignment with one another. I worked to develop consensus through iterative, collaborative planning exercises, then patiently oversaw implementation plans. Calibrating plans, guiding the process, cajoling the constituents, keeping an eye on the big picture, communicating with internal and external communities, carrying through on promises, and reiterating often the common ground—the shared values and aspirations that inspired allegiance and support—were all components of my work. Juggling all these balls could be at once exhausting and exhilarating.

To advance the plans that would enrich, develop, and improve the colleges, I tried to keep above the fray of petty campus politics, to handle all issues with candor, fairness, and steadiness, to hold no secrets, to play no favorites, and to frame issues in a way understandable to all constituencies in the community. I delegated responsibilities by hiring exceptionally strong people and by giving them lots of independence, while also drawing them together around me as a team. I tried to be inclusive, to leave no constituents out in the cold, to be visible on and get out and about the campus, to think big but also mind the store, to be a good steward of institutional resources.

Most fundamentally, my administrative work sought to make the parts and the people function effectively as a whole. The object was always to advance the College's mission.

But as important as the mission was to me, there was the market—always the market. As I discussed in chapter 6, an unfortunate consequence of the U.S. Supreme Court's decision that outlawed discussions among institutions of higher learning about financial aid was the increased competition among them essentially to "buy" students with financial aid packages. Also interjecting and intensifying competitive marketing in higher education were the insidious ratings inflicted on them—most infamously—by *US News and World Report* and its imitators. In dismay, I watched this influence, so destructive to and meaningless in higher learning, build over the course of my career. I remember my surprise when I first encountered the preoccupation with rankings among the officers' group at Wesleyan. I commented with some amusement: "I thought we were about education, not status." But others quickly disparaged and challenged the self-evident naiveté of that view. They pointed out the tremendous influence and consequence of these rankings for the "elite" liberal arts colleges in the United States.

At the time, I was a newcomer to that sector of higher education and somewhat uncomfortable with the concept of elitism within it. I found a disjuncture between how these institutions, such as Wesleyan, privately depended on *privilege* and *selectivity* and how they publically condemned them as values. Some faculty and administrators were preoccupied with status and rank in the hierarchy of "elite" institutions, and their colleges were dependent on the patronage of wealthy donors. At the same time, their typically left-leaning faculties were often outspokenly critical of the abuses and inequities generated by class-conscious, moneyed, commoditized culture.

I knew *US News* ratings were influential, but I believed that colleges and universities should not just capitulate to this regrettable interjection of consumer capitalism, based on fallacious methodology, into the academy but should take a principled stand against them. When I was president of Mount Holyoke, I wrote several op-eds and letters to the editor deriding these spurious rankings and banned reference to them in published materials or on the College website. Make no mistake—I was being both pragmatic and realistic: I knew that over the long run, Mount Holyoke would necessarily fall in the rankings not through declining merit of its education but because the ratings were so strongly and demonstrably correlated with wealth. In truth, a great divide between the very rich colleges and all the others was opening at the time and getting wider every year, at the same time that the disparities in wealth and income between the very rich and the rest in society were likewise growing in the United States. I thought it was foolish to give any credence to such a specious measure of excellence, especially when the odds were stacked against nearly all colleges—including ours—in the competition.

But I learned that fighting against college rankings is quixotic tilting at windmills. They were neither going away nor declining in influence. American consumer culture is addicted to ranked lists. Everything, from washing machines and aspiring American idols to colleges and universities, can be seen in competition with one another to be "the best." Never mind that different schools have distinct missions that suit the needs and temperaments of diverse, unique students. One size does not fit all in higher education. But capitalism invades every facet of our thinking and commodifies education itself. In this frame, students and parents are "customers" to whom universities and colleges sell their wares with ever-more corporate-like marketing and compete with one another with ever-more country club–like facilities and by being ever-more "selective" (that is, by attracting and then rejecting more applicants) than our competitors. In other words, far from being purist, ethereal ivory towers, liberal arts colleges are full-blown participants in the capitalist culture and markets of the larger world.

Despite those misgivings, I saw one significant benefit to the *US News* rankings: the annual list valorized the category of *liberal arts college* and kept it in view as a significant sector of higher education in the United States. And given what a vast enterprise American higher education had become and what a tiny sector the liberal arts colleges represented, the rankings helped showcase the top-tier liberal arts colleges as "elite" exemplars of excellent higher learning and facilitated their "competition" with larger, better-known universities. So this annual exercise, however indulgent and overblown, was a valuable marketing tool, after all.

In this way my idealism about higher education confronted the realities of the capitalist marketplace. Liberal arts education was not just about mission—it was also about market or market share. For however capacious its educational aims, the college was also a nonprofit "business." It had to cultivate "customers," and it had to make ends meet. The cost structure of running a small college was increasingly problematic. With no "public trough" to draw from, these colleges depended largely on tuition and fees supplemented by endowment and gift income. Rising labor costs; expensive physical plants, utilities, and technology; ever-more-extensive student services and amenities; increased regulatory bureaucracy; and other costs compelled colleges to raise student tuition and fees to staggering levels, which then had to be subsidized annually by ever-larger financial aid packages. Tuition and fees were exceeding what most families, even those of upper-middle income, could afford, and institutions were also encouraging poorer, more-diverse students to enroll as well. With no relief other than minimal support from governmental grants, financial aid subsidies grew to a larger and larger percentage of tuition revenue. The model seemed unsustainable. Yet year after year, we struggled with these intractable and frustrating realties, wrestled budgets into submission, and, at the same time, enrolled increased numbers of high-need students. Of course, we worried about and tried to hold down rising student indebtedness. These daunting and vexing financial challenges were and would continue to be the steady diet of college administrators into the foreseeable future.

Still, I became somewhat philosophical about the fact that budgets were always stretched, no matter where I was serving. Invariably, we looked enviously at institutions that enjoyed endowments several multiples greater than ours and that tapped wealthier alumni bodies as well. Clearly, other colleges were much worse off, too. In truth, the three liberal arts colleges I was affiliated with had extraordinary resources and advantages in comparison to the vast majority of similar institutions. I also drew solace from their venerable history and longevity, knowing that previous generations often surmounted greater challenges. Each was founded and led by persons who had battled incredible odds. Just think of Mount Holyoke's remarkable founder, Mary Lyon, a woman with profound vision, powerful ambition, and no money, who went around collecting modest donations in her little green purse. Through perseverance and persuasion, economy and creativity, she prevailed. And so would we—so would our successors continue to struggle with the challenges of high aspirations confronted by limited resources.

Then again, maybe one shouldn't rely on historical precedent too much. The liberal arts college, and the women's college in particular, are in some ways remnants of an earlier era. They could go extinct. They had been in the vanguard of spreading educational opportunity in the nineteenth century, but in the twenty-first, this sector is in the rearguard, a tiny proportion of the whole. The increasingly vast enterprise of American higher education now included hundreds of public and private universities, professional schools, colleges, and countless community colleges. The omnivorous for-profit sector enrolls prodigious numbers of students with massive online, weekend, adult, and nonresidential options. Indeed, some fear that technology has made education so accessible that it threatens the very existence of the residential college.

Although technology has radically transformed the nature, delivery, and accessibility of knowledge, I don't think it will put the residential college out of business any more than the printing press eclipsed the venerable universities that predated it. The liberal arts college offers something entirely different from the impersonal delivery of online education. It is grounded in close student-faculty relationships, in a residential living and learning community, in the intellectual and ethical development of young people at a formative time in their lives, and, most fundamentally, in liberal arts education. This classic collegiate experience is still valued by students and their parents as representing "education at its best." It is the gold standard in higher learning. Applicant pools are robust and competitive for all top-tier colleges. Undoubtedly, in recent years some families, shaken by a troubling economy, want to see a more-direct correlation between a degree and a job. Liberal arts colleges have responded by increasing their attention to internships, providing career development centers, and cultivating linkages between the curriculum and the world of work. All this they must do, but nonetheless, they must also continue to be tireless advocates for and defenders of the ineffable, life-enhancing benefits of an excellent liberal arts education. It is no overstatement to say that the liberal arts education is our civilization's best hope.

An education is not, after all, just a means to getting a job. It opens up a young person to the life of the mind, because it is certainly true that the "soul selects her own society and then shuts the door," as Emily Dickinson said.[1] Lily Tomlin wryly adds, "Remember we're all in this alone."[2] But we—all of us—are also in this life *together* on our fragile earth, united by a vast, rich, stunning legacy of science, arts, and letters, and by an awesome history of human struggle and achievement. Institutions of higher education are the primary vehicles through which that heritage is reflected upon, added to, and passed on to succeeding generations.

To be sure, majoring in art, ancient history, philosophy, dance, physics, or any other liberal arts subjects might seem downright impractical. "What are you going to do with that degree?" people will ask. But a liberal arts education is paradoxically both nonutilitarian—a disinterested pursuit of learning for learning's sake—and highly "useful": it develops the skills, knowledge, critical thinking, quality of mind, reflective habits, and ethical perspectives needed to daily pursue a productive and fulfilling life. Moreover, at its best, a liberal arts education fosters what John Henry Newman called a "philosophical habit of mind"—skepticism, confidence, self-reliance—useful in all sorts of practical and pragmatic ways, and these qualities inform the best kind of democratic citizenry.[3] Now more than ever, we need these educated individuals as a bulwark against the ignorance, gullibility, and abuses of power prevalent in American society and the world. In sum, the best way to prepare our young people for the inevitable and far-reaching changes that they will experience in their personal and civic lives is to encourage them to take up and to extend the incredibly rich legacy of human knowledge encapsulated in the liberal arts and sciences.

However strong the case can be made for the liberal arts education, the fact remains that the liberal arts sector as a whole is under duress, and many liberal arts colleges lower in the pecking order are metamorphosing into more-comprehensive, more-professional, and more vocationally oriented institutions offering weekend, night, and online educational options. While the devaluation of the liberal arts is lamentable and, in my mind, deplorable, I still admire the survival instinct and entrepreneurial spirit of these institutions that are evolving to meet market needs in their communities. I don't blame them for scrambling to save themselves and find markets they can serve and thrive in. I just hope they don't strip away the liberal arts foundation of their programs and shortchange students with too much short-term and shortsighted vocational training.

The challenges are even more daunting for women's colleges. I enjoyed working with the presidents of women's colleges as part of the Women's College Coalition, a membership organization of North American women's colleges. I can only celebrate their scrappy determination to save their women's college mission in the face of diminishing applicant pools. Some now meet the needs of older or neighborhood women or offer professional and graduate options in their curriculum. Even more inspiring was my work with Women's Education Worldwide, an organization that we at Mount Holyoke founded, along with Smith College, and that brought together for the first time women's colleges from around the world. At our first meeting we drew participants from twenty-nine countries and four continents. Represented at the our meetings were long-established institutions such as our American, British, and Australian "sisters" as well as major Asian universities, such as Japan Women's University and Ewha Women's University of Korea, and newly emerging institutions in Bangladesh, Kenya, Zimbabwe, Saudi Arabia, the United Arab Emirates, and Bahrain.

While recognizing wide variation in age, size, wealth, and circumstances among our institutions, we still found much common ground. For example, all acknowledged the need to develop our students' self-confidence and leadership capabilities and to combat inequality, discrimination, and cultural barriers based on gender— matters much more severe, of course, in some parts of the world than in the United States and Western Europe. I remember the response of the Sudanese representative to the question on our initial survey: "What is your major challenge?" "Civil war," he replied, putting our challenges in startling perspective.

In his provocative keynote address at our inaugural conference of Women's Education Worldwide, Nobel laureate Amartya Sen asserted that "few subjects match the social significance of women's education" and argued that basic education for women holds the potential for "facilitating radical social and economic changes that are so badly needed in our problem-ridden world."[14] Yet, despite all the good work of women's colleges to fulfill the education and advancement of women—what I called "the great unfinished agenda"—women's colleges are becoming increasingly anomalous in a coeducational world. Indeed, except for the Middle East and South Asia, coeducation is now the norm worldwide.

In this country the steady trickle of women's colleges going coed continues year after year. From a high of three hundred or so women's colleges before the widespread coeducational movement, fewer than forty women's colleges remain in the United States, and every year more coeducate, assimilate, or close. The decision to go coed, while often highly contested by their students and alumnae, seemed to make good business sense for most, if not all, institutions that made the change. The hardest part was living through the initial fury that this change engendered. I served as the chair of the reaccreditation teams at Skidmore and Wheaton colleges, both of which had strengthened markedly after embracing coeducation. The same appears to be true of Vassar College, one of the Seven Sisters, which had made the switch in 1969.

Unquestionably, the educational situation for women in this country has changed dramatically in my lifetime and is changing still, thanks in large part to the civil rights and women's movements of the 1960s and 1970s. Far from being excluded from educational establishments as they had been throughout the millennia of human history, women are now welcomed into institutions of all kinds, although whether they are treated fairly and equitably is sometimes an open question. But we should not lose sight of the fact that now women are a majority of students both in this country and around the world. That statistic—that fact—represents a dramatic sea change and gain over the span of about sixty years. While in earlier decades women's colleges produced a disproportional number of women who went on to leadership positions in government, education, and the professions, that situation is changing. As more women enter the educational pipeline, the very best women students now have the choice of attending the best institutions of higher learning, whether coed or single-sex.

In 2007, I gave a lecture at Harvard and published an op-ed with this query: "If a woman can now be president of Harvard, do we still need women's colleges?"[5] I answered with a resounding yes! They are still relevant and there is still a need. Now that more years have passed and women have been president not only of Harvard but also of Princeton, Penn, Yale, Brown, and other great institutions of higher education, the glass ceiling most definitely shows cracks, although it is far from shattered. The number of women college presidents, 26 percent of the total in 2014, has risen at one percent a year since 1980, when it was 10 percent.[6] This is progress, but the pace is slow, and today comparatively few women hold positions of leadership and power in any sector of our society. Seemingly intractable gender discrimination persists in compensation levels across our society. Women in the United States earn on average only eighty-one cents for every dollar their male counterparts receive for comparable work (according to 2010 U.S. census).

Fortunately, the recent #MeToo movement is bringing to public awareness the shocking degree of sexism and sexual harassment embedded in what are still predominantly patriarchal corporate, political, public, and educational institutions. This movement shows how far women have yet to go and also reminds those of us who have lived comfortably on campuses where women are valued and treated equitably of how different it can be in the larger world. I would like to be able to assert that women's colleges are blissfully free of this sexism and harassment, but, alas, human nature being what it is, occasionally they rear their ugly heads on these campuses too, but, in my experience, they are comparatively rare and completely antithetical to the dominant ethos and culture. The picture is altogether bleaker elsewhere in the world. In virtually every country large numbers of women are still subjected to sexism, discrimination, or much worse. In a world shaped and still overwhelmingly dominated by patriarchy and with shocking examples of male power gone pathological, it is good—even critical—to have colleges proudly carrying on a "tradition of her own," institutions that inspire, encourage, and empower women. It will be a terrible loss if they give up their great cause to educate, advance, and empower women.

So there might well remain a significant place in higher education for standard bearers at the top of the pecking order to remind the world of the unfinished agenda of women's education and equity worldwide. I'm thinking of colleges such as the five remaining "Seven Sisters"—Wellesley, Smith, Bryn Mawr, Barnard, and Mount Holyoke—among other fine schools. The historic mission of these women-only institutions is palpable and motivating. Yet no one should underestimate the considerable costs and challenges of maintaining that single-sex mission. However inspirational, resourceful, and downright scrappy a women's college may be in sustaining itself, I am not sanguine that it can go on indefinitely defying the disinclination of the vast majority of young women to apply and the hard realities of the educational marketplace—without degrading the quality of its education. The sad truth is that the market is comparatively weak, because young women are ruling out women's colleges when they survey potential colleges and universities. Inexorably, single-sex colleges over time will be less competitive in student recruitment and thus in reputation and resources with the best American liberal arts colleges and universities. Indeed, that market erosion is already happening. Rather than retaining the luster of past glory, women's colleges may become niche schools. Certainly, they will continue to be attractive to some students, including the large percentage who choose them because of their excellent academic reputation and *despite* their single-sex status (although most become converts after being there a while). These brilliant institutions will continue to give great value in education and life to the students they serve.

Fundamentally each women's college will need to weigh mission and market. Sometimes the trade-off is stark: is the college's highest priority to be single-sex or is it to survive? For top-tier women's colleges, the question is whether the highest priority is the single-sex mission or whether it is to be competitive with the best colleges in the land. It will become harder to do both in the future. There is no simple choice. Competitiveness can be overrated, to be sure, and it is a stereotypically male trait, after all, and the preoccupation with status is certainly one of the more insidious dimensions of "elite" private education. But more critically and personally, during my presidency I saw how deeply engrained the gender identity is at Mount Holyoke—it occupies the very heart of the College's mission. As I have been arguing throughout this book, *mission* is the energetic core, the motivating force, of an institution. Going coed would be heart-wrenching, disruptive, and costly. The losses would be as great as the gains, at least in the first years. If a women's college such as Mount Holyoke is still attracting enough good students to fill beds and pay the bills, should it hang on? That is certainly the choice of the heart.

But the head says that maybe the issue needs reframing: Isn't the fact that women are now welcomed into institutions of all kinds in this country and across the world a tremendous victory for women and a validation of the success of women's colleges in pioneering the way? If so, is now the time to welcome young men into these institutions? Surely, young men, as much as young women, would benefit from the life-sustaining intellectual and moral values that infuse women's colleges. Indeed, it could be argued that young men need them more—that growing up male in this world of dizzying change, heartbreaking injustices and inequities, and crazed demagoguery that uses and abuses the idealism and lifeblood of young men is even more complicated than growing up female.

I find the case for going coed logically compelling, especially from the outside looking in. And it is the smarter, long-term business decision. But I have also seen from the inside the extraordinary power of a passionately held mission to energize and motivate students and alumnae to achieve towering moral, ethical, and educational greatness inside and outside the institution. In truth, I remain in conflict with myself about whether market trumps mission or vice versa at this point in history. I struggled with this vexing issue throughout my presidency. I'm glad not to be sitting in that chair. To be or not to be coed is an issue that will not go away.

As a young woman I neither had a women's college education nor, in truth, wanted one. Rather, I sought to get away from the small-town world of my upbringing and see the larger world—and what better place to begin that quest that at a vibrant, large, state university such as the University of Wisconsin? Now the limitations of my undergraduate experience are more apparent. Although I had professors who encouraged me and the English honors program gave me a small community of like-minded students, many of my classes were large lecture courses in which I was just one of scores of anonymous, silent students. I know that at a single-sex liberal arts college like Mount Holyoke, I would have received more attention, along with fuller and better mentoring, from the faculty than I did at the University of Wisconsin. I would have been excited and nurtured by intellectual life and energized by the "women can do it" culture. But, in truth, if given the choice again, and remembering what it is like to be an eighteen-year-old woman, I would probably again, with restless energy, choose to "light out to the Territory" and opt for the challenges, stimulations, and pulsating culture of a larger university (and, not incidentally, all those interesting young men). So I understand the choice that so many young women are making today.

I am enormously grateful for my belated women's college education—my nearly fifteen years at Mount Holyoke—which connected me to untapped dimensions of my own female identity and to a supportive community of remarkable women and the women and men who supported them. It helped me to see myself not as a singular woman making it on my own but rather as the lucky recipient of centuries of struggle and frustration, of defeat and triumph, of the power of mothers and sisters who had come before me, and of achievements of the women's colleges that pioneered the way. I faced gender discrimination over the course of my career, much more than young women do now, but not in the debilitating way that it afflicted and crippled previous generations, including my mother's cohort. Mostly I feel lucky for the way that I moved along in the wake of the women's liberation movement and slipped through slightly cracked doors that were previously shut tight to women. Still, at times I was well aware of my chilly reception by the male-dominated world of the professoriate and administration and felt the loneliness and isolation of being the first, or one of the first, women to do this or that, and invariably, my gender was remarked upon. As more women take the lead in education, business, and the professions, perhaps a woman's gender will be seen as less remarkable; then perhaps we can drop "woman" when we refer to her position.

I have tried to show in this book my complicated maternal and paternal heritage and the influential role of my sister and other "sisters" real and fictional in charting the whole new territory of being a woman over the decades of the mid- to late-twentieth and early twenty-first centuries. It was a big leap in one generation from Mother's eighth-grade education in rural Wisconsin to my service as provost and president of three of the finest colleges in the land. I experienced painful tension, conflict, and misunderstanding, as well as belated growth, greater understanding, and appreciation. This book is about recognizing and valuing all the disparate parts that make up the whole of a life.

NOTES

PREFACE

1. "Who saw life steadily and saw it whole," in the sonnet, "To a Friend," *The Poems of Matthew Arnold, 1840–1867* (London: Oxford University Press, 1922), 40. First published in The *Strayed Reveller, and Other Poems* (London: B. Fellowes, 1849).

2. William Faulkner, quoted in *Faulkner in the University: Class Conferences at the University of Virginia*, ed. Frederick L. Gwynn and Joseph L. Blotner (Charlottesville: University of Virginia Press, 1959), 84.

3. Joyce Carol Oates, "(Woman) Writer: Theory and Practice," in *(Woman) Writer: Occasions and Opportunities* (New York: Dutton, 1989), 22–32.

CHAPTER 1

1. Margaret Drabble, *Realms of Gold* (New York: Knopf, 1975), 116.

2. Thomas Wolfe, *You Can't Go Home Again* (New York: Harper & Brothers, 1941).

3. Kate Chopin, "The Story of an Hour," originally published as "The Dream of an Hour," *Vogue*, December 6, 1894. *KateChopin.org*, Kate Chopin International Society. www.katechopin.org/the-story-of-an-hour/.

4. Stephen J. Dedalus, in James Joyce, *A Portrait of the Artist as a Young Man* (New York: Macmillan, 1916), v, 238.

CHAPTER 2

1. Nancy Chodorow, *The Reproduction of Mothering: Psychoanalysis and the Sociology of Gender* (Berkeley: University of California Press, 1978), 200.

2. Margaret Drabble, *The Waterfall* (New York: Knopf, 1969), 114.

3. Joanne V. Creighton, "Sisterly Symbiosis: Merging and Separating Identities in Margaret Drabble's *The Waterfall* and A. S. Byatt's *The Game*," *Mosaic: An Interdisciplinary Critical Journal*, 21, no. 1 (winter 1987): 15–29.

4. A. S. Byatt, *The Game: A Novel* (1967; reprint, Harmondsworth, Middlesex, England: Penguin, 1983), 96.

5. Byatt, *The Game*, 97.

6. Drabble, *The Waterfall*, 128.

7. Ann Tyler, *Dinner at the Homesick Restaurant* (New York: Knopf, 1982), 21.

8. Byatt, *The Game*, 148.

9. Didion quoted in Susan Braudy, "A Day in the Life of Joan Didion," *MS*, 8 February 1977, 109.

10. Rich, quoted by her sister Cynthia Glauber in Elizabeth Fishel, *Sisters: Love and Rivalry inside the Family and Beyond* (New York: Morrow, 1979), 13.

11. Margaret Drabble, "A Woman Writer," *Books* 11 (spring 1973): 6.

12. Iris Rozencwajg, "Interview with Margaret Drabble," *Women's Studies* 6 (1979): 335, 339.

13. Susan Gubar and Sandra Gilbert, *The Mad Woman in the Attic: The Woman Writer and the Nineteenth-Century Literary Imagination* (New Haven: Yale University Press, 2000).

14. Rosamond Smith [Joyce Carol Oates], *Lives of Twins* (New York: Simon and Schuster, 1987), *Kindred Passions* (Waukegan, Ill.: Fontana Press, 1989), *Soul/Mate* (New York: Dutton, 1989), *Nemesis* (New York: Dutton, 1990), *Snake Eyes* (New York: Dutton, 1992), *You Can't Catch Me* (New York: Dutton, 1995), *Double Delight* (New York: Plume, 1997), and *Starr Bright Will Be With You Soon* (New York: Plume, 2000).

15. Virginia Woolf, *A Room of One's Own* (1929; reprint, New York: Harcourt, 1989).

CHAPTER 5

1. W. B. Yeats, "The Fascination of What's Difficult" and "Easter, 1916," *The Collected Poems of W. B. Yeats*, ed. Richard J. Finneran, 2d rev. ed. (New York: Scriber, 1996), 93, 180.

2. Machiavelli, in *The Prince: The Historical, Political, and Diplomatic Writings of Niccolo Machiavelli*, trans. Christian E. Detmold (Boston: Osgood, 1982), 35.

3. Roy Chamberlin, letter to the editor, *The Independent*, 10 March 1909, quoted in Louise Wilby Knight, "The Quails: The History of Wesleyan University's First Period of Coeducation, 1872–1912," (honors thesis, Wesleyan University, 1972), 150. I'm indebted to this informative thesis which is accessible at http://wesscholar.wesleyan.edu/cgi/viewcontent. cgi?article=1386&context=etd_hon_theses_

4. *Wesleyan Literary Monthly*, May 1909, copy in The Wesleyan Collection, Special Collection & Archives, Wesleyan University Library, Middletown, Connecticut. Clippings from the *Wesleyan Argus* and other materials are collected in "Coeducation at Wesleyan, 1867-1912,"

http://www.sscommons.org/openlibrary/welcome.html#3|collec-
tions|7730296||Wesleyan20University3ACoeducation20at20Wesley-
an2C20313836372D31393132|||.

5. NEASC Evaluation Team Report, Wesleyan University, John Chandler, Chair, *et al.*, 1992.

6. Robert Bellah, *et al.*, *Habits of the Heart: Individualism and Commitment in American Life* (Berkeley: University of California Press, 2007).

CHAPTER 6

1. Mount Holyoke, Amherst, Hampshire, and Smith Colleges and the University of Massachusetts joined together 1965 to form Five Colleges, Inc., the longest standing and largest consortium in the country, which interlinks and enriches the campuses and towns within the Pioneer Valley.

2. "Ivy Universities Deny Price-Fixing but Vow to Avoid It in the Future," *New York Times*, 23 May 1991.

CHAPTER 9

1. http://www.nytimes.com/2001/02/22/us/boston-globe-prints-apology-on-article-on-murder-inquiry.html.

2. "The Lies of Joseph Ellis," *New York Times*, 21 August 2001; David Abel, "College Suspends History Professor: Ellis's Lying Brought 'Hurt' President Said," *Boston Globe*, 18 August 2001; Elizabeth Mehren, "College Suspends Professor," *Los Angeles Times*, 18 August 2001; Pamela Ferden, "Professor Suspended for Lying," *Washington Post*, 18 August 2001.

3. B. B. Burke and Glenda Whitley, *Stolen Valor: How the Vietnam Generation Was Robbed of Its Heroes and History* (Dallas: Verity Press, 1998).

4. F. Scott Fitzgerald, *The Great Gatsby* (New York: Scribner's, 1925), 110.

5. William Faulkner, *Absalom, Absalom! The Corrected Text* (New York: Vintage, 1990), 212.

6. "Historians Say Borrowing Was Wider Than Known," *New York Times*, 23 February 2002.

CHAPTER 10

1. Mary Lyon to Zilpah Grant, 8 October 1836, Mount Holyoke College Library Archives, South Hadley, Massachusetts, http://clio.fivecolleges.edu/mhc/lyon.

2. Jim Collins, *Good to Great: Why Some Companies Make the Leap and Others Don't* (New York: Harpers Business, 2001), 96.

3. Some of these ideas are discussed in my essay, "Orchestrating Shared

Governance," *Remaking College: Innovation and the Liberal Arts*, ed. Rebecca S. Chopp, Susan Frost, and Daniel H. Weiss (Baltimore, Md.: The Johns Hopkins University Press, 2014), 69–73.

4. Richard P. Chait, Thomas P. Holland, and Barbara E. Taylor, *Improving the Performance of Governing Boards*, American Council on Education (Phoenix, Ariz.: Oryx Press, 1996).

5. Barbara E. Taylor, Richard P. Chait, and William P. Ryan, *Governance as Leadership: Reframing the Work of Nonprofit Boards* (Hoboken, N.J.: Wiley, 2005), 97.

CHAPTER 11

1. Isaac Sharpless, http://www.archive.org/details/haverfordcollege-1972have.

CHAPTER 12

1. "The Soul Selects Her Own Society," 1862, in *The Complete Poems of Emily Dickinson*, ed. Thomas H. Johnson (Boston: Little, Brown, 1960), 143.

2. Lily Tomlin, *Wikiquote: https://en.wikiquote.org/wiki/Lily_Tomlin#Metro_Weekly_interview_.282006.29*.

3. John Henry Newman, *The Idea of a University* (London: Longman, Green, 1907).

4. Amartya Sen, "What Is the Point of Women's Education" (keynote address at the inaugural meeting of Women's Education Worldwide: The Unfinished Agenda, South Hadley, Mass., June 2004).

5. "Why We Need Women's Colleges," *Boston Globe*, 21 May 2007. Adapted from a speech delivered at Harvard University's Graduate School of Education, 16 April 2007.

6. Bryan J. Cook, "The American College President Study: Key Findings and Takeaways," *The Presidency*, spring 2012 (supplement), 3–5.